# Freud

# Freud

## *From Individual Psychology to Group Psychology*

M. Andrew Holowchak, PhD

**JASON ARONSON**
*Lanham • Boulder • New York • Toronto • Plymouth, UK*

Published by Jason Aronson
A wholly owned subsidiary of The Rowman & Littlefield Publishing Group, Inc.
4501 Forbes Boulevard, Suite 200, Lanham, Maryland 20706
www.rowman.com

10 Thornbury Road, Plymouth PL6 7PP, United Kingdom

British Library Cataloguing in Publication Information Available

**Library of Congress Cataloging-in-Publication Data**
Holowchak, Mark, 1958–
  Freud : from individual psychology to group psychology / M. Andrew Holowchak.
     p. ; cm.
  Includes bibliographical references and index.
  ISBN 978-0-7657-0945-5 (cloth : alk. paper)—ISBN 978-0-7657-0946-2 (electronic)
  I. Title.
  [DNLM: 1.  Freud, Sigmund, 1856–1939. 2.  Freudian Theory—history. 3.  Mental
Disorders—psychology. 4.  Psychoanalysis—history. 5.  Psychotherapy, Group—history.
WM 11.1]

    616.89'152—dc23                                                        2012025508

To friend and colleague Allan Back

# Contents

# Acknowledgments

I would like to thank the good people at Jason Aronson for making possible this work. I would especially like to thank acquisitions editor Amy King and production editor Stephanie Brooks (for doing well the dirty work).

# Preface

"Identification is known to psycho-analysis as the earliest expression of an emotional tie with another person." Sigmund Freud, *Group Psychology*

WITHIN THE LAST TWO DECADES OF HIS LIFE, there is a noticeable shift in Freud's thinking. No longer does his clinical work take center stage. In works such as *Totem and Taboo, Beyond the Pleasure Principle, Group Psychology and the Analysis of the Ego, The Ego and the Id, The Future of an Illusion, Civilization and Its Discontents,* and *Moses and Monotheism,* Freud returns to larger, social issues that dominated his thinking in his early life. He writes in a postscript to his *Autobiographical Studies* of his "detour" and "return."

> [A] significant change has come about. Threads which in the course of my development have become entangled have now begun to separate; interests which in the course of my development had become intertangled have now begun to separate. Interests which I have acquired in the later part of my life have receded, while the older and original ones become prominent once more. . . . My interest, while making a lifelong detour through the natural sciences, medicine and psychotherapy, returned to the cultural problems which had fascinated me long before. . . (1935, *S.E.,* XX: 71-2).

Freud's return to and professional focus on the thoughts of his early life is perhaps especially notable in his 1920 work *Beyond the Pleasure Principle.* With the introduction of his death drive in that work, Freud goes beyond his own pleasure-zone, as it were, and that enables him, through psychoanalysis, to undertake such prodigious social issues as human unhappiness, death, war, religion, and human suffering. Like the brook trout's tortuous return to her spawning grounds to lay her eggs and die in the river where her life began, Freud too returns to his early-life preoccupations, as if to give closure to his life before his own death.

Nevertheless, Freud is uneasy about his "return" to social or group issues, because it marks a speculative shift in his thinking that seems characteristic more of philosophical thought, which he avowedly abhors, than of science (1920, *S.E.,* XX: 57). No idea, Freud says, any longer comes to him; he now goes "half-way to meet it."[1] He is uneasy because, as he reputedly said to Helene Deutsch, "I have allowed myself to leave the pure empyrean of psychology." He is uneasy, Roazen states, because he has become a philosopher, seer, and artist as well as scientist.[2] Consequently, his assessment of important social issues in works like *The Future of an Illusion* and *Civilization and Its Discontents* is hostile, even self-deprecating.[3]

## Three Senses of "Psychoanalysis"

Freud's later-life social works are indeed more speculative, but that does not necessarily mean that he takes himself to don the hat of anyone other than a scientist. Freud's foray into issues outside of the clinic is a consequence of his deeper penetration into clinical issues through further work, often of a speculative sort, on depth psychology. That "research" showed him that group-psychology issues were a natural extension of and complement to individual-psychology issues. In other words, the speculative turn to which Freud admits when he takes on group issues is due to adoption of a more expansive conception of "psychoanalysis" qua science—a conception which requires, for the sake of comprehensiveness and completeness, some speculative risk-taking.

Freud's 1925 essay "Autobiographical Study" ends with a statement of the ambiguity of "psychoanalysis":

> [T]he word "psycho-analysis" has itself become ambiguous. While it was originally the name of a particular therapeutic method, it has now also become the name of a science—the science of unconscious mental processes. By itself this science is seldom able to deal with a problem completely, but it seems destined to give valuable contributory help in the most varied regions of knowledge. The sphere of application of psycho-analysis extends as far as that of psychology, to which it forms a complement of the greatest moment (1925, *S.E.*, XX: 70).

Here Freud states expressly that psychoanalysis had begun in the clinic as a method for treating hysterical patients, but it has developed into a science of "unconscious mental processes."

Three years earlier, in a 1922 encyclopedia article appropriately titled "Psycho-Analysis," Freud is more precise about the ambiguity of "psychoanalysis."

> Psycho-Analysis is the name (1) of a procedure for investigating unconscious mental processes which are almost inaccessible in any other way, (2) of a method (based on that investigation) for the treatment of neurotic disorders and (3) of a collection of psychological information obtained along those lines, which is gradually being accumulated into a new scientific discipline (numbers added; 1922, *S.E.*, XVIII: 235).

Consequently, "psychoanalysis" has evolved over time to have three distinct meanings, which I flesh out as three theses. I shall refer to the three hereafter as $\Psi A_1$ (the depth-psychology thesis), $\Psi A_2$ (the analytic thesis), and $\Psi A_3$ (the comprehensive thesis).

- Depth-Psychology Thesis ($\Psi A_1$): Psychoanalysis is a procedure for investigating unconscious mental processes.
- Analytic Thesis ($\Psi A_2$): Psychoanalysis is an analytic method, using data from $\Psi A_1$, for treating individual clients with neurotic disorders.
- Comprehensive Thesis ($\Psi A_3$): Psychoanalysis is a comprehensive collection of psychological data that are being accumulated to form a new science.

Freud's ordering is certainly not arbitrary. It is especially noteworthy that the analytic thesis is second to the depth-psychology thesis, not conversely, though the analytic thesis, as the opening quote from "Autobiographical Study" indicates, claims temporal priority. What that shows is that psychoanalysis, for Freud, was fundamentally a science of the unconscious and that the many posits that Freud adopted over the years to spell out that depth-psychology—e.g., his topographical and structural models, his *Eros-* and death-drives, and his employment of dynamic and economic language—were not dispensable. They were deemed to be part of a theoretical superstructure without which Freud could not do—a superstructure comparable to that of Newton's dynamical system. That the "laws" of the unconscious defied common understanding and that they contradicted the received notion of "unconscious" held by philosophers of his day were difficulties he had to surmount. Yet those difficulties, Freud believed, were not insuperable and they did not, he believed, challenge the scientific status of psychoanalysis. They were, for instance, no more insuperable than those challenges which Newton faced, when he posited that gravity was a force that regulated all bodily interaction in the universe without being able to explain how one body could "act" on another without being in contact with that other.

Freud's three theses in "Psychoanalysis" also neatly illustrate the development of psychoanalysis over time, roughly from *The Interpretation of Dreams* to the beginning of his mature metapsychological thoughts in *Beyond the Pleasure Principle* and his foray into group-psychology issues. After parting with Joseph Breuer, Freud could not begin serious clinical work until such time that he had developed sufficiently the depth-psychology notions of "unconscious," "repression," and his topographical model of the mind (*Cs.*, *Pcs.*, and *Ucs.*)—viz., given himself a proper or, at least, a provisionally suitable theoretical scaffolding for his clinical work. Those metempirical concepts, avowedly grounded in his analytical labors, developed over time and enabled him eventually to work his way out of the clinic and have, to his thinking, something significant to say apropos of larger social issues. He came to find that those notions, as well as his venture into analysis of social issues, required an elaboration of what came famously to be called his "metapsychology"—comprising topographical, economical, and dynamic "explanations" of psychical phenomena. Freud even ventured, in the 1910s, to write 12 metapsychological essays, yet the overall project was left unfinished and he ultimately abandoned the task, after publishing some of the proposed essays. Nonetheless, he came back to metapsychology afresh in

*Beyond the Pleasure Principle* in 1920 and *The Ego and the Id,* three years later, where he developed fully the inchoate ego-psychology of *Group Psychology and the Analysis of the Ego* (1921).

## From Individual to Group Psychology

Overall, Freud's return to larger "group" issues, often of global influence, likely began with *Totem and Taboo* in 1913, but it did not take root until around 1920. That shift occurred not only, among other things, because of a certain disaffection for and frustration with individual psychology over time,[4] but it occurred also because of a pressing need to link himself through psychoanalytic investigation to larger, less vexatious, and more substantial human issues—i.e., human unhappiness, the quick advance of technology, religiosity, morality, and war, *inter alia.*

As other writers have duly noted, one catalyst for the shift to group psychology was indeed the need to come to grips with the alienation from humanity Freud must have felt due to the senseless bloodshed of World War I, his own bout with cancer, the constant bickering among members of his psychoanalytic societies, and the deaths of loved ones and intimates like his daughter Sophie in 1920, her fragile son Heinele, Victor Tausk, and Anton von Freund. Freud, a consummate dreamer, was pressed by events to embrace willy-nilly the unrelenting, but bearable, harshness of reality.[5] The result was a personal, psychical, and moral maturation of the sort advocated by ancient Stoic philosophers, which allowed for the possibility of the development of $\Psi A_3$.

Another catalyst for the shift to group psychology, the focus of this undertaking, was simply his adoption of a more comprehensive notion of "psychoanalysis"—$\Psi A_3$—which did not merely comprise data of the clinic. That expanded conception was made possible by three Freudian purchases—Comtean progressivism, biological recapitulationism, and metapsychological explanation—and those purchases allowed Freud to link psychoanalysis with disciplines like history, philology, biology, and aesthetics. Those purchases also gave psychoanalysis, qua $\Psi A_3$, broad scope and considerable explanatory power—at least in Freud's own eyes.

Yet a question remains: What precisely is $\Psi A_3$? What are the accumulated "psychological data" of $\Psi A_3$ to which Freud refers? Are the procedural and methodological data from $\Psi A_1$ and $\Psi A_2$ part of those data? It is tempting to assert that these data are merely the mass of information from the case-study reports upon which Freud's psychoanalytic generalizations stand or fall. That, I maintain, is only part of the story. The psychological data of $\Psi A_3$ include not only case-study reports, but also Freud's observations of group normalcy and pathology, his adoption of auxiliary hypotheses (e.g., Comtean progressivism and biological recapitulationism), and his speculations on pre-historical human phylogenetic development that he takes to be factual, among other things. In moving outside of the clinic, psychoanalysis becomes a science with the conceptual tools to tackle some of the most ponderous human concerns.

## Structure of *Freud*

*Freud: From Individual Psychology to Group Psychology* concerns Freudian psychoanalysis as a full-fledged science, $\Psi A_3$, as it relates psychoanalytically to issues of individual psychology (*Individualpsychologie*) and group psychology (*Massenpsychologie*). It essays to answer questions such as these: "How effective did Freud perceive individual psychology to be?," "What is group psychology?," "To what extent did Freud think psychoanalytic investigation of group pathology could be curative of social ills?," "How seriously did Freud take metapychological explanation?," and "How important were auxiliary hypotheses, borrowed (often uncritically) from other disciplines, in the formation of group psychology?" In sketching out the development of individual psychology and group psychology, I argue that psychoanalysis for Freud was always essentially $\Psi A_1$—a procedure for investigating unconscious phenomena that allowed for explication and understanding of both individual and group issues.

Part I of *Freud* is about individual psychology. Chapter 1 traces out the development of Freud's thought on clinical therapy. Chapter 2 is a critical analysis of the various clinical methods Freud employed over the years. The third chapter covers specific issues of Freudian psychotherapy, such as transference, proper conditions for therapy, length of therapy, suitability of clients, and the end of therapy. The fourth chapter critically examines the merit of Freudian psychoanalysis as a remedy for individual pathology. Here I include Freud's own appraisal of individual therapy as well as psychoanalytic insights on morality and pedagogy as they apply to individuals.

Part II of *Freud* is about group psychology. Chapter 5 begins with the conditions influencing Freud's shift to group-psychology issues, turns to his metapsychology, and ends with his move to placing culture on the couch. Chapters 6 and 7 are a psychoanalytic examination of other disciplines—non-sciences and sciences alike. Finally, the final chapter is an analysis of the worth of Freudian psychoanalysis as a remedy for group pathology. Here dealing with larger human issues, like war and death, Freud qua philosopher is at his best.

Because of the comprehensive treatment of the development of Freud's thinking from individual psychology to group psychology—which represents not a shift in his thinking, but an applicative broadening of key, substratal concepts—the book will serve well as a primer for any course on Freud's thinking over his career. Readers, who might be unfamiliar with Freud, are given a comprehensive depiction as well as a critical analysis of the development of psychoanalysis in an easy-to-assimilate manner from Freud's early days in analytic therapy, beginning with his stays with Charcot and Bernheim in France, to his mature thinking, where he develops notions such as the death drive and the structural model (id, ego, and super-ego) to compensate for theoretical defects in his earlier thinking.

# Notes

1. Ernst Jones, *The Life and Works of Sigmund Freud,* Vol. I (New York: Basic Books, 1953), 379.

2. Paul Roazen, *Freud: Political and Social Thought* (New York: Alfred A. Knopf, 1968), 101–2.

3. E.g., see Freud, *Letters,* 389–90, and Maryse Choisy, *Sigmund Freud* (New York: Citadel Press, 1963), 84.

4. E.g., letters to colleague Wilhelm Fleiss: May 15, 1888, where Freud writes a letter to Fliess while a patient is under hypnosis, and March 15, 1898, where he admits to sleeping during afternoon sessions. Jeffrey Moussaieff Masson, *The Complete Letters of Sigmund Freud to Wilhelm Fliess: 1887–1904* (Cambridge: Harvard University Press, 1985). Also, Ferenczi in his diary quotes Freud, "neurotics are a rabble, good only to support us financially and to allow us to learn from their cases: psychoanalysis as therapy may be worthless." Sandor Ferenczi, *The Clincal Diary of Sandor Ferenczi,* ed. J. Dupont (Cambridge: Harvard University Press, 1988), 186. See Allan Frosch, "The Culture of Psychoanalysis and the Concept of Analyzability," *Psychoanalytic Psychology,* Vol. 23, No. 1, 44.

5. Writes R. J. Bocock: "Freud's analysis of groups, and of civilization as a whole, depends on the relations between these two sets of instinctual forces. One can say that his sociological theory depends, then, on the *a priori* initial postulates of two sets of instinctual forces, the sexual instincts and the death instincts. The first are life-affirming, the other are destructive of life." R. J. Bocock, "Freud and the Centrality of Instincts in Psychoanalytic Sociology," *The British Journal of Sociology*, Vol. 28, No. 4, 1977, 473–74.

# PART I
# PSYCHOANALYSIS AS INDIVIDUAL THERAPY

# Chapter 1
# Toward *Individualpsychologie*

"[T]he study of dreams is not only the best preparation for the study of neuroses, but dreams are themselves a neurotic symptom, which, moreover, offers us the priceless advantage of occurring in all healthy people." Sigmund Freud, *Interpretation of Dreams*

OVER THE COURSE OF YEARS OF CLINICAL OBSERVATIONS and daring, often extravagant speculation, psychoanalysis developed modestly from evolving approaches to individual therapy in the clinic ($\Psi A_2$) to a "science" in its own right ($\Psi A_3$) that enabled Freud to tackle global issues—such as human discontent, war, and the problem of uncritical technological advance—with awareness, intensity, and relevance.

This chapter traces out the development of $\Psi A_2$ over his lifetime—i.e., Freud's views of neurosis throughout his life, from his earliest speculations on hysteria in the mid-1880s to his mature thoughts beginning with *The Interpretation of Dreams* and developed fully in *The Ego and the Id* and later, relevant works.

## Hysteria and Hypnosis

In October 1885, under a traveling grant, Freud left for Paris to study for some six months under the celebrated neurologist Jean-Martin Charcot at the Salpêtrière asylum. At the time, Charcot was experimenting with hypnosis, thought by most to be something only charlatans would use, to treat hysteria. Freud was astonished by what he saw at the Salpêtrière. He learned under Charcot that hysteria was a genuine disorder that was conformable to laws,[1] that hysteria occurred in men as well as women, that hysteria seemed to be indifferent to anatomy, that hysterical symptoms were often brought about by trauma, and that a trained physician could use hypnosis to produce hysterical symptoms (1925, *S.E.,* XX: 13). Freud dubbed Charcot's view of hypnosis "somatic," as it was a physiologically altered condition of the nervous system brought about by external stimuli that impacted the body. The key was that a person had to be neuropathologically disposed. "[T]he mechanism of some . . . of the manifestations of hypnotism is based upon physiological changes—that is, upon displacements of

3

excitability in the nervous system, occurring without the participation of those parts of it which operate with consciousness." Hysteria, believed to be caused by trauma that would induce a hypnotic state at the time of the trauma, was found to be accessible by hypnosis, by which a therapist could use suggestions to counter the hysterical symptoms. Thus, hypnosis was a tool that allowed access to the physiological substructure of hysteria. It had no therapeutic use. Freud summed, "only neuropaths (especially hysterics) are hypnotizable" (1888, *S.E.,* I: 77-8).

Though greatly influenced by Charcot, Freud was also attracted to the rival thesis of Ambrose-August Liébeault and Hippolyte Bernheim at Nancy. Liébeault and Bernheim maintained simply that hypnosis was not a signal of a degenerative neurological state, but merely a matter of suggestion. "[A]ll the phenomena of hypnotism have the same origin: they arise, that is, from a suggestion, a conscious idea, which has been introduced into the brain of the hypnotized person by an external influence and has been accepted by him as though it had arisen spontaneously" (1888, *S.E.,* I: 77). Though thought to be a matter of suggestion, Liébeault and Bernheim used hypnosis qua suggestion to alleviate hysterical symptoms, which were themselves believed to be caused by a state of heightened suggestibility, similar to sleep. The two therapists developed a therapeutics based on suggestion.[2] They were not always successful with their method and, when successful, favorable results were not always long-lived.

Those two rival, but antipodal explanations—somatic-based versus psychic-based—would prove to be polar tugs that enticed and haunted Freud throughout his career. Though always convinced proper scientific explanation needed to be based on physiology, one of Freud's greatest contributions to science would be to show one could give scientifically legitimate explanations of human motivations and behavior without recourse to human physiology.

Freud tergiversated on the issue of hypnosis. Prior to seeing Bernheim in the summer of 1889, he was enamored of Charcot's view.[3] The visit to Nancy inclined him to hypnosis as suggestion, but the purchase was never complete. As late as 1921, he rejected hypnosis as suggestion in favor of the "naïf earlier one" (1921, *S.E.,* XVIII: 128, fn. 1). It seems that Freud wanted to believe that hypnosis was mere suggestion, but he could not quite divorce himself fully from the view that there was some physiological link between hypnosis and hysteria.

Freud learned abundantly from his trip to France—enough to pave the way for a science of the psyche. First, each of these rival schools examined the therapeutic benefits of hypnosis as a means of alleviating the symptoms of hysteria, when hypnosis was mostly in discredit. Thus, Freud saw firsthand that scientific advance often came through rejecting received views and having the daring to travel an unconventional, even barmy path—a sentiment reflected succinctly years later in a letter to friend and confidant Wilhelm Fleiss (June 30, 1896), himself a most unconventional physician: "You have taught me that a bit of truth lurks behind every popular lunacy."[4] Second, the almost theatrical impressions of these two rival schools must have been lasting on the young neuroscientist. They bolstered the notion, already implanted in him by Brentano,[5] that physical effects could be psychologically caused. Freud writes, as he reflects on the effect of his trip to France:

> With the idea of perfecting my hypnotic technique, I made a journey to Nancy in the summer of 1889 and spent several weeks there. I witnessed the moving spectacle of old Liébeault working among the poor women and children of the laboring classes. I was a spectator of Bernheim's astonishing experiments upon his hospital patients, and I received the profoundest impression of the possibility that there could be powerful mental processes which nevertheless remained hidden from the consciousness of men (1925, *S.E.*, XX: 17).

## Cathartic Theory

### "Chimney Sweeping"

The trip to France made a permanent impression on Freud and he began to work on hysteria. A critical step toward the development of his own views on the topic was his collaboration with physician and older friend Josef Breuer.

In 1880, Breuer took on, mostly as a favor to her family, a young, female patient, whom they would call "Anna O." Anna suffered from a variety of hysterical symptoms and Breuer found, quite by accident, an extraordinary, new method of cure. Freud pressed Breuer for details. What he found astonished him and would become the basis of psychoanalysis. Freud, then, convinced his reticent friend to collaborate on and publish their findings. The result was the celebrated *Studies on Hysteria*—the beginning of psychoanalysis.[6]

Freud begins the book by mentioning that certain pathological phenomena have traumatic, precipitating events that are psychical. In cases of traumatic neuroses, he adds, a patient cannot see the causal link, as "the operative cause of the illness is not the trifling physical injury but the affect of fright—the psychical trauma" (1895, *S.E.,* II: 5-6). As an example of how such a pathological phenomenon can be removed, Freud offers the analogy of a foreign body, perhaps a virus:

> [T]he causal relation between the determining psychical trauma and the hysterical phenomenon is not of a kind implying that the trauma merely acts like an *agent provocateur* in releasing the symptom, which thereafter leads an independent existence. We must presume rather that the psychical trauma—or more precisely the memory of the trauma—acts like foreign body which long after its entry must continue to be regarded as an agent that is still at work. . . .[7]
>
> For we found, to our great surprise at first, that *each individual hysterical symptom immediately and permanently disappeared when we had succeeded in bringing clearly to light the memory of the event by which it was provoked and in arousing its accompanying affect, and when the patient had described that event in the greatest possible detail and had put the affect into words* (1895, *S.E.,* II: 6).

The key here, Freud notes, is that wakening the memory of the precipitating event with complete clarity is sufficient for removal of the symptom, so long as the accompanying affect is aroused along with it. How is that possible? From his studies in France he learned two things: that forgotten memories were not lost, but capable of retrieval, and that there was a force at work that kept them from consciousness. Freud famously sums: *"[H]ysterics suffer mainly from reminiscences"*[8] (1895, *S.E.,* II: 7).

Though the book illustrates the new cathartic method with five case-studies—four by Freud and one by Breuer—the most famous case-study is Breuer's Anna O. Anna's hysteria started when she began to dote on her moribund father. She suffered from a multiplicity of symptoms through four phases of illness: a latent incubation (about six months, beginning July 1880), manifest illness (peculiar psychosis, convergent squinting, severe visual disturbances, paralyzing contractures, complete or partial paralysis of certain parts of body, and reduced muscular contracture of right extremities; about four months), a period of somnambulism (about eight months), and a gradual winding down of mental states and symptoms (in June 1882) (1895, *S.E.,* II: 21-2). What was most perplexing, Breuer discovered, was that Anna's symptoms began to disappear when she, under hypnosis, told stories to Breuer. Success in being able to recount the hallucinations of the day through hypnosis enabled her to wake up lucid, calm, and serene so that she set herself to her work in an efficient manner the next day. Breuer adds, "If for any reason she was unable to tell me the story during her evening hypnosis, she failed to calm down afterwards, and on the following day she had to tell me *two* stories in order for this to happen." That suggested a mounting of inner tension of some sort and, with it, an increase of resistance. Anna herself dubbed this method the "talking cure" and, somewhat humorously, "chimney sweeping"[9] (1895, *S.E.,* II: 29-30).

Of how such "etiological" successes occurred, Breuer writes:

> These findings—that in the case of this patient the hysterical phenomena disappeared as soon as the event which had given rise to them was reproduced in her hypnosis—made it possible to arrive at a therapeutic technical procedure which left nothing to be desired in its logical consistency and systematic application. Each individual symptom in this complicated case was taken separately in hand; all the occasions on which it had appeared were described in reverse order, starting before the time when the patient became bed-ridden and going back to the event which had led to its first appearance. When this had been described the symptom was permanently removed (1895, *S.E.,* II: 35).

Breuer's cathartic method, completely consistent and systematically implemented, can be summed as follows:

- Through hypnosis, the first instant of reproduction of an event causing a symptom is sufficient for removal of that symptom.
- Each symptom is to be treated independently of all others.

- Treatment of a symptom consists of "narrating" each occurrence of a symptom in reverse order—from latest appearance to earliest appearance.
- Efficient use of the method results in permanent removal of the symptom.

The method is "cathartic" because some sort of dammed-up emotional energy, unable to find discharge, is converted into physical symptoms—thereby making hysterical symptoms conversions of dammed-up affect. Therapy consists in talking away the symptoms to discharge the emotional energy—the result of, perhaps, some early traumatic event—and the overall effect is curative.

> The psychotherapeutic procedure . . . *brings to an end the operative force of the idea which was not abreacted in the first instance, by allowing its strangulated affect to find a way out through speech; and it subjects it to associative correction by introducing it into normal consciousness (under light hypnosis) or by removing it through the physician's suggestion, as it is done in somnambulism accompanied by amnesia* (1895, *S.E.,* II: 17).

Thus, Freud's first model of hysteria can be summed as follows:

> **Cathartic Theory:** Hysterical symptoms are conversions of dammed-up affect, mnemonically linked with pathogenic events.

### Three Forms of Mnemonic Elements

Freud went beyond giving a method for treating hysteria in *Studies on Hysteria;* he also proffered a dynamical explanation and a primitive, inchoate topography. He noted that mnemonic elements of pathogenic events have three forms— linear-chronological, concentric-pathogenic, and branching-dynamic—and expatiated on each.[10]

First, mnemonic elements display a linear, chronological arrangement.

> These files form a quite general feature of every analysis and their contents always emerge in a chronological order which is as infallibly trustworthy as the succession of days of the week or names of the month in a mentally normal person. They make the work of analysis more difficult by the peculiarity that, in reproducing the memories, they reverse the order in which these originated. The freshest and newest experience in the file appears first, as an outer cover, and last of all comes the experience with which the series in fact began (1895, *S.E.,* II: 288).

Second, mnemonic elements are stratified concentrically, around the pathogenic nucleus, in a manner that is neatly proportional to the resistances an analyst faces.

> The contents of each particular stratum are characterized by an equal degree of resistance, and that degree increases in proportion as the strata are neared to the nucleus. Thus there are zones within which there is an equal degree of modification of consciousness, and the different themes extend across these zones.

The most peripheral strata contain the memories (or files), which, belonging to different themes, are easily remembered and have always been clearly conscious. The deeper we go the more difficult it becomes for the emerging memories to be recognized, till near the nucleus we come upon memories which the patient disavows even in reproducing them (1895, *S.E.,* II: 289).

Finally, mnemonic elements form a logical and dynamic branching arrangement of converging lines "according to thought-content."

This arrangement has a dynamic character . . . the course of the logical chain would have to be indicated by a broken line which would pass along the most roundabout paths from the surface to the deepest layers and back, and yet would in general advance from the periphery to the central nucleus, touching at every intermediate halting-place—a line resembling the zig-zag line in the solution of Knight's Move problem, which cuts across the squares in the diagram of the chess-board. . . . The logical chain corresponds not only to a zig-zag, twisted line, but rather to a ramifying system of lines and more particularly to a converging one. It contains nodal points at which two or more threads meet and thereafter proceed as one; and as a rule several threads which run independently, or which are connected at various points by side-paths, debouch into the nucleus. To put this in other words, it is very remarkable how often a symptom is determined in several ways, is "overdetermined" (1895, *S.E.,* II: 289-90).

The linear, concentric, and branching patterns used by Freud neatly illustrate some of the difficulties in applying the cathartic method as a treatment for hysteria—e.g., complexity of symptom-formation, overrepresentation in the symptom, and resistance.

Perhaps the largest difficulty was that the cathartic method was merely symptomatic, not causal.[11] As a symptomatic method, it "does not influence the basic causes of hysteria and is therefore unable to prevent new symptoms developing in the place of those that have been removed" (1895, *S.E.,* II: 262-4). That limitation would eventually lead Freud to a more nuanced, deeper view of pathogenic explanation, which would ultimately entail a fuller and historically richer account of hysteria, such that a trained therapist would have access to substratal causes.

The need for a more nuanced view was Freud's belief, based on his own clinical observations, that the pathogens of hysteria were essentially sexual. Here he parted company with Breuer, who was all along, at best, a disobliged participant in their collaborative efforts.[12] In short, while Breuer, who spoke only of Anna O.'s underdeveloped sexuality in his case-study (1895, *S.E.,* II: 21), did not see sexuality as a factor in Anna's hysteria,[13] Freud saw a sexual pathogen in each of the four cases he analyzed in the *Studies on Hysteria* and presumed different sexual factors to result in different sorts of neurosis. "In the first place I was obliged to recognize that, in so far as one can speak of determining causes which lead to the *acquisition* of neuroses, their aetiology is to be looked for in *sexual* factors. There followed the discovery that different sexual factors, in the most general sense, produce different pictures of neurotic disorders" (1895, *S.E.,* II: 257).

## Hysteria and Seduction

Given Freud's observation of a connection between sexuality and neuroses, the next step for Freud was to posit that the link between pathogen and symptom was essentially sexual and physical. As early as November 27, 1893, he writes to Wilhelm Fleiss: "Altogether I have hit upon the idea to tie anxiety not to a psychic but rather to a *physical* consequence of sexual abuse. I was led to this by a wonderfully pure case of anxiety neurosis following *coitus interruptus* in a totally placid and totally frigid woman. Otherwise it does not make any sense."[14]

Three years later, Freud formally endorses a sexual etiology through an early childhood seduction in "Aetiology of Hysteria" in 1896. Childhood seduction, often in the form of molestation by a parent or close relative, is a *conditio sine qua non* for neurosis and that marks a pronounced therapeutic change from Freud's days with Breuer. With Breuer, Freud was symptom-oriented—i.e., therapy continued until symptoms ceased. Experience showed, however, that symptoms often returned and the method was not curative. By the time of "Aetiology of Hysteria," therapy became etiological and prophylactic: It aimed at getting at the underlying causes of the sexual symptoms, thereby offering promise of complete cure, and even offered suggestions for prevention. He writes, "The symptoms of hysteria (apart from the stigmata) are determined by certain experiences of the patient's which have operated in a traumatic fashion and which are being reproduced in his psychical life in the form of mnemonic symbols" (1896, *S.E.,* II: 192-3).

Freud then lists two operative principles for proper etiological recapitulation, which I label the principles of idoneity and force (1896, *S.E.,* II: 194).

- **Principle of Idoneity:** A suspected pathogen must be relevantly idoneous as a causal determinant of a hysterical symptom.
- **Principle of Force:** A suspected pathogen must have sufficient traumatic force to bring about a hysterical symptom.

Given the vagueness of these two conditions, Freud offers the following test:

If the memory which we have uncovered does not answer our expectations (i.e., the two principles), it may be that we ought to pursue the same path a little further; perhaps behind the first traumatic scene there may be concealed the memory of a second, which satisfies our requirements better and whose reproduction has a greater therapeutic effect; so that the scene that was first discovered only has the significance of a connecting link in the chain of association. And perhaps this situation may repeat itself; inoperative scenes may be interpolated more than once, as necessary transitions in the process of reproduction, until we finally make our way from the hysterical symptom to the scene which is really operative traumatically and which is satisfactory in every respect, both therapeutically and analytically (1986, *S.E.,* II: 195).

Freud here develops a causal scheme and adds the following principles to idoneity and force. I use his words.

- **Mnemonic Principle:** "We have learned that *no hysterical symptom can arise from a real experience alone, but that in every case the memory of earlier experiences awakened in association to it plays a part in causing the symptom*" (1896, *S.E.,* II: 197) and "*hysterical symptoms can only arise with the co-operation of memories*" (1896, *S.E.,* II: 202).
- **Principle of Sexual Etiology:** "Whatever case and whatever symptom we take as our point of departure, *in the end we infallibly come to the field of sexual experience*" (1896, *S.E.,* II: 199).
- **Principle of Unconscious Etiology:** "[T]he matter is not merely one of the existence of the sexual experiences, but that a psychological precondition enters in as well. The scenes must be present as *unconscious memories*; only so long as, and in so far as, they are unconscious are they able to create and maintain hysterical symptoms. . . . *[H]ysterical symptoms are derivatives of memories which are operating unconsciously* (1896, *S.E.,* II: 211-2).
- **Principle of Childhood Etiology:** "Our view then is that infantile sexual experiences are the fundamental precondition for hysteria, are, as it were, the disposition for it and that it is they which create the hysterical symptoms, but that they do not do so immediately, but remain without effect to begin with and only exercise a pathogenic action later, when they have been aroused after puberty in the form of unconscious memories. . ." (1896, *S.E.,* II: 212).
- **Principle of Overdetermination:** "[T]he idea which is selected for the production of a symptom is one which has been called up by a combination of several factors and which has been aroused from various directions simultaneously. . . . [That is], *hysterical symptoms are overdetermined*" (1896, *S.E.,* II: 216).

Of the various principles, the principles of childhood aetiology and sexual aetiology—the chief components of the seduction theory—were the most difficult to justify. Freud anticipated and got resistance and rebuff, which he attempted to overcome through four main arguments. First, there is uniformity in the verbal reports of his patients which is necessary, if there is regularity to hysteria (i.e., if it is conformable to psychical laws) and if the preconditions of such experiences are the same. Second, patients not only often describe horrifying early sexual events as harmless—a sure sign that they misconstrue their significance—but they also mention details of their experiences without grasping their significance. Third, the infantile sexual scenes relate to the content of the whole "exactly like" a child's picture-puzzle. He states, "after many attempts, we become absolutely certain in the end which piece belongs in the empty gap; for only that one piece fills out the picture and at the same time allows its irregular edges to be fitted into the edges of the other pieces in such a manner as to leave no free space and to entail no overlapping"[15] (1896, *S.E.,* II: 205). Finally, he gasconades of his patience, perseverance, and inductive successes as a clinical therapist:

[T]he singling out of the sexual factor in the aetiology of hysteria springs at least from no preconceived opinion on my part. The two investigators as whose pupil I began my studies of hysteria, Charcot and Breuer, were far from having any such presupposition; in fact they had a personal disinclination to it which I originally shared. Only the most laborious and detailed investigations have converted me, and that slowly enough, to the view I hold to-day. If you submit my assertion that the aetiology of hysteria lies in sexual life to the strictest examination, you will find that it is supported by the fact that in some eighteen cases of hysteria [six men and twelve women] I have been able to discover this connection in every single symptom, and, where the circumstances allowed, to confirm it by therapeutic success (1896, *S.E.,* II: 199, see also 207-8).

Freud sums his analytic attitude at this point in his career thus, "At bottom of every case of hysteria there are *one or more occurrences of premature sexual experience,* occurrences which belong to the earliest years of childhood but which can be reproduced through the work of psycho-analysis in spite of the intervening decade" (1896, *S.E.,* II: 203). He arrives at what is commonly called his "Seduction Theory."

**Seduction Theory:** Early childhood seduction (generally by a close relative) is necessary causal condition for neurosis.

# Neurosis and Wish-Fulfillment

## Abandonment of Seduction

In *Three Essays on a Theory of Sexuality,* Freud tells his readers that he has formally abandoned his seduction model on account of examining case-studies that others have compiled (1905, *S.E.,* VII: 140 and 190-1). That was some eight years after Freud had this to say about the seduction model in a now-famous letter of September 21, 1897, to friend Wilhelm Fleiss.

The continual disappointment in my efforts to bring a single analysis to a real conclusion; the running away of people who for a period of time had been most gripped [by analysis]; the absence of the complete successes on which I had counted; the possibility of explaining to myself the partial successes in other ways, in the usual fashion—this was the first group. Then the surprise that in all cases, the father, not excluding my own, had to be accused of being perverse—the realization of the unexpected frequency of hysteria, with precisely the same conditions prevailing in each, whereas surely such widespread perversions against children are not very probable. The [incidence] of perversion would have to be immeasurably more frequent than the [resulting] hysteria because the illness, after all, occurs only where there has been an accumulation of events and there is a contributory factor that weakens the defense. Then, third, the certain insight that there are no indications of reality in the unconscious, so that one cannot distinguish between truth and fiction that has been cathected with affect. (Accordingly, there would remain the solution that the sexual fantasy invariably seizes upon the theme of the parents.) Fourth, the consideration that in the most deep-reaching psychosis the unconscious memory does not break through, so that the secret of childhood experiences is not disclosed even in the most confused delirium. If one thus sees that the unconscious never overcomes the resistance of the conscious, the expectation that in treatment the opposite is bound to happen, to the point where the unconscious is completely tamed by the conscious, also diminishes.[16]

Though Freud says that there are four main reasons, there are several given:

- the incompleteness of every case of analysis,
- patients, under the grip of analysis, quitting treatment,
- seemingly more plausible explanations other than actual seduction (e.g., Freud's reason three: the unconscious cannot tell truth from untruth),
- implication of the father (Freud's own too?) as seducer in all cases,
- given the prevalence of hysteria, the much greater prevalence of seduction, and
- failure of unconscious memories to break through conscious barriers, even in cases of deepest psychosis.

Critics have varied takes on Freud's letter and the time Freud took before formally endorsing his abandonment. Jeffrey Masson, on the one extreme, argues that abandonment occurs not because of "theoretical or clinical reasons but because of a personal failure of moral courage" on Freud's part—a sort of caving into the pressures of the scientific community in an effort to gain acceptance.[17] Patricia Kitcher says more modestly that abandonment of seduction did not occur at the time of Freud's letter to Fleiss. The letter signaled doubts, not a definite change of mind. Abandonment occurred slowly over the years, due to accumulated evidence against it.[18] Joel Kupfersmid maintains, earlier than and consistent with Kitcher, that the abandonment of the seduction hypothesis and slow acceptance of the Oedipus complex were due to Freud's intrapsychic conflict. By supplanting seduction with fantasy, Freud was able to exonerate his father from perverse behavior, since the reports of seduction were wish-based, as well as himself for perverse wishes, since such wishes were universal.[19] Following Kitcher, personal communication of abandonment of a position to an intimate friend need not be taken as a decided abandonment of that position. Freud was expressing doubts, though expressing them firmly. Once Freud abandoned seduction as a needed condition for neurosis, the only other plausible avenue to pursue was that the "seductions" related to him by patients must often, though not always, be wish-fantasies based on real, childhood events.[20] He writes in a later letter to Fleiss (January 13, 1899): "What is rising out of the chaos this time is the connection to the psychology contained in the *Studies on Hysteria*—the relation to conflict, to life: clinical psychology, as I should like to call it. *Puberty is becoming ever more central; fantasy as the key holds fast.*"[21] The key insight for Freud was recognition that childhood "memories" are always reconstructions of some sort—what Freud would dub "screen memories."

Our childhood memories show us our earliest years not as they were but as they appeared at the later periods when the memories were aroused. In these periods of arousal, the childhood memories did not, as people are accustomed to say, *emerge*; they were *formed* at that time. And a number of motives, with no concern for historical accuracy, had a part in forming them, as well as in the selection of the memories themselves (1899: *S.E.,* III: 322).

## Interpretation of Dreams

Acknowledgement of screen memories was the *coup de main* that led to Freud's wish-fulfillment theory of dreams in his monograph *The Interpretation of Dreams*. In this work, which contains the germ of Freud's subsequent thought, he boasts that "dreams really have a meaning and that a scientific procedure for interpreting them is possible"[22] (1900, *S.E.,* IV: 100). A dream, as it is dreamt, is the manifest content, while its meaning is the underlying, unconscious wish that generates it or its latent content. Thus, the latent content is the underlying unconscious wish that is responsible for generating the dream, while the manifest content is the fulfillment of that wish.

- **Generational Thesis:** Every dream is generated by an unconscious, childhood (usually sexual) wish.
- **Fulfillment Thesis:** Every dream is the fulfillment of an unconscious, childhood (usually sexual) wish.

The process, usually heavily censored, by which latent dream becomes manifest dream Freud calls "dream work"—comprising the defense-mechanisms of condensation, considerations of representation, displacement, and secondary revision—which allows for economy of expression through a mitigated expression of unconscious fantasies.[23] Interpretation of dreams is thus a matter of retracing the process of dream work in reverse order to get at the unconscious tensions that generate them. Like slips of tongue and jokes, disguised manifest dreams allow people, while asleep, some measure of release of unconscious tension. Thus, the process of dreaming is, in part, a cathartic process that allows the wish generating it to find fulfillment in fantasy. Freud summarizes: *"[A] dream is a (disguised) fulfillment of a (suppressed or repressed) wish"* (1900, *S.E.,* IV: 160).

The main method for interpreting dreams, discussed fully in chapter 2, Freud dubs "free association." He elaborates: "My patients were pledged to communicate to me every idea or thought that occurred to them in connection with some particular subject; amongst other things they told me their dreams and so taught me that a dream can be inserted into the psychical chain that has to be traced backwards in the memory from a pathological idea" (1900, *S.E.,* IV: 100-1). For dreams, free association can proceed by asking a dreamer to associate from elements in the dream as they happened in the dream, from any element in the middle of the dream, or from events of the previous day that are related to the dream. For patients familiar with the process of free association, an analyst may leave it to the patient to decide where to begin (1923, *S.E.,* XIX: 109).

Since dreams can be "inserted into the psychical chain" linked to pathological ideas, Freud maintains that dreams are manifestations of everyday neuroses.

> We will demonstrate the sense of dreams by way of preparing for the neuroses. This reversal is justified since the study of dreams is not only the best preparation for the study of neuroses, but dreams are themselves a neurotic symptom, which, moreover, offers us the priceless advantage of occurring in all healthy people. Indeed, supposing all human begin were healthy, so long as they dreamt we could arrive from their dream at almost all the discoveries which the investigation of neuroses has led to (1915, *S.E.,* XV: 83).

Freud's theory of dreams would become the keystone of his psychoanalytical theory—the "royal road to . . . knowledge of the unconscious activities of the mind" (1900, *S.E.,* V: 608), though the massive book, in which it was housed, did not bring him the instant éclat for which he wished.

With *The Interpretation of Dreams,* Freud proposes his first model of the mind—the "topographical model," comprising the systems Conscious (*Cs.*) or that of which one is immediately aware, Preconscious (*Pcs.*) or that which is readily accessible to *Cs.,* and Unconscious (*Ucs.*) or that which is directly inaccessible to *Cs.* The latent dream, housed in *Ucs.,* slips into *Cs.,* through a censoring agency between systems *Ucs.* and *Pcs.,* and finds expression in the manifest dreams, which allows for some release of unconscious tension.

With the wish-fulfillment function of dreams, Freud has moved beyond early childhood seduction as a necessary condition for neurosis. Believing now that no recollections from childhood are without the taint of fantasy, Freud is forced to the conclusion that early childhood is sexually vigorous—i.e., children, like adults, have pronounced sexual wishes and intense sexual feelings and they act on them. Sexuality is no longer adult-exclusive. By abandoning childhood seduction and endorsing wish-fulfillment, Freud is also now able to modify his thoughts on neurosis. The wish-fulfillment thesis would become the keystone of psychoanalysis.

**Wish-Fulfillment Theory of Neurosis:** Repressed childhood wishes (of a sexual nature) give rise to neurosis.

## Neurosis and Sexuality

### Freud and Fleiss

One finds the roots of Freud's seduction theory in certain of his letters to Wilhelm Fleiss,[24] a younger friend whose unconventional views of the human condition had a marked influence on Freud's developing thoughts on psychoanalysis. The two doctors were introduced to each other in a consultation with one of

Breuer's patients in Vienna in 1887. The impression Fleiss left on Freud was so striking that the latter wrote Fleiss thereafter in an effort to begin a correspondence. The two would correspond affectionately for well over a decade—what might truly be called the formative years of psychoanalysis—until they split abruptly in 1902.

Fleiss's views on human beings were outré—perhaps even absurdly so. He believed in human bisexuality and that each male had a 23-day sexual cycle to correspond with females' menstrual cycle.[25] He also believed that the nose was the dominant sexual organ and that a certain type of neurosis was determined by the mucous membrane of the nose and treatable by operations on it. Freud took on board certain of Fleiss's ideas, especially bisexuality. For instance, on August 1, 1899, Freud writes: "The farther the work of the past year recedes, the more satisfied I become. But bisexuality! You are certainly right about it. I am accustoming myself to regarding every sexual act as a process in which four individuals are involved."[26] The correspondence with Fleiss helped Freud to develop his views on infantile sexuality and to ground psychoanalysis in a sexual etiology. It is likely correct to say that the influence of Fleiss was in the main very positive, in spite of Fleiss's eccentricities and his own, now widely known failures as a physician.[27]

There were other important progenitors for Freud's sexual etiology.

First, I mention two early scenes that, Freud himself notes, strongly impressed him. In Paris, he witnessed a conversation between Charcot and Brouardel, a professor of Forensic Medicine in Paris, where Charcot iterated that the hysterical symptoms of a particular woman were genitally linked. "*Mais, dans des cas pareils c'est toujours la chose génitale, toujours—toujours—toujours.*" While still a medical student at Vienna, Freud had a conversation with Richard Chrobak, a Professor of Gynecology at Vienna, concerning a hysterical woman, who was still a virgin, though married eighteen years. Chrobak told Freud that the sole prescription was: "*R: Penis normalis dosim repetatur.*"

Second, there were key historical figures that influenced Freud's thought. Charles Darwin's *Descent of Man and Selection in Relation to Sex* certainly affected Freud as it did many others.[28] So too did J. G. Frazer's speculations on the sexual behavior of primal human hordes.[29] In addition, Richard Krafft-Ebing, a senior colleague of Freud, studied sexuality from an anthropological perspective and published his observations—many of which were similar to those published by Freud later—in his great and massively influential work *Psychopathia Sexualis*. Havelock Ellis followed in Krafft-Ebbing's footsteps. Those persons Freud read and many others, whom Freud did not formally acknowledge.[30] Schopenhauer, Nietzsche, Rousseau, and Feuerbach philosophically paved the way for a sexual etiology by helping to weaken the link, in published works, between human nature and rationality.

## "Three Essays on Sexuality"

As we have seen, Freud's sexual etiology was grounded in his early clinical observation of eighteen cases of observed sexual etiologies and eighteen cases of avowed successes. After abandoning his seduction theory, infantile sexuality came to the fore and the large number of reported sex-abuse cases now was taken principally as youthful wish-fantasies of patients. In his case-study *Dora* in 1905, he writes:

> According to a rule which I had found confirmed over and over again by experience, though I had not yet ventured to erect it into a general principle, a symptom signifies the representation—the realization—of a phantasy with a sexual content, that is to say, it signifies a sexual situation. It would be better to say that at least one of the meanings of a symptom is the representation of a sexual phantasy, but that no such limitation is imposed upon the content of its other meanings (1905, *S.E.,* VII: 46-7).

Sexual scenes in patients' dreams reinforced sexual wish-fantasy. Thus, it was natural for Freud to follow his work on dreams with a work on sexuality that focused on infantile sexuality.

That work was *Three Essays on the Theory of Sexuality* (1905-1925), considered by many to be his *magnum opus* next to *Interpretation of Dreams.*[31] The work began humbly—an opuscule of some 80 pages. By the sixth edition, published in 1925, the humble booklet was expanded to some 120 pages.

The work is broken into three parts—sexual aberrations, infantile sexuality, and transformations of puberty. Freud begins with sexual aberrations such as inversion (homosexuality) and bisexuality. Inversion, he states, is neither a degenerative human condition nor is it purely, if at all, innate.[32] Following Kraft-Ebbing, he adds that every person has masculine and feminine brain centers that are under the guidance of the sex-gland at puberty. Prior to puberty, individuals are entirely at the mercy of a sexual drive—defining "instinct" (*Trieb,* better translated as "drive") provisionally here as "a measure of the demand made upon the mind for work"—independent of the sex-gland. He concludes that abnormal cases show that sexual drive and sexual object are merely contingently "soldered together" and that "the sexual instinct is in the first instance independent of its object" and not due to its object's inherent attractions (1905, *S.E.,* VII: 136-48). True deviations, perversions, are activities that go beyond the sexual regions of the body—genitals, mouth, and anus—and linger over improper, substitutive regions. Extreme forms are sadism, a biological urge to overcome a sexual object other than by wooing, and masochism, a condition that seems to be nothing other than sadism turned back on oneself. These tend to confirm bisexuality—the presence of maleness (i.e., activity) in persons as well as femaleness (i.e., passivity) (1905, *S.E.,* VII: 149-60). From such observations, Freud concludes that resistance is at play to restrain the sexual drive and that the sexual drive itself is not simple, but complex (1905, *S.E.,* VII: 162).

The final two sections, "Infantile Sexuality" and "Transformations of Puberty," I examine together, since together they comprise Freud's stages of sexuality.

Freud begins "Infantile Sexuality" by mentioning that the view that sexuality begins with puberty is wrong. Memories of the formative years of childhood lag behind other mental activities, though the impressions of those early events have "left the deepest traces on our minds and have had a determining effect upon the whole of our later development" (1905, *S.E.,* VII: 259-60). Development involves sexual diphasism as well as the Oedipus complex[33]—a critical point in the psychosexual stages of sexual development. I begin with the pregenital, autoerotic phase—comprising the oral, anal, and phallic stages.

*Oral (Cannibalistic) Stage (roughly, b. to 1½ years).* Suckling at a mother's breast and deriving needed nourishment are pleasurable for an infant and, thus, sexual. Here the link between sexuality and self-preservation is obvious. Over time, the lips become an erotogenic zone through taking in warm milk and sucking itself becomes a substitutive source of erotic satisfaction through association. "The need for repeating the sexual satisfaction now becomes detached from the need for taking nourishment—a separation which becomes inevitable when the teeth appear and food is no longer taken in only by sucking, but is also chewed up" (1905, *S.E.,* VII: 181-2).

*Anal (Sadistic) Stage (roughly, 1½ to 3 years).* At this stage, there develop a tension between active and passive states—"the opposition between two currents . . . that runs through all sexual life." Activity is the need for mastery through somatic musculature; passivity is the need for mastery through the erotogenic mucous membrane of the anus. Erotogenic stimulation here consists of use of violent muscular contractions to hold back stool to produce painful and pleasurable sensations—i.e., ambivalence (1905, *S.E.,* VII: 185-7). Here the child learns control of pleasure and pain through control of anal tension.

*Phallic (Oedipal) Stage (roughly, 3 to 5-6 years).* As the boy's first object is his mother's breast, the mother, by caring for her child's body, becomes his first seducer. However long the child is weaned, it is too little and too short. He sees himself as his mother's lover, the rival of his father, and eventually shows his organ to her. As an undersized rival—since his father has a larger member—he envies and hates his father.[34]

Shortly the mother becomes aware of the rivalry and forbids the boy's handling of his organ. The boy is threatened with castration. The threat causes him extraordinary anxiety; it is the most severe trauma of his life.

*Latency (5-6 years to puberty).* The latency phase, a period of dormant sexuality, is caused by the anxiety of the prior stage. The threat of castration changes the boy's relations with both parents. To preserve his organ, he renounces his mother and his own masculinity and becomes passive apropos of his father. Threat of castration, in effect, feminizes the boy. He gives up masturbation, fantasies more about his mother, and enters into a period of latency. He identifies with his father through sublimation and takes on his father's moral scheme as his own. That results in the formation of the boy's sense of conscience (later, "super-ego") and the repression of his lost love—more precisely, the smashing of his former lust for his mother. As Freud writes, "One of the clearest indications that a child will later become neurotic is to be seen in an insatiable demand for his parents' affection"—a demand fueled by an excess of parental affection (1905, *S.E.,* VII: 194-7, 223).

*Genital Stage (puberty-adulthood).* The second sexual phase is the hetero-erotic phase—the focus of "Transformations of Puberty," the final section of Freud's *Three Essays on Sexuality.* Proper genital mastery comes in proper substitutive satisfaction—i.e., sublimation. Writes Freud:

> A good portion of the symptomatology of the neuroses which I have traced to disturbances of the sexual processes, is expressed in disturbances of other, non-sexual, somatic functions; and this circumstance, which has hitherto been unin-telligible, becomes less puzzling if it is only the counterpart of the influences which bring about the production of sexual excitation (1905, *S.E.,* VII: 206).

Here we arrive at Freud's libido theory—a 1915 addition to the third part of the book. "Libido" he defines as "a quantitatively variable force which could serve as a measure of processes and transformations occurring in the field of sexual excitation." It is to be distinguished from the energy that underlies other forms of psychical activity, though libido is not derived from the sexual parts of the body only. "Ego-libido" he calls the mental representation of that quantity of libido, whose production, increase or diminution, and distribution or displace-ment enables the psychotherapist to explain psycho-sexual phenomena. Ego-libido is, thus, the "great reservoir" from which object-attachments are formed. "The narcissistic libidinal cathexis of the ego is the original state of things, rea-lized in earliest childhood, and is merely covered by the later extrusions of libi-do, but in essentials persists behind them. When one develops object-attachments, ego-libido is cathected to objects—i.e., it becomes object-libido" (1905, *S.E.,* VII: 217-8). The motivation for libido theory here is likely Darwi-nian: Animal behavior betrays fundamentally self-preservative and erotic beha-viors and humans are animals.

We can sum Freud's key points in his *Three Essays on Sexuality* for his de-veloping thoughts on neurosis.

- Sexual development begins in infancy and is diphasic: a pregenital phase (oral, anal, phallic stages), and a genital phase (genital stage).
- The aim of infantile sexuality is to stimulate erotogenic zones by replacing unpleasure of tension with the pleasure of release of tension.
- The earliest years are marked by amnesia and autoeroticism, though those years are chief determinants of later behavior.
- Neuroses are disturbances of early sexual life.
- Failure to traverse the stages of psycho-sexual development in a managea-ble fashion—failure especially to moderate a child's erotic affection for par-ents—increases the likelihood of psycho-sexual disturbances and later neurosis.
- Sexual aberrations (e.g., homo- and bisexuality) show that object choice and sexual drive are, at the beginning of sexual life, independent of each other and determinable principally by the years of childhood experience.
- Bisexuality corresponds to active, sadistic components and passive, maso-chistic components that may be biologically rooted.
- Sexual perversion is finding satisfaction outside of bodily erotogenic

zones.

- Perversion shows that the sexual drive struggles against the resistance of sexual conventions and that the sexual drive may be complex, not simple.

We may summarize the contribution of his *Three Essays on Sexuality* for his theory of neurosis as follows:

**Neurosis as Sexual Disturbance:** Neuroses occurs through disturbances in the normal development of early sexual life.

# Neurosis and the Structural Model

## Problems with Topographical Model

Over the years, difficulties with his topographical model became apparent. I mention two: the problem of consciousness as a differentiator of systems and the problem of censorship in dreams.[35]

First, in his 1915 paper "The Unconscious," Freud says that consciousness, as the only part of the psyche to which we have direct access, "is in no way suited to serve as a criterion for the differentiation of systems" (1915, *S.E.,* XIV: 192). By that, he means it is too gauzy, too unstable, to be the prominent psychical system that allows for some sense of psychical unity.

Second, in *The Interpretation of Dreams*, Freud maintains that censorship in dreams is mostly at the hands of *Pcs.* (1900, *S.E.,* IV: 567-8, 617). That entails that one can readily be aware of one's own resistance, but not of the content of that resistance. Clinical experience, for Freud, suggests that that is false. In most cases of resistance, patients are both unaware of the content of resistance and resistance itself (1923, *S.E.,* XIX: 8). Consequently, Freud believes that a new topography is needed.

## Ego and Id

Freud's structural model in *The Ego and the Id* in 1923 was an attempt to solve the problems of differentiation and censorship through positing a different, more versatile and stable, psychical entity—the ego. He writes:

We have formed the idea that in each individual there is a coherent organization of mental processes; and we call this his *ego.* It is to this ego that consciousness is attached; the ego controls the approaches to motility—that is, to the discharge of excitations into the external world; it is the mental agency which supervises all its own constituent processes, and which goes to sleep at night, though even then it exercises the censorship on dreams (1923, *S.E.,* XIX: 8).

Later he adds that "ego" is the name of that psychical agency that takes in stimuli for internal processes and orients an organism to the external world—that "single superficial system *Pcpt.-Cs.* (1923, *S.E.,* XIX: 14). "I propose to take it into account by calling the entity which starts out from the system *Pcpt.* and begins by being *Pcs.* the 'ego', and . . . in calling the other part of the mind, into which this entity extends and which behaves as though it were *Ucs.*, the 'id'" (1923, *S.E.,* XIX: 17).

Id Freud describes fully in "Dissection of the Personality" from *New Introductory Lectures on Psycho-Analysis*:

> We approach the id with analogies: we call it a chaos, a cauldron full of seething excitations. We picture it as being open at its end to somatic influences, and as there taking up into itself instinctual needs which find their psychical expression in it. It is filled with energy reaching it from the instincts, but it has no organization, produces no collective will, but only a striving to bring about the satisfaction of the instinctual needs subject to the observance of the pleasure principle. The logical laws of thought do not apply to the id, and this is true above all of the law of contradiction. Contrary impulses exist side by side, without canceling each other out or diminishing each other: at the most they may converge to form compromises under the dominating economic pressure towards the discharge of energy. There is nothing in the id that could be compared with negation; and we perceive with surprise an exception to the philosophical theorem that space and time are necessary forms of our mental acts. There is nothing in the id that corresponds to the idea of time; there is not recognition of the passage of time, and . . . no alteration in its mental processes is produced by the passage of time. Wishful impulses which have never passed beyond the id, but impressions, too, which have been sunk into the id by repression, are virtually immortal; after the passage of decades they behave as though they had just occurred. . . . The id of course knows no judgements of value: no good and evil, no morality. The economic or . . . the quantitative factor, which is intimately linked to the pleasure principle, dominates all its processes. Instinctual cathexes seeking discharge—that, in our view, is all there is in the id (1933, *S.E.,* XXII: 73-4).

How precisely are the id and the ego related? The ego literally springs forth out of the id over time. It is that part of the id that has been altered through an organism's direct experience with the external world through the medium of the system *Pcpt.-Cs.* It essays to bring the id in accord with reality through adaptation to or change of the external world and to substitute the reality principle for the id's own pleasure principle (1926, *S.E.,* XX: 201). While the id represents human passions, the ego represents human reason or common sense. In an analogy that hearkens back to Plato's comparison of the rational soul to a charioteer and the spirited and appetitive souls as white, obedient and black, disobedient horses in *Phaedrus*,[36] Freud writes:

> The functional importance of the ego is manifested in the fact that normally control over the approaches to motility devolves upon it. Thus in its relation to the id it is like a man on horseback, who has to hold in check the superior

strength of the horse; with this difference, that the rider tries to do so with his own strength while the ego uses borrowed forces. The analogy may be carried a little further. Often a rider, if he is not to be parted from his horse, is obliged to guide it where it wants to go; so in the same way the ego is in the habit of transforming the id's will into action as if it were its own[37] (1923, *S.E.,* XIX; 19).

## Super-Ego

From the perspective of neurosis, Freud also acknowledges another difficulty with his early topographical model—unconscious self-criticism, which requires the super-ego, another psychical agency.

> From the point of view of analytic practice, the consequence of this discovery [of an unconscious ego that produces effects without one's awareness] is that we land in endless obscurities and difficulties if we keep to our habitual forms of expression and try, for instance, to derive neuroses from a conflict between the conscious and the unconscious. We shall have to substitute for this antithesis another, taken from our insight into the structural conditions of the mind— the antithesis between the coherent ego and the repressed which is split off from it (1923, *S.E.,* XIX: 9; also 21).

Two factors drive the formation of the super-ego: one, historical; the other, biological. Historically, Freud mentions the sexual diphasism of the sort mentioned in *Three Essays on Sexuality.* Libidinal development in the course of a child's first three stages—oral, anal, and phallic—is interrupted by a period of latency, brought on by the Oedipus complex. Biologically, Freud mentions the lengthy duration of childhood helplessness and dependence (1923, *S.E.,* XIX: 31).

The super-ego is thus to be considered "heir of the Oedipus complex." It is the expression of the id's most powerful impulses and most significant libidinal vicissitudes as well as the ego's mastery of the Oedipus complex. As representative of the internal world, it also sets itself up as an antagonist to the ego, representative of the external world (1923, *S.E.,* XIX, 32).

## Benefits of Structural Model

Overall, Freud's "structural model" allows for a fuller sense of functional unity for an organism, acting in the external world, through positing the existence of ego. The ego is an organism's sense of self and link to reality. Writes Paul Roazen:

> The development of ego psychology serves as a bridge to the social sciences precisely because of its attention to processes of adaptation: in terms of the example of social cohesion, the splits within the superego are not looked on solely from the standpoint of individually regressive acts, but rather from that of the consequences for the individual's relationship to the social unit as a whole.[38]

However, the ego is easily incapacitated, as it is continually assailed in three directions. First, the id makes unrelenting demands on it. Second, the super-ego makes sure that in gratifying the id's demands, the ego follows the dictates of conscience. Third, the exigencies of reality constantly make the gratification of id-impulses difficult (1923, *S.E.,* XIX, 59-60). Thus, the ego is not only the psychical link to reality, but it is also the "seat of anxiety."

We may sum the function of each of Freud's new psychical agencies thus:

- **Id:** The id is the human psychic apparatus. It harbors from birth phylogenetic memories and later repressed memories. The id is wholly unconscious and functions in accordance with the pleasure principle. Failure to discharge libido results in neurosis.
- **Ego:** The ego functions in accordance with the reality principle and delays gratification of id-impulses for the sake of preservation of the organism. The ego develops out of the id at the time a child distinguishes between itself and other objects. The major function of the ego is to effect compromises for defensive purposes. Ego-operations are commonly called "defense mechanisms."
- **Super-ego:** The super-ego is an organism's moral agency that is independent of the ego. The super-ego develops around the age of five or six—just as latency begins and the Oedipal complex is resolved. It is a massive defensive effort directed towards Oedipal impulses and a child's sense of guilt.

With the structural model and the three new "agencies," repression is more than an overpowering anticathexis of the unconscious and, thus, Freudian psychotherapy aims beyond disclosure of repressed ideas in the unconscious. Neurosis now comprises unresolved conflicts between the parts of the psychic apparatus. Specifically, the ego—given the demands of the id, the censorship capacities of the super-ego, and the limitations or boundaries of reality—does what it can to stand its ground. With focuses on Oedipal (castration) anxiety, Freud now maintains that anxiety results in repression, whereas earlier he maintained that repression is the cause of anxiety (1926, *S.E.,* XX: 85). Therapy consists in strengthening the ego to empower it to "achieve progressive conquest of the id" (1923, *S.E.,* XIX: 56). In a late work, "Analysis, Terminable and Interminable," Freud sums:

The aetiology of every neurotic disturbance is, after all, a mixed one. It is a question either of the instincts being excessively strong—that is to say, recalcitrant to taming by the ego—or of the effects of early (i.e., premature) traumas which the immature ego was unable to master. As a rule there is a combination of both factors, the constitutional and the accidental. The stronger the constitutional factor, the more readily will a trauma lead to a fixation and leave behind a developmental disturbance; the stronger the trauma, the more certainly will its injurious effects become manifest even when the instinctual situation is normal (1937, *S.E.,* XXIII, 220).

Of how this relates to neurosis, Freud writes, "the ego has made an attempt to suppress certain portions of the id in an inappropriate manner, this attempt has failed, and the id has taken it revenge" (1926, *S.E.,* XX: 203). We might sum Freud's final thoughts on neurosis thus:

**Neurosis and the Structural Model:** Neurosis is a result of conflicts among the various psychical agencies, whereby the ego is weakened or overwhelmed by powerful instincts or early traumata.

Analytic cure for Freud's mature etiological views involves strengthening the ego to handle the demands of reality and of other internal psychical agencies.

# Notes

1. In spite of the fact that there were no known physiological correlates. This sentiment is conveyed by Freud's metaphorical use of a crystal, thrown to the ground. When it breaks, it does not break arbitrarily, but according to lines of cleavage, predetermined by the structure of the crystal (1933, *S.E.,* XXII: 1933: 58–59).

2. For a fine account of the *fin-de-siècle* treatments for nervous disorders, see Sonu Shamdasani, "'Psychotherapy': The Invention of a Word," *History of the Human Sciences,* Vol. 18, No. 1, 2–3.

3. See his letter to Fliess of August 29, 1888, in Sigmund Freud and Wilhelm Fleiss, *The Complete Letters of Sigmund Freud to Wilhelm Fliess: 1887–1904,* ed. Jeffrey Moussaieff Masson (Cambridge: Harvard University Press, 1985), 24, and "Preface to the Translation of Bernheim's *Suggestion*" (1888, *S.E.,* I: 97–98).

4. Sigmund Freud et al., *The Complete Letters of Sigmund Freud to Wilhelm Fliess,* 193.

5. Brentano writes, "Not only may psychical states be aroused by physical states and mental by mental, but it is also the case that physical states have mental consequences and mental states have physical consequences." Franz Brentano, *Psychology from an Empirical Standpoint,* trans. A. C. Rancurello, D. B. Terrell, and L. L. McAllister (New York: Humanities Press, 1973), 6.

6. Shamdasi argues that one must see Freud's nomination of "psychoanalysis" within the wider framework of the nomination of "psychotherapy." As such, he is a part of the psychotherapeutic movement and not its founder, as Freudian apologists claim. Sonu Shamdasani, "'Psychotherapy,'" 13.

7. An analogy he would later reject (1895, *S.E.,* II: 292).

8. Freud illustrates this earliest view of hysteria keenly in the first of his *Five Lectures on Psychoanalysis,* years later with an analogy. There he talks of the queerness one would experience at watching a Londoner pause and fall into deep melancholy at the richly carved Gothic column called "Charing Cross," which adorns the resting spot of Queen Eleanor of the thirteenth century. It is the same with one who is neurotic. He sums, "This fixation of mental life to [early] pathogenic traumas is one of the most significant and practically important characteristics of neurosis" (1910, *S.E.,* XI: 16–17).

9. Upon cessation of treatment, Breuer claimed Anna was completely cured, but he himself referred her to the famous sanitarium Bellevue in Switzerland for additional treatment years later.

10. For more on these three, see Malcolm Macmillan, "The Sources of Freud's Methods for Gathering and Evaluating Clinical Data," *Freud and the History of*

*Psychoanalysis*, eds. Toby Gelfand and John Kerr (Hillsdale, NJ: The Analytic Press, 1992), 114–24.

11. Causal therapies were said to be unable to remove extant symptoms and were merely prophylactic.

12. Due it seems to his uneasiness with Anna's dependence on him, which turned sexual, during his sessions with her. For Freud's own account of his break with Breuer in his own words, see "History of the Psycho-Analytic Movement" (1914, *S.E.*, XIV: 11–12), "Autobiographical Study" (1925, *S.E.*, XX: 22–23), and "Psycho-Analysis" (1922, *S.E.*, XVIII, 237).

13. In a letter to Fliess dated November 10, 1895, Freud states that Breuer gave a formal speech on Freud and noted his "conversion" to sexual etiology. Later that day, he said to Freud, "But all the same, I don't believe it." Freud et al., *Letters of Freud to Fliess*, 151.

14. Freud et al., *Letters of Freud to Fliess*, 61.

15. See M. Andrew Holowchak, "The Problem of Unassailability: Freud, Analogy, and the Adequacy of Constructions in Analysis," *Psychoanalytic Psychology*, Vol. 19, No. 2, 255–66.

16. Masson, *Letters of Freud to Fliess*, 264–65.

17. Jeffrey M. Masson, *The Assault on Truth* (New York: Farrar, Straus & Giroux, 1984), 192.

18. Patricia Kitcher, *Freud's Dream: A Complete Interdisciplinary Science of Mind* (Cambridge: MIT Press), 87–88.

19. Joel Kupfersmid, "The 'Defense' of Sigmund Freud," *Psychotherapy*, Vol. 29, No. 2, 1992, 297–309.

20. For more on abandonment of seduction theory, see the exchange between Holowchak and Kupfersmid in chaps. 3 and 4 of M. Andrew Holowchak, ed., *Radical Claims in Freudian Psychoanalysis*.

21. Freud et al., *Letters of Freud to Fliess*, 342.

22. Ellenberger has shown that Freud's boasts that he alone of contemporaries has discovered that dreams have a meaning are false. From 1896 to 1899, almost all the ideas put forth by Freud were anticipated by others. H. E. Ellenberger, *The Discovery of the Unconscious* (New York: Basic Books, 1970), 311.

23. Mitigated because they would cause emotional harm to the dreamer, if uncensored.

24. Beginning roughly on December 6, 1986. See Freud et al., *Letters of Freud to Fliess*.

25. The father of biorhythms.

26. Jeffrey M. Masson, *Letters of Freud to Fliess*, 364.

27. A particularly inept operation on one of Freud's patients, Emma Eckstein, nearly resulted in her death. Freud was quick to absolve Fliess of wrongdoing. For more on the break between Fliess and Freud and the role played by bisexuality, see Peter Gay, *Freud: A Life for Our Time* (New York: W.W. Norton & Company, 2006), chapter 4.

28. Frank J. Sulloway, *Freud: Biologist of the Mind* (New York: Basic Books, 1979), 252.

29. Writes Freud in *Totem and Taboo*, "They [the arguments of Frazer] have shown, on the contrary, that the earliest sexual excitations of youthful human beings are invariably of an incestuous character and that such impulses when repressed play a part that can scarcely be over-estimated as motive forces of neuroses in later life" (1913, *S.E.*, XII: 123–24).

30. See Frank Sulloway, *Freud: Biologist of the Mind*, chapter 8.

31. Freud wrote in a letter (1908) to disciple Karl Abraham, "The resistance to infantile sexuality strengthens me in my opinion that the three essays are an achievement of comparable value to the *Interpretation of Dreams.*" Sigmund Freud, *The Letters of Sigmund Freud,* ed. Ernst Freud (London: The Hogarth Press, 1961), 145.

32. See also an anonymous letter, dated April 9, 1935. See also Freud's letter to Leon Steinig, June 6, 1932. Sigmund Freud, *The Letters of Sigmund Freud,* ed. Ernst Freud (New York: Basic Books, 1961).

33. A term first employed by Freud in 1910. For more, see Peter Hartcollis, "Origins and Evolution of the Oedipus Complex as Conceptualized by Freud," *Psychoanalytic Review,* Vol. 92, No. 3, 2005, 315–34.

34. For a complete account of the Oedipus complex in this and other of Freud's works, see M. Andrew Holowchak, *Radical Claims in Freudian Psychoanalysis,* chapter 1.

35. This new model was also likely a way of incorporating the thoughts of the secessionists Adler and Jung into a new psychoanalytic framework.

36. Plato, *Phaedrus,* 246a–b.

37. In "Analysis Terminable and Interminable," Freud states that the id has such an affect on the defensive posture of the ego that "the result of this in the sphere of psychical events can only be compared to being out walking in a country one does not know and without having a good pair of legs" (1937, *S.E.,* XXIII: 237).

38. Paul Roazen, *Freud: Political and Social Thought* (New York: Alfred A. Knopf, Inc., 1968), 240.

# Chapter 2
# Methods of Therapy

> "It was to be expected—though this was still unproved and not until later confirmed by wide experience—that everything that occurred to a patient setting out from a particular starting-point must also stand in an internal connection with that starting-point." Sigmund Freud, "Psycho-Analysis"

ONCE CONVINCED HYSTERIA WAS NOT A FLUCTUANT, inexplicable phenomenon, Freud experimented with various methods of treatment in search of a cure. He started by experimenting with hydrotherapy and electrotherapy, but found them to be unavailing. On hydrotherapy, Freud elaborates:

> My knowledge of electrotherapy was derived form W. Erb's textbook, which provided detailed instructions for the treatment of all the symptoms of nervous diseases. Unluckily I was soon driven to see that following these instructions was of no help whatever and that what I had taken for an epitome of exact observations was merely the construction of phantasy. The realization that the work of the greatest name in German neuropathology had no more relation to reality than some "Egyptian" dream-book, such as is sold in cheap bookshops, was painful, but it helped to rid me of another shred of the innocent faith in authority from which I was not yet free. So I put my electrical apparatus aside, even before Mobius had solved the problem by explaining that the successes of electric treatment in nervous disorders (in so far as there were any) were the effect of suggestion on the part of the physician (1925, *S.E.*, XX: 16).

The passage illustrates plainly three things. First, it situates Freud and illustrates the confusion that existed in his day vis-à-vis the nature of nervous disorders and suitable methods of treatment. Second, it enables us to see that the first step to progress toward a science of psychoanalysis for Freud was having the daring to doubt the foremost authorities of his day. Last, it shows that Freud considered no remedy to be scientific if its successes are merely placebo-based—viz., science is more than mere suggestion.

This chapter is about Freud's variegated methods of therapy over the years. I follow the template Freud gives in "Remembering, Repeating and Working-Through," where the development of psychoanalytic technique, he says, goes through a series of three phases: a cathartic phase, an associative phase, and a phase of working through resistances.

# Cathartic Phase

## Abreacting

The first phase of psychoanalytic technique was Breuer's cathartic method—what Freud in "Beginning of Treatment" calls the "intellectualist view" of therapy (1913, *S.E.,* XII: 141). Cathartic technique consists of etiologically tracing a symptom back to its moment of origin, through inducing a hypnotic state in a patient and then persisting to reproduce the mental processes to discharge them in conscious activity. It is, therefore, a matter of "remembering and abreacting, with the help of the hypnotic state" (1913, *S.E.,* XII: 147). Thus, the cathartic method, though called "intellectualist," has both cognitive and affective dimensions, which would be staples of all further methods for Freud.

> The investigations which lay at the root of Breuer and Freud's studies led above all to two results, and these have not been shaken by subsequent experience: first, that hysterical symptoms have sense and meaning, being substitutes for normal mental acts; and secondly, that the uncovering of this unknown meaning is accompanied by the removal of the symptoms—so that in this case scientific research and therapeutic effort coincide. . . . From the very beginning the factor of *affect* was brought into the foreground: hysterical symptoms . . . came into existence when a mental process with a heavy charge of affect was in any way prevented from equalizing that charge by passing along the normal paths leading to consciousness and movement (i.e., from being "abreacted"), as a result of which the affect, which was in a sense "strangulated," was diverted on to the wrong paths and found its discharge into the somatic innervation (a process named "conversion"). The occasions upon which "pathogenic ideas" of this kind arose were described . . . as "psychic traumas," and, since these often dated back to the very remote past, it was possible . . . to say that hysterics suffered to a large extent from reminiscences (which had not been dealt with). *Under the treatment, therefore, "catharsis" came about when the path to consciousness was opened and there was a normal discharge of affect* (1922, *S.E.,* XVIII: 235-6).

Freud states that no analyst can have any hope of penetrating directly to the nucleus of the pathogen. Every analyst must be prepared to overcome substantial resistance along the way. In consequence, analysis begins at the periphery. "It is at first as though we were standing before a wall which shuts out every prospect and prevents us from having any idea whether there is anything behind it, and if so, what" (1895, *S.E.,* II: 293).

The key to penetrating the "wall" is to trigger recollection. Freud here describes remembering, facilitated by Bernheim's famous pressure technique. An analyst presses on a patient's forehead and then asks his patient to relate what he remembers. It is the act of pressing, mere suggestion, which facilitates remembering and breaks through the initial, weakest resistances—thereby allowing for some advance of recollection, before new resistances crop up.

After we have worked in this way for some time, the patient begins as a rule to co-operate with us. A great number of reminiscences now occur to him, without our having to question him or set him tasks. What we have done is to make a path to an inner stratum within which the patient now has spontaneously at his disposal material that has an equal degree or resistance attaching to it. . . . . The things that he brings up in this way often seem disconnected, but they offer material which will be given point when a connection is discovered later on (1895, *S.E.*, II: 292).

The analyst, as it were, advances in a radial manner, as he essays to grab a portion of a peripheral "logical thread" and work his way inward. Even so, he finds gaps, imperfections, and false connections in the account, given by a patient. If one thread takes an analyst only so far, he drops it temporarily and takes up another.[1] The process is laborious and slow, and it sometimes involves hunches to move it forward. Nonetheless, a therapist has at his disposal one clue to the strength of the resistances he is encountering: The time that a thought, once brought up, remains in conscious awareness is in proportion to its significance (1895, *S.E.*, II: 292-6).

In spite of the suggestive manner of Bernheim's pressure technique and a therapist's use of guesses, Freud assures his readers that there is never concern about misleading a patient, because the wealth of reminiscences in the end will confirm or disconfirm any mistaken guess.

I have never once succeeded, by foretelling something, in altering or falsifying the reproduction of memories or the connection of events; for if I had, it would inevitably have been betrayed in the end by some contradiction in the material. If something turned out as I had foretold, it was invariably proved by a great number of unimpeachable reminiscences that I had done no more than guess right. We need not be afraid, therefore, of telling the patient what we think his next connection of thought is going to be. It will do no harm (1895, *S.E.*, II: 295).

The suggestion here is not that a therapist should often use guesses to expedite cure, for Freud was insistent that therapy was always lengthy and laborious, but instead that guesses will do a therapist no harm, if used now and again, when resistance is great.

Overall, all reminiscences that surface spontaneously, during the course of analysis, have significance of some sort. If a particular memory is not in itself significant, it likely functions as a bridge between two memories that are (1895, *S.E.*, II: 195-6).

Remembering, merely the first part of cathartic therapy, ought not to be taken as curative, as many amateurish psychoanalysts believe it to be. Freud elaborates in "Wild Psycho-Analysis:

If knowledge about the unconscious were as important for the patient as people inexperienced in psychoanalysis imagine, listening to a lecture or reading books would be enough to cure him. Such measures, however, have as much influence on the symptoms of nervous illness as a distribution of menu-cards in a time of famine has upon hunger. The analogy goes even further than its immediate application; for informing the patient of his unconscious regularly results in an intensification of the conflict in him and an exacerbation of his troubles (1910, *S.E.,* XI: 225).

As the last line suggests, though remembering is the first step toward catharsis, it must be induced only when a patient is affectively ready for it. Otherwise, disclosure of something for which a patient is unprepared consciously to handle can add to the ponderous resistances that a therapist already faces.

Abreacting, which involves the affect associated with the memory, comes next and is, in essence, curative. Returning to *Studies on Hysteria,* Freud states: *"[Psychotherapy] brings to an end the operative force of the idea, which was not abreacted in the first instance, by allowing its strangulated affect . . . a way out through speech."* It does so by subjecting the strangulated affect to associative correction through speech by means of normal consciousness (1895, *S.E.,* II: 17).

## Cathartic Techniques

The cathartic methods Freud employed for abreaction early in his analytic career were predominately two: hypnosis and Bernheim's hand-on-head pressure technique.[2]

### *Hypnosis*

As I note in chapter 1, Freud ping-ponged on the issue of the psychoanalytic merit of hypnosis. At times, following Charcot, he considered it an efficacious technique for disclosing underlying pathogens, because the physiological state of a hysterical person made that person hypnotizable. At other times, following Bernheim, he considered hypnotism to be nothing other than suggestion. He writes in his "Autobiographical Study":

> In Paris [with Charcot] I had seen hypnotism used freely as a method for producing symptoms in patients and then removing them again. And now the news reached us that a school had arisen at Nancy [with Bernheim] which made an extensive and remarkably successful use of suggestion, with or without hypnosis, for therapeutic purposes. It thus came about, as a matter of course, that in the first years of my activity as a physician my principal instrument of work, apart from haphazard and unsystematic psychotherapeutic methods, was hypnotic suggestion (1925, *S.E.,* XX: 16-7).

Irrespective of his waffling on the merit of hypnosis over time, early in his analytic career especially, Freud considered it a useful analytic tool.

At the start of *Studies on Hysteria,* Freud says that hypnoid states, to use the language of Charcot, share with each other and with hypnosis one feature: The ideas, emerging in them, are intense and associatively disconnected from consciousness. He says, "[T]he nature of these states and the extent to which they are cut off from the remaining conscious processes must be supposed to vary just as happens in hypnosis, which ranges from a light drowsiness to somnambulism, from complete recollection to total amnesia." Stated more precisely, hypnoid states are "the basis and *sine qua non* of hysteria" (1895, *S.E.,* II: 12).

Though Freud early on found hypnosis serviceable—in "Autobiographical Study," for illustration, he states he used hypnosis to inquire about causes of hysterical symptoms (1925, *S.E.,* XX: 19)—its use, he acknowledged, was limited. In his case-study of Lucy R. in *Studies on Hysteria,* Freud confessed that his own capacity to induce a hypnotic state was inferior to Bernheim's. Some of his patients, he admits, remonstrated against undergoing hypnosis, because of his lack of success with it (1895, *S.E.,* II: 108 and 268). Such continual failures left him embarrassed and undermined his authority as a doctor. He elaborates:

> I soon dropped the practice of making tests to show the degree of hypnosis reached, since in quite a number of cases this roused the patients' resistance and shook their confidence in me. . . . Furthermore, I soon began to tire of issuing assurances and commands such as: "You are going to sleep! . . . sleep!" and of hearing the patient, as so often happened when the degree of hypnosis was light, remonstrate with me: "But, doctor, I'm *not* asleep," and of then having to make highly ticklish distinctions: "I don't mean ordinary sleep; I mean hypnosis. As you see, you are hypnotized, you can't open your eyes," etc., "and in any case, there's no need for you to go to sleep," and so on (1895, *S.E.,* II: 108).

In "Psychotherapy," written 10 years after *Studies on Hysteria,* Freud lists several of the defects of hypnosis. Hypnosis is suggestive and, therefore, cosmetic, not etiological and substantive—i.e., it does not concern itself with the origin, strength, and meaning of hysterical symptoms. Instead, it "superimposes a suggestion" with the hope that the suggestion will be sufficiently strong to keep the pathogenic idea from expressing itself. It conceals the play of underlying mental forces and, thereby, conceals a patient's resistances. Consequently, instead of facilitating recovery, hypnosis guards against recovery (1905, *S.E.,* VII: 260-1).

Shortly after *Studies on Hysteria,* Freud abandons hypnosis as a fruitful method of pathogenic disclosure, though it is likely that he never stopped tinkering with it throughout his life.

### *Pressure Technique*

Whereas Freud had limited success with hypnosis, he professes in his case-study of Lucy R., to have found a friendlier suggestive alternative in the "pressure" technique of Bernheim.

Freud overcame the difficulties with hypnosis by recalling something he had seen Bernheim do. Bernheim showed Freud that memories of events, which would crop up during somnambulism, were not forgotten while awake. Such memories could be revived during wakefulness by a mild command and slight pressure of the hand on the head of a patient. For instance, Bernheim once convinced a woman in a state of somnambulism that he was no longer standing before her. He then essayed to draw her attention to him in a variety of ways—some quite assertive—but he did not succeed. On waking her, he asked her to relate to him all that had just transpired. The woman could recall nothing. Bernheim did not accept her express ignorance, however. Insisting that she could remember everything, he placed his hand on her forehead to aid recall. Amazingly, she recalled everything that she had claimed had escaped her notice (1895, *S.E.,* II: 108-10).

Thus, when faced with a patient's express ignorance of underlying pathogenic events, Freud persevered. "I placed my hand on the patient's forehead or took her head between my hands and said, 'You will think of it under the pressure of my hand.[3] At the moment at which I relax my pressure you will see something in front of you or something will come into your head. Catch hold of it. It will be what we are looking for" (1895, *S.E.,* II: 109-10).

The suggestive technique, in all cases, yielded just those results Freud needed. "I can safely say that it has scarcely ever left me in the lurch. . . . It has always pointed the way which the analysis should take and has enabled me to carry through every such analysis to an end without the use of somnambulism." So cocksure was Freud of the efficacy of the suggestive technique that he could readily dismiss patients' responses such as "I see nothing" as signs of resistance, due to tension in their critical faculty. Something had surely surfaced in every case of pressure, he insisted, but was immediately judged by the patient to be unserviceable or irrelevant and so it was not related to the analyst. Overall, the suggestive method gave Freud insight into the motives behind forgetting. It showed that "forgetting is often intentional and desired; and its success is never more than *apparent*" (1895, *S.E.,* II: 110-2 & 268-70).

In sum, Freud learned much from Bernheim's technique.

- In spite of professed ignorance, patients know everything that is of any pathogenic significance.
- What patients know about pathogenicity can be brought out through mild suggestion.
- Persistence in the suggestive method is always profitable.
- The suggestive method ultimately gives an analyst insight into psychical mechanisms, like resistance, underlying pathology.

In spite of its avowed superiority over hypnosis and its superb track record, the pressure technique, he says, was operose (1895, *S.E.,* II: 111) and Freud would abandon it not long after *Studies on Hysteria.* We cannot say precisely when, but 1904 is a likely year.[4]

## Limits of the Cathartic Method

Problems with the cathartic method were several and they did not escape Freud's notice, even in *Studies on Hysteria*. I list merely the most pressing difficulties and Freud's responses to them.

First, Freud notes that the cathartic method is symptomatic, not causal. It can remove present symptoms, but cannot be responsible for preventing new ones from emerging. Still, it has one advantage over causal therapy.

> The cathartic method is not to be regarded as worthless because it is a symptomatic and not causal one. For causal therapy is in fact as a rule only a prophylactic one; it brings to a halt any further effects of the noxious agency, but does not therefore necessarily get rid of the results which that agency has already brought about. As a rule a second phase of treatment is required to perform this latter task, and in cases of hysteria the cathartic method is quite invaluable for this purpose (1895, *S.E., II*: 262).

Symptomatic therapy has a second benefit. Through eliminating present symptoms, patients are given the "whole amount of their capacity for resistance, so that they can successfully withstand the effects of the noxious agency" (1895, *S.E., II*: 64).

Second, given its symptomatic nature, cathartic method is time- and labor-intensive. The demands on an analyst are prodigious. So are the demands on a patient. An analyst's first task is to recognize the dilatoriness of the cathartic process; success is achievable slowly and step-by-step. Patience is required (1895, *S.E., II*: 282). Acknowledging the difficulty of time, Freud advocates guessing to expedite analysis. Whereas a correct guess would accelerate analysis, an incorrect guess would compel "the patient to take sides . . . by enticing him into energetic denials which betray his undoubted better knowledge" (1895, *S.E., II*: 296). Either way, he vaunts, no harm would be done.

Third, the cathartic method might not remove all the symptoms of hysteria. To that objection, Freud notes, first, that a patient's personal circumstances, inaccessible to an analyst, might intervene to help the analyst and, second, that some symptoms, as mere residues of "complete and permanent successes," are harmless. Nonetheless, pathogenicity is, as a rule, over-determined and relapses are always possible (1895, *S.E., II*: 262-3).

Fourth, during periods of acute hysteria, an analyst, like a physician faced with an acute infectious disease, is often handcuffed. Cure, in such instances, can come about only when malady has run its course (1895, *S.E., II*: 263-4).

Freud needed a new method with greater potential for permanency of cure.

## Abandonment of Cathartic Method

Defects notwithstanding, the cathartic method was not without its merits, which Freud summarized in "Autobiographical Study," numerous years after he abandoned it. First, it stressed the role of emotions in psychopathology. Second, it distinguished between conscious mental acts and those beneath the surface of consciousness. Third, it introduced a dynamic factor, by positing that a symptom arises through the damming-up of an effect. Fourth, it introduced an economic factor, by regarding that same symptom as the product of a quantity of energy that would otherwise have been employed in some other way (1925, *S.E.,* XX: 21-2).

Nonetheless, those successes were mostly of the theoretical sort, insofar as the cathartic method helped to advance Freud's own grasp of the etiology of hysteria. In practice, however, the cathartic method scarcely went further than direct description of symptoms. In doing so, it did not address the problem of etiology in a manner serviceable to hysterical patients. In addition, it failed to recognize the sexual origins of hysteria. "I now learned from my rapidly increasing experience that it was not *any* kind of emotional excitation that was in action behind the phenomena of neurosis but habitually one of a sexual nature, whether it was a current sexual conflict or the effect of earlier sexual experiences" (1925, *S.E.,* XX: 21-22).

The cathartic method, in spite of recognizing cognitive and affective dimensions to hysteria, was ultimately too cognitive for Freud. In "Beginning of Treatment," Freud reflects:

> It is true in the earliest days of analytic technique we took an intellectualist view of the situation. We set a high value on the patient's knowledge of what he had forgotten, and in this we made hardly any distinction between our knowledge of it and his. We thought it a special piece of good luck if we were able to obtain information about the forgotten childhood trauma from other sources— for instance, from parents or nurses or the seducer himself—as in some cases it was possible to do; and we hastened to convey the information and the proofs of its correctness to the patient, in the certain expectation of thus bringing the neurosis and the treatment to a rapid end. It was a severe disappointment when the expected success was not forthcoming. How could it be that the patient, who now knew about his traumatic experience, nevertheless still behaved as if he knew no more about it than before? Indeed, telling and describing his repressed trauma to him did not even result in any recollection of it coming into his mind (1913, *S.E.,* XII; 141).

In short, Freud began to notice that the affective aspect of hysteria played a greater role in cure than he had thought it played and that cathartic therapy was ill-suited to handle that aspect.

In addition to those things, Freud came to see that the affective aspect of therapeutic cure was more complex than he had originally thought it was. He came to see that therapeutic success was also influenced profoundly by a patient's affective relationship to his psychoanalyst. As Freud says in "Psycho-Analysis":

> It soon appeared that the therapeutic hopes which had been placed upon cathartic treatment in hypnosis were to some extent unfulfilled. It was true that the disappearance of the symptoms went hand-in-hand with the catharsis, but total

success turned out to be entirely dependent upon the patient's relation to the physician and thus resembled the effect of "suggestion." If that relation was disturbed, all the symptoms reappeared, just as though they had never been cleared up (1922, XVIII: 237).

All in all, Freud was coming to see the significance of transference in therapeutic success.

I turn now to the second phase of the development of analytic technique—the associative phase.

## Associative Phase

The associative phase comprises chiefly the method of free association, first mentioned in *The Interpretation of Dreams,* but also a second, ancillary method, the method of dream-symbol interpretation, emphasized in later editions of the same book.

### Free Association

The cathartic method quite naturally led Freud to the method of free association (*freier Einfall* or, literally, "free irruption" in the sense of an idea, suddenly popping into mind[5]). Freud's own difficulties with hypnosis led him to Bernheim's pressure technique, and from there the step to free association was short.

> The abandonment of hypnosis seemed to make the situation hopeless, until [I] recalled a remark of Bernheim's to the effect that things that had been experienced in a state of somnambulism were only *apparently* forgotten and that they could be brought into recollection at any time if the physician insisted forcibly enough that the patient knew them. [I] therefore endeavored to press [my] *unhypnotized* patients into giving [me] their associations, so that from the material thus provided [I] might find the path leading to what had been forgotten or warded off. [I] noticed later that such pressure was unnecessary and that copious ideas almost always arose in the patient's mind, but that they were held back from being communicated and even from becoming conscious by certain objections put by the patient in his own way. It was to be expected—though this was still unproved and not until later confirmed by wide experience—that everything that occurred to a patient setting out from a particular starting-point must also stand in an internal connection with that starting-point; hence arose the technique of educating the patient to give up the whole of his critical attitude and of making use of the material which was thus brought to light for the purpose of uncovering the connections that were being sought. A strong belief in the determination of mental events certainly played a part in the choice of this technique as a substitute for hypnosis (1922, *S.E.,* XVIII: 237-8).

As the passage shows, there are three assumptions fundamental to free association.[6]

- **Principle of Psychical Determinism:** Mental events are (in some sense) determined.
- **Principle of Etiological Concatenation:** Everything occurring to a patient from a particular starting-point must stand in an internal connection to that starting-point.
- **Principle of Recall:** Somnabulant experiences can be brought to recollection at any time through a trained analyst's persistence.

So radical was the inclusion and dependence on "free association" that Freud gave a new name to his analytic therapy to distinguish it from that of Breuer. He writes, "The new technique [of free association] altered the picture of the treatment so greatly, brought the physician into such a new relation to the patient and produced so many surprising results that it seemed justifiable to distinguish the procedure from the cathartic method by giving it a new name . . . *psycho-analysis*." Free association was a matter of taking the material gained through its use to be linked—via associative links through a patient's experiences, real or fantasized—to hidden pathogens and then essaying to discover those pathogens (1922, *S.E.*, XVIII: 238-9).

To get at the underlying "meaning" of associations in that manner, Freud argued that the analyst and the patient, as it were, had to bring something to the table—what Freud called the "fundamental rule of psycho-analysis."

A patient must relate everything that his self-observation can detect, and keep back all the logical and affective objections that seek to induce him to make a selection from among them, while the doctor must put himself in a position to make use of everything he is told for the purposes of interpretation and of recognizing the concealed unconscious material without substituting a censorship of his own for the selection that the patient has forgone (1912, *S.E.*, XII: 115).

On the one hand, a patient must be in a position of "attentive and dispassionate self-observer." Thus, he must relate what is on the surface of his conscious thoughts with utmost candor. All ostensibly disagreeable, nonsensical, unimportant, and even irrelevant thoughts are to be related to an analyst. Freud says, "It is uniformly found that precisely those ideas which provoke these last-mentioned reactions [disagreeableness, nonsensicality, unimportance, and irrelevance] are of particular value in discovering the forgotten [unconscious] material" (1922, *S.E.*, XVIII: 238).

On the other hand, an analyst must meet his patient, who surrenders himself uncritically to his unconscious, halfway. An analyst's attitude too must also be one of surrender to his own unconscious mental activity—in a state of *"evenly suspended attention"*—without fixating on anything in particular that a patient relates.[7] In such circumstances, a patient's associations emerge like "allusions" to one theme, which, over time and through repetition, prove to be the key to his pathology (1922, *S.E.*, XVIII: 239). "To put it in a formula: he must turn his own unconscious like a receptive organ towards the transmitting unconscious of the patient. . . . [Thus], the doctor's unconscious is able, from the derivatives of the unconscious which are communicated to him, to reconstruct that unconscious, which has determined the patient's free associations." He adds that the most successful cases of treatment are ones that proceed without any purpose in view and where the analyst, with evenly suspended attention, swings from one mental attitude to another (1912, *S.E.*, XII: 114-6).

In short, meeting the patient unconscious to unconscious was needed for the sort of neutrality Freud thought was essential for proper analysis. Deviation from the neutral state would likely result in suggestion on the part of the analyst and contaminated material. Freud elaborates:

> For as soon as anyone deliberately concentrates his attention to a certain degree, he begins to select from the material before him; one point will be fixed in his mind with particular clearness and some other will be correspondingly disregarded, and in making this selection he will be following his expectations or inclinations. This, however, is precisely what must not be done. In making the selection, if he follows his expectations he is in danger of never finding anything but what he already knows; and if he follows his inclinations he will certainly falsify what he may perceive. It must not be forgotten that the things one hears are for the most part things whose meaning is only recognized later on (1912, *S.E.*, XII: 111-12).

The analyst's attitude, cool and dispassionate, he likens to that of a surgeon, "who puts aside all his feelings, even his human sympathy, and concentrates his mental forces on the single aim of performing the operation as skillfully as possible." That prevents an analyst from projecting his own emotions into analysis and it allows the patient maximal assistance on the road to recovery (1912, *S.E.*, XII: 115).

## Limits of Free Association

There are several difficulties with free association. I focus on four: neutrality, psychical determinism, etiological concatenation, and faulty constructions.

First, let us consider the principle of neutrality—the therapist's pledge to meet his patient unconscious to unconscious. Writes psychotherapist Stephen Ellman:

> The issue of neutrality is not only extremely important for the practice of analysis, but it is also the issue that frequently divides contemporary psychoanalysts. . . . [T]he analyst [like Freud] who tends to see neutrality as an essential component of the analytic situation tends to see interpretation as the main avenue of analytic communication. Interpretation stimulates insight, and insight is the vehicle of change in the analytic process.[8]

Many analysts today—Charles Brenner and Mark Kanzer among them—strive for neutrality, even though it may be an unobtainable ideal.[9] Others—Ellman himself as well as M.M. Gill and Mark Grunes—view neutrality as impossible or undesirable.[10] Gill maintains that everything in analysis is a matter of transference and argues that neutrality is an illusion. Grunes states that neutrality is perceived by patients as a signal that a therapist is amoral and that impedes the aim of analysis—the resolution of psychical conflict.[11]

Some variants of psychoanalytic thought—object-relations theory and, especially, interpersonal-relational theory—view neutrality as counterproductive, as the relationship between analyst and patient is interactive, not analyst-driven. Peter Rudnytsky considers the relationship between patient and analyst and the primary transference to be foremost in object-relations theory.[12] Peter Fonagy refers to an "interpersonal-relational approach" in which the analytic setting is co-constructed between therapist and patient—each an active participant that has a role in determining the success or failure of therapy. With co-construction, neutrality is not just obstructive; it is impossible.[13]

A second difficulty is the issue of psychical determinism: All psychic events have causes. Just what does Freud mean by this? Brenner and Fancher give what is likely the received view: All psychic events are determined by prior psychic events.[14]

That interpretation is, however, not what Freud had in mind. First, it is not clear just what a "psychic event" is. Many events that Freud *explained* psychically were not themselves psychical events, but physical events—i.e., a nervous twitch or numbness of a particular part of one's body. Second, since Freud often states that psychical explanation will one day likely be replaced by physiological explanation, it seems likely that Freud is only essaying to explain *certain types of phenomena*—like dreams, neurotic symptoms, jokes, and slips of the tongue—by reference to psychical causes. Behavior that cannot be explained by constitutional mechanisms, states Wes Salmon, *"alone constitutes indirect inductive evidence for the existence of conscious or unconscious psychic mechanisms for which other indirect inductive evidence is also theoretically available."* Such psychical mechanisms might be of a deterministic or a probabilistic sort and their existence is a matter of experience. Nonetheless, these psychical mechanisms are entirely consistent with neurophysiological mechanisms, yet are at least provisionally indispensable for psychoanalysts.[15]

A third difficulty is the assumption of etiological concatenation—roughly the view that pathological phenomena are causally linked, cognitively and affectively, to pathogenic memories that are early and sexual and, most importantly, still operable. Given etiological concatenation, Freud believes that free association is the best method for access to these early pathogenic experiences.

Etiological concatenation is problematic, merely because it is posited metempirically and in an *ad hoc* manner. Whatever a patient relates through free association, Freud seems to be saying, is relevant to his pathology either as a mask, indicative of repression, or a step toward a solution, indicative of attenuation of repression. All his clinical behavior, then, is rooted in abnormal childhood sexuality. Moreover, what of the immeasurable number of events which have occurred between childhood trauma and later-life neurosis? As Ernest Nagel writes, "For even if one grants that such a childhood experience is an indispensable condition for an adult neurosis, the assumption that the repressed wish has continued to operate essentially unmodified in the subject's unconscious, despite the countless number of more proximate happenings in the subject's life, cannot be accepted as a matter of course."[16] One must show, not merely posit, that the precipitating event in early childhood is etiologically operative and operative in an unmodified manner.

Adolf Grünbaum has also addressed etiological concatenation and the purported efficacy of free association in *The Foundations of Psychoanalysis.* He draws from a passage in "Analytic Therapy," in which Freud writes: "[A patient's] conflicts will only be successfully solved and his resistances overcome if the anticipatory ideas he is given tally with what is real in him. Whatever in the doctor's conjectures is inaccurate drops out in the course of the analysis; it has to be withdrawn and replaced by something more correct" (1917, *S.E.,* XVI: 452). For Freud, remission of pathogenic symptoms, according to Grünbaum, demands correct analytic assessment and cannot come about spontaneously or by any method other than psychoanalysis, in which free association takes pride of place.[17]

What are the implications of the Tally Argument on the merit of free association? When there is remission of symptoms, the associations prior to remission, gleaned through free association, must be rightly related to the real pathogenic notions. That is presumptuous. Because cure is often fugacious, certain alternative remedies are equally effective and there is always spontaneous remission, for which Freud does not account. Thus, free association must be called into question. *"[T]he attribution of therapeutic success to the removal of repressions not only was but remains to this day, the sole epistemic underwriter of the purported ability of the patient's free associations to certify causes."*[18]

The final difficulty—the problem of faulty constructions—is a matter I cover fully at this chapter's end.

## Symbolic Interpretation

The method of interpreting symbols in dreams was mentioned in the first edition of *The Interpretation of Dreams,* though it played a small part in the overall program of the book. Because of the work of several colleagues on symbols in dreams thereafter, most notably Wilhelm Stekel's *The Interpretation of Dreams* in 1911, Freud expanded the meager section on symbols in early editions of his book. That section, called "Typical Dreams" in early editions, would become the beefy Section E, "Representation by Symbols in Dreams," of Chapter VI in 1914. This elaborate treatment of symbolic interpretation, which was to function as a corrective to works like that of Stekel, was unsurprisingly sexual-based.

Vis-a-vis the nature of symbols in dreams, Freud states that dreams use symbols as disguised representations of latent thoughts and that many might be interpreted universally, or nearly so. Yet he cautions, "Often enough a symbol has to be interpreted in its proper meaning and not symbolically; while on other occasions a dreamer may derive from his private memories the power to employ as sexual symbols all kinds of things which are not ordinarily employed as such." Condensation—the notion that the symbol of a dream can mean many, often divergent things—confounds the difficulty of interpreting symbols, independently of a dreamer's associations (1900, *S.E.,* V: 352-3).

Freud then goes on to list several common symbolic themes, of which I list a few.

**Symbolic Theme → *Meaning***
Emperor or King, Empress or Queen → *Dreamer's parents*
Prince, Princess → *Dreamer him- or herself*
Elongated objects (sticks, tree-trunks, umbrellas) or long, sharp objects, and
     weapons (knives, daggers, pikes, ploughs, hammers, rifles, revolvers, dag-
     gers, sabers, etc.), key to room, little brother → *Penis*
Boxes, cases, chests, cupboards, ovens, hollow objects, ships, vessels → *Uterus*
Rooms → *Women*
Walking on steps, ladders, staircases → *Sexual act*
Climbing smooth walls, descending façade of houses → *Climbing erect bodies*
Smooth walls → *Men*
Tables, boards → *Women*
Wood → *Female*
Man's genital organ → *Woman's hat, overcoat (Mantel)*

Then there are some tricky symbols. "Tables" and "boards" represent *women* "by antithesis," because they are straight and flat in contrast to the curvaceous bodies of women. "Wood" symbolizes *female material*, because the island called "Madeira" is Portuguese for "wood." An "overcoat" (*Mantel*) symbolizes a *man's genital organ*, likely because of assonance.

Given his insistence on the sexual etiology of neurosis and his notion that dreams are symptoms of everyday neurosis, Freud looked for a sexual interpretation of every oneiric symbol. For instance, he says of Marcinowski's collection of drawings of dreams:

> Marcinowski has published a collection of dreams illustrated by their dreamers
> with drawings that ostensibly represent landscapes and other localities occur-
> ring in the dreams. These drawings bring out very clearly the distinction be-
> tween a dream's manifest and latent meaning. Whereas to the innocent eye they
> appear as plans, maps, and so on, closer inspection shows that they represent
> the human body, the genitals, etc., and only then do the dreams become intel-
> ligible (1900, *S.E.,* V: 356).

There is here no critical discussion of why such landscapes must have a sexual interpretation, which seems gratuitous.

He then gives other symbols, each of a sexual nature (1900, *S.E.,* V: 356-7).

> Playing with a child or beating a child → *Masturbation (oftentimes)*
> Baldness, cutting hair, teeth falling out, and decapitation → *Castration*
> Fishes, snails, cats, mice or snakes; airplane; hand or foot → *Penis*
> Small animals or vermin → *Children undesired*

Mouth, ear, or eye → *Uterus*

Freud then goes on to consider several of the insufficiently verified interpretations of colleague Wilhelm Stekel. "Many of these show penetration, and further examination has proved them correct. . . . But this author's lack of a critical faculty and his tendency to generalization at all costs throw doubts upon others of his interpretations or render them unusable; so that it is highly advisable to exercise caution in accepting his conclusions." He gives a few illustrations. "Relatives" symbolize *the genitals,* but Freud adds, "I can only confirm this in the case of sons, daughters and younger sisters . . . only so far as they fall into the category of 'little ones.'" "Luggage" symbolizes *a load of sin* that weighs one down, but it often turns out to be "an unmistakable symbol of the dreamer's own genitals" (1900, *S.E.,* V: 357-8). Of course, what counts here as confirmation and disconfirmation is uncertain. Ultimately, Freud's critique is refragable and dictated by his own ineluctable proclivity toward sexual etiology.

Why do most dreams require sexual interpretation? Freud gives two answers in the 1909 edition:

> The more one is concerned with the solution of dreams, the more one is driven to recognize that the majority of the dreams of adults deal with sexual material and give expression to erotic wishes. A judgement on this point can be formed only by those who really analyse dreams, that is to say, who make their way through their manifest content to the latent dream-thoughts, and never by those who are satisfied with making a note of the manifest content alone. . . . No other instinct has been subjected since childhood to so much suppression as the sexual instinct with its numerous components; from no other instinct are so many and such powerful unconscious wishes left over, ready to produce dreams in a state of sleep. In interpreting dream we should never forget the significance of sexual complexes, though we should also, of course, avoid the exaggeration of attributing exclusive importance to them (1900, *S.E.,* V: 396).

His assertion that those who do not "really analyse dreams" cannot pass judgment is tendentious and, as we shall in chapter 4, illegitimate. To steer clear of the charge of pan-sexualism, he adds with prepossession in 1919, "The assertion that all dreams require a sexual interpretation . . . occurs nowhere in my *Interpretation of Dreams*" (1900, *S.E.,* V: 397).

Nonetheless Freud is clear that the method of interpretation by symbols is ancillary and knuckles under to free association. He thus offers the cautionary words, often ignored by hasty critics of Freudian interpretation of dreams:

> I should like to utter an express warning against over-estimating the importance of symbols in dream-interpretation, against restricting the work of translating dreams merely to translating symbols and against abandoning the technique of making use of the dreamer's associations. The two techniques of dream-interpretation must be complementary to each other; but both in practice and in theory the first place continues to be held by the procedure which I began by describing and which attributes a decisive significance to the comments made

by the dreamer, while the translation of symbols . . . is also at our disposal as an
auxiliary method (1900, *S.E.,* V: 359-60).

For Freud, symbol interpretation is not to be used independently of free association, but rather as a complementary method that "fills the gaps" left
through association. The reason is that the method of symbol interpretation is a
relatively recent advance in psychoanalysis and, as such, is only incompletely
understood. It is also complicated by condensation (1900, *S.E.,* V: 353). In "Additional Notes on Dream Interpretation as a Whole," Freud writes, "No one can
practise the interpretation of dreams as an isolated activity [i.e., through symbols
alone]; it remains a part of the work of analysis. . . . But dream-interpretation of
such a kind, without reference to the dreamer's associations, would in the most
favourable case remain a piece of unscientific virtuosity of very doubtful value"
(1925, *S.E.,* XIX: 128).

It is fruitful briefly to compare Freudian interpretation with that of the
second-century oneirocritic, Artemidorus of Daldis, who gives us the only complete book of interpretation of dreams from antiquity. Defending the principle,
*Anything that appears in agreement with nature, law, custom, profession, names
or time bodes a good outcome, while anything contrary to them bodes ill,* Artemidorus states, "You must bear in mind, however, that this principle is not universally and irrevocably valid even though it holds good for the majority of
cases." He gives as an illustration a man who dreams of beating his mother,
which is contrary to law. The dream boded well for the man, who was a potter,
for potters work by beating into shape earth, which is also called "mother."[19] For
Artemidorus, as it is for Freud, circumstances predominate in interpretation;
symbolic meaning takes second place.

Last, Freud insists symbols in dreams are products of everyday-life neurosis.

> Now psycho-analytic research finds no fundamental, but only quantitative, dis-
> tinctions between normal and neurotic life; and indeed the analysis of dreams,
> in which repressed complexes are operative alike in the healthy and sick, shows
> a complete entity both in their mechanisms and in their symbolism. The naïve
> dreams of healthy people actually often contain a much simpler, more perspi-
> cuous and more characteristic symbolism than those of neurotics; for in the lat-
> ter, as a result of the more powerful workings of the censorship and of the con-
> sequently more far-reaching dream-distortion, the symbolism may be obscure
> and hard to interpret (1900, *S.E.,* V: 373-4).

The suggestion here is that neurotics are not substantially different from normal
people. What differentiates pathology from normalcy is a matter of degrees—
generally manifest in the symbols of dreams.

## Working through Resistances

### Remembering, Repeating and Working Through

The final phase of the development of psychoanalytic technique over time involves recognition of resistances and emphasizes transference. As Freud elaborates in "Remembering, Repeating, and Working Through":

> Finally, there was evolved the consistent technique used today, in which the analyst gives up the attempt to bring a particular moment or problem into focus. He contents himself with studying whatever is present for the time being on the surface of the patient's mind, and he employs the art of interpretation mainly for the purposes of recognizing the resistances which appear there, and making them conscious to the patient. From this there results a new sort of division of labour: the doctor uncovers the resistances which are unknown to the patient; when these have been got the better of, the patient often relates the forgotten situations and connections without any difficulty (1914, *S.E.,* XII: 147).

Though "Remembering, Repeating, and Working Through" might be considered one of Freud's middle works, prior to the introduction of his structural model, it marks a turning point in therapeutic technique. Here psychoanalytic technique focuses on transference—the interplay between analyst and patient—and free association is employed less rigidly. Here also Freud first mentions "compulsion to repeat," which plays such a significant role in *Beyond the Pleasure Principle* six years later.

The technique sketched here is essentially the same technique employed throughout the remainder of his life, though his theoretical framework would undergo significant modifications. It should not be considered for Freud a method that supplanted free association, for Freud never abandoned the associative method. Throughout his life, free association was the preferred method for his discoveries concerning the psychical mechanisms of psychopathology.

New patients begin treatment, Freud says, feeling shame that is based on their newly discovered helplessness from prior sexual activities, which they cannot now recall. New patients are silent and unaware that their silence is caused by inner resistance—a "repetition of a homosexual attitude which comes to the fore as a resistance against remembering anything" (1914, *S.E.,* XII: 150).

> What interests us most of all is naturally the relation of this compulsion to repeat to the transference and to resistance. We soon perceive that the transference is itself only a piece of repetition, and that the repetition is a transference of the forgotten past not only on to the doctor but also on to all the other aspects of the current situation. We must be prepared to find, therefore, that the patient yields to the compulsion to repeat, which now replaces the impulsion to remember, not only in his personal attitude to his doctor but also in every other activity and relationship which may occupy his life at the time. . . (1914, *S.E.,* XII: 150-1).

A patient's resistance, he adds, is quickly recognized by his inability to remember and by extensive "repetitions" in analysis. In fact, the greater the resistance that a therapist encounters, the more extensively will a patient's acting out (repetition) replace remembering. The repetitions here are mnemonic symptoms—where repetition takes the place of remembering—which are intensified due to elements of transference.

> Remembering, as it was induced [cathartically] in hypnosis, could not but give the impression of an experiment carried out in the laboratory. Repeating, as it is induced in analytic treatment according to the newer technique, on the other hand, implies conjuring up pieces of real life; and for that reason it cannot always be harmless and unobjectionable. This consideration opens up the whole problem of what is so often unavoidable—"deterioration during treatment" (1914, *S.E.,* XXII; 152).

Complications may arise. First, a patient, aware of his illness, might adopt a new, contemptible attitude that inhibits analytic treatment.[20] Second, as a therapist breaks down a patient's resistance, new and more severe symptoms might form as signs of greater resistance. Last, a patient might engage in activities in his personal life, again signs of resistance, which cause him great harm and even make recovery impossible. The magnitude of the resistance is a measure of the work an analyst has yet to do as well as a measure of the distortion of unconscious material (1916, *S.E.,* XV: 117). An analyst best protects his patient by asking him not to make significant decisions while under analysis, though he leaves to his patient as much personal freedom as the patient can handle (1914, *S.E.,* XII: 152-3).

The catalyst for repetition and remembering is a patient's transference relationship with his analyst.

> The main instrument, however, for curbing the patient's compulsion to repeat and for turning it into a motive for remembering lies in the handling of the transference. We render the compulsion harmless, and indeed useful, by giving it the right to assert itself in a definite field. We admit it into the transference as a playground in which it is allowed to expand in almost complete freedom and in which it is expected to display to us everything in the way of pathogenic instincts that is hidden in the patient's mind (1914, *S.E.,* XII: 154).

The analytic setting offers a setting in which a patient's compulsion to repeat can express itself and, thus, allows for the possibility of transference.

What is the key to a successful transference? A patient must comply with the needed conditions of analysis. If so, then a patient is in position to replace his regular neurosis, which is independent of the therapist, with a transference neurosis, which essentially involves the therapist. "The transference thus creates an intermediate region between illness and real life through which the transition from the one to the other is made. The new condition has taken over all the feature of the illness; but it represents an artificial illness which is at every point accessible to our intervention" (1914, *S.E.,* XII: 154). This new condition, this transference-neurosis, is provisional. It allows repetitive reactions that awaken memories, once resistance has been broken.

Yet repetition and remembering are only two stages of analytic work and are not sufficient for therapeutic success. A therapist must also allow a patient to work through the resistance, by continuing analysis, according to the fundamental rule. That often involves great patience on the part of the analyst. Thus, working through "effects the great_st changes in the patient and ... distinguishes analytic treatment from any kind of treatment by suggestion" (1914, *S.E.,* XII: 155-6).

## "Heads I Win, Tails You Lose"

### *Constructions and Jigsaw Puzzles*

I now return to the problem of false constructions of psychoanalysts.[21]

In his 1937 essay "Constructions in Analysis," Freud considers an objection of a "fair-minded critic." Psychoanalysis, objects the critic, is in a no-lose position. If a patient agrees with a construction, the construction is thereby confirmed. If a patient disagrees with a construction, he is repressed and the construction is also confirmed (1937, *S.E.,* XXII: 257). "Heads I win, tails you lose," sums the critic. This criticism, or some form of it, was in Freud's day and still is a constant complaint of dissenters.[22]

Freud begins by noting a distinction between "construction" (*Konstruktion*) and "interpretation" (*Deutung*). An analyst *interprets* when he takes a single element from some material and gives its meaning—i.e., when he explains a slip of the tongue or an element in a dream. An analyst *constructs* when he ties together multiple elements in a manner that allows him to reconstruct a piece of a patient's early history. Therapy is more a matter of construction than interpretation (1937, *S.E.,* XXIII: 260-1).

The problem is how to know that a construction is correct. A patient's "yes" nor a "no" shows that the construction is false or is a signal of postponement of reaction to be gotten later. The danger of suggestion here has been greatly exaggerated (1937, *S.E.,* XXIII: 261-2).

"Yes" and "no" answers are not to be taken at face value. Both are polysemous. "Yes" can be a symptom of resistance. Consider a patient who agrees with a construction to eschew or delay disclosure of some painful unconscious truth. "Yes" can also signify above-board agreement. "No" is generally a symptom of resistance. Consider a patient who disagrees with a construction to stymie further penetration by an analyst. "No" can also signify above-board disagreement or an incomplete construction (1937, *S.E.,* XXIII: 262-3).

We have what appears to be an irresolvable imbroglio. A therapist, Freud asserts, surmounts this imbroglio through use of indirect confirmations—inferences drawn from patient's verbal behavior "that are in every respect trustworthy." For instance, the utterance "I didn't ever think" can be unmistakably translated as "Yes, you're right this time—about my *unconscious*." In the main, for negative therapeutic reactions, correct inference is measured by resistance; incorrect inference, by perfunctory responses. "If the construction is wrong," Freud says, "there is no change in the patient; but if it is right or gives an approximation to the truth, he reacts to it with an unmistakable aggravation of his symptoms and of his general condition" (1937, *S.E.,* XXIII: 263-5).

Indirect confirmations, however, are hypotheses, not truths, and hypotheses must be confirmed or disconfirmed. Thus, a correct construction requires the confirmation of recalled memories. That does not always happen. "Quite often we do not succeed in bringing the patient to recollect what has been repressed. Instead of that, if the analysis is carried out correctly, we produce in him an assured conviction of the truth of the construction which achieves the same therapeutic result as a recaptured memory" (1937, *S.E.,* XXIII: 265-6). The answer is not satisfactory, if construction is not to be guided merely by suggestion.

In an earlier paper titled "Remarks on the Theory and Practice of Dream-Interpretation" (1923), Freud deals with the interpretation of dreams and the labyrinthine problem of "corroborative" dreams. These dreams, referring to the dreamer's forgotten childhood experiences, are dreamt after an analyst has made a construction and, consistent with that construction, seemingly offer confirmation of it. Are such dreams dreamt just to comply with and "confirm" a physician's construction or are they unconscious, pathogenic thoughts? (1923, *S.E.,* XIX: 115).

The labyrinthine problem is soluble. If analysis of such a dream immediately brings to light feelings of remembering, those feelings are likely evidence of confirmation of a construction. Freud advises caution, however, as the feelings might be the result of a compliant unconscious fantasy, accompanied by subjective conviction, not of an actual memory. Thus, suggestion cannot be ruled out altogether and an analyst cannot be completely sure that his construction is correct (1923, *S.E.,* XIX: 115-6).

We are at a standstill, it seems. An analyst can never be sure of a construction, because a patient might, at each step, supply an analyst with "confirmatory evidence" in keeping with the construction. In such a manner, a patient, through resistance, might mislead an analyst through consistent, but deceptious constructions that lead to mistaken analytic conclusions that are the result of suggestion.

Freud is unfazed. He offers a jigsaw-puzzle, analogical argument.

What makes [an analyst] certain in the end is precisely the complication of the problem before him, which is like the solution of a jigsaw puzzle. A coloured picture, pasted upon a thin sheet of wood and fitting exactly into a wooden frame, is cut into a large number of pieces of the most irregular and crooked shapes. If one succeeds in arranging the confused heap of fragments, each of which bears upon it an unintelligible piece of drawing, so that the picture acquires a meaning, so that there is no gap anywhere in the design and so that the whole fits into the frame—if all these conditions are fulfilled, then one knows that one has solved the puzzle and that there is no alternative solution (1923, *S.E.,* XIX: 116).

The jigsaw-puzzle argument here gives three needed conditions for correctness of a dream's interpretation, which together are presumably jointly sufficient for it. I call these the intelligibility, fittingness, and correspondence conditions of interpretation.

> **Intelligibility Condition:** A construction must be intelligible—i.e., meaningful.
>
> **Fittingness Condition:** All the elements of a construction, like pieces of a puzzle, must tie together perfectly well.
>
> **Correspondence Condition:** The construction must match the (screen) memory of the patient.

When all these needed conditions are met, an analyst can be certain—and certainty can only be guaranteed by the conditions being jointly sufficient and met—his interpretation of a dream must be its real meaning— its latent content.

When under the spell of his seduction theory, Freud employed the jigsaw-puzzle argument in a much earlier work, "Aetiology of Hysteria" (1896), to demonstrate the reliability of an analyst's construction of an early childhood seduction.

> But another and stronger proof of this [actual childhood seduction] is furnished by the relationship of the infantile scenes to the content of the whole of the rest of the case history. It is exactly like putting together a child's picture-puzzle; after many attempts, we become absolutely certain in the end which piece belongs in the empty gap; for only that one piece fills out the picture (i.e., intelligibility condition) and at the same time allows its irregular edges to be fitted into the edges of the other pieces (i.e., fittingness condition) in such a manner as to leave no free space and to entail no overlapping (i.e., completeness condition?). In the same way, the contents of the infantile scenes turn out to be indispensable supplements to the associative and logical framework of the neurosis, whose insertion makes its course of development for the first time evident, or even, as we might often say, self-evident (1896, *S.E.,* III: 205).

### A Puzzle about Analogical Arguments

As Freud himself recognized with his frequent use of archeological comparisons, analogical arguments are never without flaws. When one takes the time to look for reasons why an analogy could be faulty, one generally finds them. There are almost always good reasons for dismissing any analogy that is proposed to shed light on some phenomenon. Analogies, used inductively as arguments, are generally bad arguments.[23]

What analogical arguments aim to do is make probable some conclusion, say "Dreams have attribute $\delta$," by showing some other thing, say the group of all jigsaw puzzles, has attribute $\delta$ and that jigsaw puzzles are similar to dreams in importantly relevant ways. Schematically:

Jigsaw puzzles have attributes $\alpha$, $\beta$, and $\gamma$.

Dreams have attributes α, β, and γ.
Jigsaw puzzles have attribute δ.
So, dreams have attribute δ.

Elsewhere, I give fuller examination of this problem. Now I merely iterate that there are good reasons the analogy, if given as justificatory—and I maintain it is given justificatorily and not heuristically—is unpersuasive. There are important points of disanalogy. First, the pieces of any jigsaw puzzle are unalterable and unvaried. That is not so with the data of constructions. They will vary from therapist to therapist, in keeping with varying orientations of therapists. Second, individual pieces of a jigsaw puzzle must fit together into a coherent whole, as they were cut from a coherent whole. Consider Freud's own imagery involving etiological patterns of mnemonic elements in *Studies on Hysteria* (chapter 1)—i.e., linear, concentric, and branching patterns. Such varied causal imagery creates difficulties for the jigsaw-puzzle analogy. Third, the number of pieces to any given puzzle is fixed. That is not the case with the elements of analysis, whose data depend on the therapist. Ten minutes of woolgathering, due to boredom, might result in data irretrievably lost. Sessions with a different therapist will result in different, though not necessarily inconsistent, data.

One question redounds: Did Freud really believe that the puzzle analogy and its intelligibility, fittingness, and correspondence conditions, taken together, were sufficient guarantors of the truth of a well-formed construction?

In "Remarks on Dream Interpretation," Freud says that the jigsaw-puzzle analogy gives an analyst assurance, but, he adds, that assurance can be confirmed only when analysis is completed. In short, these needed conditions are together insufficient to justify an analyst's construction. In "Aetiology of Hysteria" years earlier, the jigsaw-puzzle analogy does not seem to require the confirmation of analysis taken to completion. It is meet to assume that Freud had a change of mind over the years and that the status of the puzzle argument in his "Remarks on Dream Interpretation," written almost thirty years later, is the view on which he settled. If so, assurance, or the greatest degree of it, can only come with the completion of analysis.

A final question remains. Can a therapist know at the end of analysis that his constructions all along were correct and his treatment was effective? I call this the problem of unassailability, to which I return at the end of chapter 3.

# Notes

1. A technique made possible by three assumptions: that at least one memory in the "thread" has been repressed, that the hysterical symptom was the result of a summation of affects of several successively occurring traumata, and that there likely was an incubation period between the trauma and hysterical symptom. See Malcolm Macmillan, "The Sources of Freud's Methods for Gathering and Evaluating Clinical Data," *Freud and the History of Psychoanalysis*, eds. Toby Gelfand and John Kerr (Hillsdale, NJ: The Analytic Press, 1992), 119.

2. Both techniques were made possible, according to Macmillan, by a newly adopted belief of Freud in psychical continuity. Prior to the *Studies,* Freud held the view that "conscious" was psychical, while what was unconscious was physiological. See Malcolm Macmillan, "The Sources of Freud's Methods for Gathering and Evaluating Clinical Data," 117.

3. Freud elsewhere states that recall will occur "at the moment of the pressure" and "all the time the pressure lasts" (1895, *S.E.,* II: 145 & 170, respectively). As the pressure technique is purely suggestive, these methodological inconsistencies are inconsequential.

4. See Strachey's fn. 1, 1895, *S.E.,* II: 110.

5. For Freud's thoughts on the history of free association, see "Note on the Prehistory of the Technique of Analysis" (1920, *S.E.,* XVIII, 263–65).

6. Macmillan believes that the first two were believed by Freud sufficient to prevent the problem of suggestion—i.e., an analyst's convincing a patient that a memory, constructed by the analyst, must be true. Macmillan goes on to say that most of the avowed "reports" of childhood seductions by patients that gave rise to the seduction theory were likely a "foisting of [Freud's] reconstructions onto them." Malcolm Macmillan, "The Sources of Freud's Methods for Gathering and Evaluating Clinical Data," 133–34.

7. See also 1909, *S.E.,* X: 23.

8. Steven J. Ellman, *Freud's Technique Papers: A Contemporary Perspective* (Northvale, NJ: Jason Aronson, 1991), 333.

9. Charles Brenner, *Psychoanalytic Technique and Psychic Conflict* (New York: International University Press, 1976), and Mark Kanzer, "Past and Present in the Transference," *Journal of the American Psychological Association* 1: 144–54.

10. In Freud's day, Oskar Pfister objected to the neutrality of a therapist, when it comes to transference. He says, "[A]ccording to my observations, it is also important that the analyst should transmit values which over-compensate for the patient's gain from illness or guilt feelings." Sigmund Freud and Oskar Pfister, *Psychoanalysis and Faith,* 112.

11. M.M. Gill, *Analysis of Transference, Vol. 1: Theory and Technique* (New York: International Universities Press, 1982) and Mark Grunes, "The Therapeutic Object Relationship," *Psychoanalytic Review,* 71: 123–43.

12. Peter L. Rudnytsky, "A Psychoanalytic Weltanschauung," *Psychoanalytic Review,* 79(2), 1992, 295–302.

13. Peter Fonagy, *Attachment Theory and Psychoanalysis* (New York: Other Press, 2001).

14. Charles Brenner, *An Elementary Textbook of Psychoanalysis,* (New York: Doubleday/Anchor, 1973), 2, and Raymond E. Fancher, *Psychoanalytic Psychology: The Development of Freud's Thought* (New York: W.W. Norton & Co., 1973), 6.

15. Wes Salmon, "Psychoanalytic Theory and Evidence," *Psychoanalysis, Scientific Method, and Philosophy,* ed. Sydney Hook (New York University Press, 1958), 256–60. Salmon's comments line themselves up neatly with the dual-aspect-monism theory of mind advocated by Wallace. Edwin R. Wallace, "Mind-Body: Monistic Dual-Aspect Interactionism," *Journal of Nervous Mental Disorders,* 176: 4–21. See also Graham McFee, "Why Doesn't Sports Psychology Consider Freud?" *Philosophy and the Sciences of Exercise, Health and Sport,* ed. Mike McNamee (London: Routledge, 2005), 85–116.

16. Ernest Nagel, "Methodological Issues in Psychoanalytic Theory," *Psychoanalysis, Scientific Method, and Philosophy,* ed. Sydney Hook (New York University Press, 1958), 54.

17. Adolf Grünbaum, *The Foundations of Psychoanalysis: A Philosophical Critique* (Berkeley: University of California Press, 1984), 139–40.

18. Adolf Grünbaum, *The Foundations of Psychoanalysis*, 185. Richardson maintains that Grünbaum's Necessary Condition Thesis (NCT) is untenable. He offers instead what can be dubbed the "Superiority Thesis" (ST). ST commits Freud only to the view that psychoanalytic cures are superior to other sorts of cures in that they are more stable, which is sufficient to rule out suggestion. As Grünbaum essays to vindicate psychoanalysis through its clinical successes, Freud has no such intention. Instead, he merely wishes to show psychoanalysis is not suggestive therapy. This response, though spirited, is unavailing, as it is too liberal of a reading of "Analytic Therapy." Robert Richardson, "The 'Tally Argument' and the Validation of Psychoanalysis," *Philosophy of Science,* 57, 1990, 673–75.

19. Artemidorus, *Oneirocritica,* trans. Robert J. White (Torrance, CA: Original Books, Inc.), IV.2

20. In "Beginning of Treatment," Freud says no analyst begins to communicate findings to a patient until transference has taken place (1913, *S.E.,* XII: 139).

21. For a fuller discussion, see M. Andrew Holowchak, "The Problem of Unassailability: Freud, Analogy, and the Adequacy of Constructions in Analysis," *Psychoanalytic Psychology,* Vol. 19, No. 2, 255–66.

22. E.g., Sydney Hook, "Science and Mythology in Psychoanalysis," *Psychoanalysis, Scientific Method, and Philosophy,* 212-24; Lawrence Kubie, "Psychoanalysis and Scientific Method," *Psychoanalysis, Scientific Method, and Philosophy* (New York University Press, 1959), 57-80; and Ernest Nagel, "Methodological Issues in Psychoanalytic Thought," *Psychoanalysis, Scientific Method, and Philosophy* (New York University Press, 1959), 38-56; and J. O. Wisdom, "Testing of a Psycho-Analytic Interpretation," *International Journal of Psycho-Analysis,* 48, 1967, 44–52.

23. Adolf Grünbaum, *Foundations of Psychoanalysis,* 237.

# Chapter 3
# *Individualpsychologie* as Praxis

"Nothing in life is so expensive as illness—and stupidity." Sigmund Freud, "On the Beginning of Treatment"

REUD'S *STUDIES ON HYSTERIA,* PUBLISHED IN 1895, set the stage for $\Psi A_2$ by giving a detailed account of the analytic method of the earliest stage of psychoanalysis. Freud's cathartic method, which I have detailed in chapter 2, required that a therapist return a patient to the moment at which the symptom was formed, reproduce the mental processes involved in that moment, and direct the discharge of those processes in conscious activity. Put succinctly, it was a matter of remembering and abreacting.

After *Studies on Hysteria,* Freud turned away from technical aspects of psychoanalysis, only to return to them in 1911, when he began a series of papers on dream interpretation, the relationship of patients to their analyst, and recommendations for analysts. Here, transference took center stage.

In this chapter, I examine issues more specific to psychoanalytic therapy as it relates to the development of $\Psi A_2$. I examine Freud's mature view of analytic therapy, based on transference, as well as other conditions applying to the analytic setting, such as suitable conditions for therapy, its length, rules for patients and analysts, the requirement of a therapist's neutrality, and the end of therapy. I begin with a fuller look at transference.

## Transference

### Lifting Repressions

The twenty-seventh lecture of Freud's *Introductory Lectures on Psychoanalysis* is "Transference"—a topic he broached in *Studies on Hysteria* and developed more fully in "Dynamics of Transference" in 1912 and "Observations on Transference Love" in 1915. Here Freud brings to bear two new factors for therapeutic success: the ego, which now is seen to house resistance, and transference, which is now seen to be the key to analytic success in dementia praecox.

Freud begins by suggesting that psychoanalysis, by helping a patient achieve a full sexual life, goes against the trends of conventional morality, which tends toward sexual abstinence. In such a manner, psychoanalysis "casts a shadow on analytic treatment for not serving general morality." He adds, "What it has given to the individual it will have taken from the community" (1917, *S.E.,* XVI, 432). The implicit argument can be constructed as follows:

1. Psychosexual frustration causes neurosis through sexual repression.
2. Neurosis can only be cured by lifting the repressions and allowing libido suitable outlets.
3. Lifting the repressions requires not only knowledge of sexual pathogens, but also the complete libidinal release of repressed sexual impulses through licentiousness.
4. Conventional morality disallows sexual licentiousness.
5. Therefore, psychoanalysis is at odds with conventional morality.

Yet to construe the problem thus is to commit the fallacy of bifurcation—i.e., to construct the problem in such a manner that only two polar alternatives are possible—which Freud himself disallows. On the one hand, the ascetical solution of conventional morality is unavailing, as it completely suppresses sexuality, which results in neurotic symptoms. On the other hand, the sensual solution that psychoanalysis seems to be advocating is also unavailing, as the demands of conventional morality result in neurotic symptoms. "Neither of these two alternative decisions could end the internal conflict; in either case one part to it would remain unsatisfied" (1917, *S.E.,* XVI, 432-3).

In addition, Freud notes, one must guard against failure to distinguish between normal conflicts and pathogenic conflicts. In pathogenic conflicts, the conflicting mental impulses are not on the same footing, as they are in normal conflicts. In pathogenic conflicts, one power is preconscious or conscious, while the other power is repressed. "For that reason the conflict cannot be brought to an issue; the disputants," he says, "can no more come to grips than [can], in the familiar simile, a polar bear and a whale." Pathogenic conflicts can only be resolved when a therapist brings out and enables the psychical conflicts to fight on the same ground—the "sole task" of psychotherapy. Thus, neither can one explain the therapeutic effect of psychoanalysis by allowing a full sexual life nor can one explain it by caving into the suppressive demands of conventional morality. Therapeutic success essentially involves compromise (1917, *S.E.,* XVI, 433-5).

The key to lifting repressions is to bring what is unconscious to consciousness. In that way, an analyst removes the preconditions of formation of symptoms and thus transforms the pathogenic conflict into one that is normal.

By carrying what is unconscious on into what is conscious, we lift the repressions, we remove the preconditions for the formation of symptoms, we transform the pathogenic conflict into a normal one for which it must be possible somehow to find a solution. All that we bring about in a patient is this single psychical change: the length to which it is carried is the measure of the help we

provide. Where no repressions (or analogous psychical processes) can be un-
done, our therapy has nothing to expect (1917, *S.E.,* XV: 435).

Thus, lifting the repressions is formulaically equivalent to making conscious
what is unconscious and filling in gaps in one's memory. The process overall is
lengthy and operose.

Here one might object, Freud adds, that the "tedious labours" of psychoanalysis, when successful, transform a person into someone completely different.
Freud objects. Psychoanalysis is not a matter of transmutation, but a matter of
fully bringing oneself back to oneself. The result is merely much less that is unconscious and much more that is conscious.

> The fact is that you are probably under-estimating the importance of an internal
> change of this kind. The neurotic who is cured has really become another man,
> though at bottom, of course, he has remained the same; that is to say, he has
> become what he might have become at best under the most favourable condi-
> tions. But that is a very great deal. If you now hear all that has to be done and
> what efforts it needs to bring about this apparently trivial change in a man's
> mental life, you will no doubt begin to realize the importance of this difference
> in psychical levels (1917, *S.E.,* XV: 435).

Freud then turns to a rather nettly issue: Is psychoanalysis a causal therapy?
On the one hand, insofar as it does not aim, in the first instance, at the removal
of symptoms, it is. On the other hand, insofar as it might be possible some day
to increase or diminish the quantity of libido chemically to strengthen or weaken
one instinct as it relates to another, it is not. Such a chemical intervention, he
flatly asserts, would be "a causal therapy in the true sense of the word," inas-
much as it should get to the real roots of the neurotic symptoms (1917, *S.E.,* XV:
436). Freud's purchase of physic-chemical reductionism is evident here.

How does a therapist lift repressions? Referring back to the cathartic method, Freud relates that there was a time when he thought that lifting a repression was principally a matter of disclosing unconscious material and making it
conscious.

> *Our* knowledge about the unconscious material is not equivalent to *his* know-
> ledge; if we communicate our knowledge to him, he does not receive it *instead
> of* his unconscious material but *beside* it; and that makes very little change in it.
> We must rather picture this unconscious material topographically. We must
> look for it in his memory at the place where it became unconscious owing to a
> repression. The repression must be got rid of—after which the substitution of
> the conscious material for the unconscious can proceed smoothly (1917, *S.E.,*
> XVI: 436).

Lifting a repression is not just a manner of etiological disclosure. A new method, which gets rid of the repression, is needed.

**Strengthening the Ego**

What is that new method? It begins like the old one: It interprets, discovers, and communicates, just like the cathartic method, but it aims to interpret, discover, and communicate at the right place and at the right time, unlike the cathartic method. Freud writes: "The anticathexis or the resistance does not form part of the unconscious but part of the ego, which is our collaborator, and is so even if it is not conscious. . . . We expect that this resistance will be given up and the anti-cathexis withdrawn when our interpretation has made it possible for the ego to recognize it" (1917, *S.E.,* XVI: 437).

How does recognition occur? Here a therapist must give his patient the appropriate anticipatory ideas. Freud bids us to imagine a balloon, visible in the sky. It is better for an analyst to act like one who tells another to look in the sky and see the balloon, instead of one who tells another to look in the sky and relate what is seen. Thus, an analyst acts no differently than a teacher who instructs his student, looking through a microscope for the first time, about what he can expect to see. Without such instruction, the student will see nothing, though indeed there is something in front of his very eyes (1917, *S.E.,* XVI: 437). Such a procedure, of course, smacks of suggestion.

Overall, since neurosis is the result of an enfeebled ego, the new method is a matter of strengthening or bolstering a weakened ego for the fight ahead.

> The new material that we produce includes, first, the reminder that the earlier decision led to illness and the promise that a different path will lead to recovery, and, secondly, the enormous change in all the circumstances that have taken place since the time of the original rejection. Then the ego was feeble, infantile, and may perhaps have had grounds for banning the demands of the libido as a danger. To-day it has grown strong and experienced, and moreover has a helper at hand in the shape of the doctor (1917, *S.E.,* XVI: 438).

This new method of aiming to strengthen a weakened ego comes about through the successes Freud has had in hysteria and the obsessional and anxiety neuroses.[1]

**Clouds in the Sky**

At some decisive point in the analytic setting, a second factor enigmatically becomes salient—the patient's development of a special interest in the doctor.[2] "Everything connected with the doctor seems to be more important to him than his own affairs and to be diverting him from his illness," Freud asserts. "For a time, accordingly, relations with him become very agreeable; he is particularly obliging, tries wherever possible to show his gratitude, reveals refinements and merits in his nature which we should not, perhaps, have expected to find in him." With the unexpected turn of his patient, the analyst too forms a favorable impression of the patient and there is considerable progress in sessions. There is a flood of associations and memories and, along with them, measurable improvement (1917, *S.E.,* XVI: 439-440).

The favorable results are unenduring. Fine weather soon turns cloudy. Affirmance turns to disaffirmance. The patient's flood of associations and memories ceases and he is now an unwilling participant in the process of analysis. Here an analyst recognizes a formidable resistance at work. He equally recognizes that the situation is now dangerous. "We find that the cause of the disturbance is that the patient has transferred on to the doctor intense feelings of affection which are justified neither by the doctor's behaviour nor by the situation that has developed during treatment" (1917, *S.E.,* XVI: 440-1).

To an untrained analyst, the obstacle seems a chance event. Yet the "chance event," as it is repeated in every new case, is a sign of underlying pathology.

[W]hen it comes to light again and again, under the most unfavorable conditions and where there are positively grotesque incongruities, even in elderly women and in relation to grey-bearded men, even where, in our judgement, there is nothing of any kind to entice—then we must abandon the idea of a chance disturbance and recognize that we are dealing with a phenomenon which is intimately bound up with the nature of the illness itself (1917, *S.E.,* XVI: 441-2).

That new fact is "transference."

## Positive and Negative Transference

"Transference" (*Übertragung*) is a literal transmission of feelings, derived outside of the analytic session, on to the doctor. Women generally experience *positive transference*—a passionate love for the analyst or, more tamely, a wish to be taken in as a favorable daughter or even as a non-sensual friend. All the same, it is straightforwardly a manifestation of libido on to the therapist. Men generally experience *negative transference*—a similar libidinal attachment to the analyst that is, because of the constraints of homosexuality, not openly affectionate, but instead hostile. Thus, at some point in therapy, libido manifests itself toward the therapist openly through ostensible love or, in disguised fashion, through hostility (1917, *S.E.,* XVI: 442-3).

How does a therapist respond to transference love or transference hostility? Acquiescence to a patient's demands is impossible. So too is complete repudiation of them. Instead, Freud says, the therapist should tell his patient that the latter's feelings of affection or hostility are not caused by the doctor, but rather are a repetition of something that has happened early on in his life. He writes, "In this way we oblige him to transform his repetition into a memory. By that means the transference, which . . . seemed in every case to constitute the greatest threat to the treatment, becomes its best tool, by whose help the most secret compartments of mental life can be opened" (1917, *S.E.,* XVI: 444).

A patient's illness grows like a living organism. Beginning of treatment does not mitigate such growth. It is only when the analyst has begun to master the illness that there is the opportunity for abatement and cure. "What happens is that the whole of his illness's new production is concentrated upon a single point—his relation to the doctor." Thus, Freud likens transference to a tree's cambium layer, between wood and bark, where new tissue forms to allow for increase in girth. At this point in treatment, a patient's memories fade to the background. The therapist no longer concerns himself with them, but is now concerned with the new neurosis, the transference neurosis, that has taken the place of the early one.

> All the patient's symptoms have abandoned their original meaning and have taken on a new sense which lies in a relation to the transference; or only such symptoms have persisted as are capable of undergoing such a transformation. But the mastering of this new, artificial neurosis coincides with getting rid of the illness which was originally brought to the treatment—with the accomplishment of our therapeutic task. A person who has become normal and free from the operation of repressed instinctual impulses in his relation to the doctor will remain so in his own life after the doctor has once more withdrawn it (1917, *S.E.*, XVI: 444-5).

Such a method works for hysteria, anxiety hysteria, and obsessional neurosis—called the "transference neuroses," whose symptoms prove to be substitutive satisfactions of libido.

In this manner, what directs therapy toward a satisfactory solution of illness is not a patient's intellectual insight, for it is neither strong enough nor free enough to work toward cure, but instead a non-cognitive, affective element—i.e., his relationship to his doctor. In positive transference, love of the therapist and its accompanying trust enable newly formed communications to occur. In negative transference, the therapist shows his patient that the therapist-directed hostility is masking genuine affection. Once positive transference occurs, a patient is enabled to direct libidinal object-cathexes toward other people, just like normal persons (1917, *S.E.*, XVI: 445-6).

Freud ends "Transference" by solving another difficulty—the explanation of Bernheim's *"suggestibilité."* The source of suggestion, Freud now confidently asserts, is nothing other than positive transference, which depends on libidinal cathexis (1917, *S.E.*, XVI: 446).

**Transference and Suggestion**

*Suggestibilité*, of course, is another problem to surmount. Freud addresses that imbroglio in "Analytic Therapy"—Lecture XXVIII of his *Introductory Lectures.* He begins by recounting his early cathartic experiences with the use of direct suggestion as a method for removing pathological symptoms. Though the method was rapid and agreeable to the patient, it was monotonous hackwork, not science, for the doctor. Moreover, it was not reliable. Patients whose symptoms had been in remission had those or other symptoms return and required further suggestion. Patients, then, often became addicts to suggestive therapy (1917, *S.E.,* XVI: 449).

Psychoanalysis, as Freud states at the end of "Transference," does not get rid of suggestion, but it uses it in a novel way. Through transference, "the patient does not suggest to himself whatever he pleases," but he is guided all along by the expertise of the therapist (1917, XVI: 451-2). That brings to mind the analogy of being told of seeing that what floats in the sky is a balloon.

How, then, can this method of transference guarantee objectivity? The question is reasonable, Freud acknowledges, as one might imagine a therapist talking a patient into believing that his symptoms have a sexual etiology, when they do not. In such a case, the sexual causes would be a manifestation of a therapist's own "depraved imagination" (1917, XVI: 452).

Freud appeals to experience to answer the objection. I return to a lengthier version of a passage quoted in the previous chapter—Freud's "Tally Argument."

> Anyone who has himself carried out psycho-analyses will have been able to convince himself on countless occasions that it is impossible to make suggestions to a patient in that way. . . . After all, his conflicts will only be successfully solved and his resistances overcome if the anticipatory ideas he is given tally with what is real in him. Whatever in the doctor's conjectures is inaccurate drops out in the course of the analysis; it has to be withdrawn and replaced by something more correct.

Here the remission of pathogenic symptoms requires accurate analytic assessment—another way of saying that eradication of pathogenic symptoms guarantees correct analytic assessment and that, without question, is a rather astonishing claim.

As Grünbaum has pointed out, that answer is gratuitous and unavailing. "Analytic Therapy," however, was not Freud's final answer to the problem. Freud's final answer, in "Analysis: Terminable and Interminable," requires reference to the end of analysis, to which I return at the end of this chapter.

## Suitable Conditions for Therapy

It is impossible to specify precisely the exact conditions that provide for the most favorable analytic setting. As in the game of chess, where opening moves and end moves can be given an "exhaustive systematic presentation," the multitude of moves in between those bookends are of an indescribably large variety and, thus, do not admit of an on-the-numbers and systematic description. One learns chess best by watching masters, not tyros, play. It is the same with psychoanalysis. Due to the extraordinary diversity of the psychical constellations" and "plasticity of all mental processes," there are no inviolable rules that govern analytic successes. Still, treatment cannot be arbitrary and so the methods employed and the means by which they are employed are not either. What one can do is to lay down "a procedure for the physician which is effective on the average" (1913, *S.E.,* XII: 123).

In this section, I draw predominantly from "Recommendations to Physicians Practicing Psychoanalysis" (1912) and "On the Beginning of Treatment" (1913).

## Recommendations for Beginning Therapy

### *Selecting Patients*

Freud first considers the selection of patients. Not every patient is suitable for psychoanalysis. Consequently, with patients about whom a therapist knows little, there is a probationary period, as it were. A therapist agrees to take on a patient provisionally for a week or two to see if his condition is suitable for psychoanalytic cure. In this period, the patient does almost all the talking. A therapist merely interjects here and there in an effort to glean information about his patient and to move along therapy. Long, preliminary discussions, prior treatment by another therapist with another method, and previous acquaintance with the patient[3] are disadvantageous to success (1913, *S.E.,* XII: 124-5).

### *Cost of and Time for Treatment*

"In regard to time, I adhere strictly to the principle of leasing a definite hour," Freud says. "Each patient is allotted a particular hour of my available working day." Yet that might not work for clients who only begin to open up toward the end of a session. Such patients might require more than an hour. Patients also meet for six days per week, excluding Sundays. For cases that are progressing well, three days per week may prove sufficient (1913, *S.E.,* XII: 126-7).

When a patient does not use the allotted time, he must still be materially responsible for it. The reasons are two. First, non-payment for non-attendance by patients threatens a therapist's material existence. Second and of equal importance, absences tend to occur most frequently whenever therapy is at a critical juncture, so excusing patients of their material responsibilities is tantamount to bolstering their repressions (1913, *S.E.,* XII: 127-8).

Should treatment be free in special cases—such as when a therapist is a beginner or when a client is materially disadvantaged? Freud's answer is no.

> Free treatment enormously increases some of a neurotic's resistances—in young women, for instance, the temptation which is inherent in their transference-relation, and in young men, their opposition to an obligation to feel grateful, and opposition which arises from their father-complex and which presents one of the most troublesome hindrances to the acceptance of medical help. The

absence of the regulating effect offered by the payment of a fee to the doctor makes itself very painfully felt; the whole relationship is removed from the real world, and the patient is deprived of a strong motive for endeavoring to bring the treatment to an end (1913, *S.E.,* XII: 132).

Thus, at the beginning of therapy, pecuniary matters must be handled frankly. "It seems to me more respectable and ethically less objectionable to acknowledge one's actual claims and needs rather than, as is still the practice among physicians, to act the part of the disinterested philanthropist." To the complaint that therapy is too costly, a therapist may roundly counter that the cost of not getting therapy is much greater. "Nothing in life is so expensive as illness—and stupidity" (1913, *S.E.,* XII: 130-1).

## Length of Therapy

To the question "How long will therapy take?" Freud offers the tale of the Philosopher and the Wayfarer from Aesop. When the Wayfarer asked the Philosopher how long a particular journey would take, the Philosopher replied flatly, "Walk!" The moral, Aesop relates, is that the Philosopher must know the length of the Wayfarer's stride before answering the question about the journey's time.[4]

In the case of the Wolf Man, Freud offers the following maxim by way of a second analogy—that of an army progressing over a stretch of land against the resistance of an enemy.

The length of the road over which an analysis must travel with the patient, and the quantity of material which must be mastered on the way, are of no importance in comparison with the resistance which is met with in the course of the work, and are only of importance at all in so far as they are necessarily proportional to the resistance (1918, *S.E.,* XVII: 11-2).

Given his etiological commitments, Freud never wavered from his stance that psychotherapy, in the majority of cases, was necessarily a lengthy process. He says, "[P]sycho-analysis is always a matter of long periods of time, of half a year or whole years—of longer periods than the patient expects." In that, he differed from many other psychotherapists, for instance Otto Rank, to whom Freud implicitly refers, when he mentions a colleague who held out hope for a short and convenient out-patient treatment for certain neuroses[5] (1913, *S.E.,* XII: 128-9). Psychoanalysis cannot be conducted pell-mell.

In a nutshell, Freud's argument is that a patient's neurosis has been developing insidiously for many years, often decades, and so it would be presumptuous and foolish to think that there could be a quick therapeutic remedy. The rationale here is sensible. Elsewhere, he gives a quasi-algorithm for length of treatment.

I turn to . . . the reproach against analytic treatment that it takes a disproportionately long time. On this it must be said that psychical changes do in fact only take place slowly; if they occur rapidly, suddenly, that is a bad sign. It is true that the treatment of a fairly severe neurosis may easily extend over several years; but consider, in cases of success, how long the illness would have lasted. A decade, probably, for every year of treatment: the illness, that is to say (as we see so often in untreated cases), would not have ended at all (1933, *S.E.*, XXII: 156).

In "Analysis Terminable and Interminable" (1937), Freud talks of others' and his own efforts to shorten analysis by given a patient a specific date for cure and why that must fail. "[W]e may be quite sure that while the force of the threat [that treatment will end on such-and-such date] will have the effect of bringing part of the material to light, another part will be held back and become buried, as it were, and will be lost to our therapeutic efforts" (*S.E.*, XXIII: 218).

Today, therapists often see patients one day per week and the cost of each session is considerable. Those without health-care coverage most often must forego therapy. Moreover, there are pharmacological alternatives, which have become a multi-billion-dollar business in the United States. Pharmacological remedies, like Prozac, are certainly quick-fixes that tend to be chosen over psychotherapy. Such "remedies," of course, are considered anything but remedies by psychotherapists today.[6]

### A "Certain Ceremonial"

There was one rule, a "certain ceremonial," that was a drawback to his early days with suggestive therapy, to which Freud insisted all analysts should adhere. That concerned the position of patients during treatment. For several reasons, he insisted that patients should lie on a sofa, while he would sit out of sight, behind them. Why? First, he loathed being stared at by his patients for eight or more hours per day. Second, he did not wish to give away the current of his unconscious thoughts through his reactions, however slight they might be, to patients' words. Finally, the purpose and result of this ceremonial are to prevent the commingling of a patient's associations with the transference, to isolate the transference, and to allow it to come to the fore at the right time as a sharply defined resistance[7] (1013, *S.E.*, XII: 134)—any of which could be hindered by being seated in plain sight.

We can now sum Freud's suggestions for beginning treatment:

- A therapist should offer new patients a probationary period of a week or two to see whether they are suited for psychoanalytic therapy.
- A therapist should shun free treatments.
- A therapist should tell patients that psychotherapy is essentially a lengthy process.
- A therapist should not be visible to his patients.

## Recommendations during Therapy

I preface this part by Freud's own caveat in "Recommendations": He states that the general technique behind the recommendations is not the only one, but merely that which is best suited to his own individuality[8] (1912, *S.E.*, XII: 111).

### *"Fundamental Rule"*

Freud begins "Recommendations" with a prodigious problem—that of trying to recall and sift through the mass of material that confronts him on a daily basis. The problem is compounded insofar as he does not recommend note-taking during a session.

The solution to such a prodigious problem is simple. It is merely a matter of a therapist doing his part to abide by the fundamental rule of psychoanalytic therapy: meeting the patient unconscious to unconscious. He gives two reasons. First, a therapist avoids the great demand of the strain of continued, focused attention. Second, focused attention requires selective attention, which impedes proper analysis. In selecting from the material before him, he follows his expectations and inclinations. Following his expectations, he runs the risk of finding only what he already knows. Following his inclinations, he will falsify what he might observe. He writes, "[A therapist] should withhold all conscious influences from his capacity to attend, and give himself over completely to his 'unconscious memory'" or, more succinctly, "He should simply listen and not bother about whether he is keeping anything in mind." As we have already seen, the fundamental rule for a therapist—giving all things equal attention—is necessarily counterweighed by "the demand made on the patient that he should communicate everything that occurs to him without criticism or selection" (1912, XII: 111-2).

### *Note-Taking*

The problem of selective attention relates equally to note-taking and that applies to dreams, noteworthy dates, and noteworthy events. In certain cases—e.g., that of a particularly significant dream—a therapist can merely ask a patient to repeat what he had said toward the end of a session so that a therapist might then have it fresh in his head.

Note-taking, Freud admits, can have particular benefit if one aims at published scientific studies, where exact reports would seem beneficial. Still, that gain is outweighed by other losses. First, note-taking could have deleterious consequences. One will be tempted to use it to piece together the structure of a study, to predict progress, or to form a picture of the precise state of affairs from time to time. To do such things is to be working on a case scientifically, not clinically. To work on a case scientifically is a matter of violating the fundamental rule of psychoanalysis, which demands evenly suspended attention. Synthesis of analytic material should happen only after a case has been concluded, not during a case (1912, *S.E.*, XII: 114). Moreover, the benefits of taking notes are insubstantial.

> [E]xact reports of analytic case histories are of less value than might be expected. Strictly speaking, they only possess the *ostensible* exactness of which "modern" psychiatry affords us some striking examples. They are, as a rule, fatiguing to the reader and yet do not succeed in being a substitute for his actual presence at an analysis (1912, *S.E.*, XII: 114).

We recall here that Freud was in the habit of seeing most patients six times each week and, consequently, the particulars of a prior session would tend to be fresh in mind at the next session. It is difficult to think that such a method would work, when one sees numerous patients—many of which meet merely once per week.

### Neutrality of Analyst

As the previous chapter showed, the proper attitude a therapist should have toward his patients and toward therapy in general would be one of neutrality. Freud offers the helpful analogy of a surgeon, which demands emotional detachment for success. "The justification for requiring this emotional coldness in the analyst is that it creates the most advantageous conditions for both parties: for the doctor a desirable protection for his own emotional life and for the patient the largest amount of help that we can give him to-day" (1912, *S.E.*, XII: 115).

Freud returns to the surgical analogy five years later in "Analyatic Therapy." He says:

> Psychoanalytic treatment may be compared with a surgical operation and may similarly claim to be carried our under arrangements that will be the most favorable for its success. You know the precautionary measures adopted by a surgeon: a suitable room, good lighting, assistants, exclusion of the patient's relatives, and so on. Ask yourselves now how many of these operations would turn out successfully if they had to take place in the presence of all the members of the patient's family, who would stick their nose into the field of the operation and exclaim aloud at every incision (1917, *S.E.*, XVI: 459).

### Moral Guidance

Freud next turns to a singularly labyrinthine concern—moral guidance. It is difficult for a doctor, guided by a natural ambition, not to suggest direction to a patient by means of sublimation, once developmental inhibitions have been resolved, but to do that is to offer the patient moral guidance. "Analysis paves the way to independence instead of a heteronomous morality," he says sharply in a letter to Oskar Pfister.[9]

It is not so much that Freud objects to a therapist wearing the hat of moral advisor, for in some cases he thinks it is advisable; it is rather that many of his patients are not capable of assuming those moral roles, through appropriate forms of sublimation.

> But here again the doctor should hold himself in check, and take the patient's capacities rather than his own desires as guide. Not every neurotic has a high talent for sublimation; one can assume of many of them that they would not have fallen ill at all if they had possessed the art of sublimating their instincts. If we press them unduly towards sublimation and cut them off from the most accessible and convenient instinctual satisfactions, we shall usually make life even harder for them than they feel it in any case. As a doctor, one must above all be tolerant to the weakness of a patient, and must be content if one has won back some degree of capacity for work and enjoyment for a person even of only moderate worth. Educative ambition is of as little use as therapeutic ambition. It must further be borne in mind that many people fall ill precisely from an attempt to sublimate their instincts beyond the degree permitted by their organization and that in those who have a capacity for sublimation the process usually takes place of itself as soon as their inhibitions have been overcome by analysis. In my opinion, therefore, efforts invariably to make use of the analytic treatment to bring about sublimation of instinct are, though no doubt always laudable, far from being *in every case* advisable (1912, *S.E.,* XII: 119).

In short, Freud does not state that an analyst should never offer moral guidance through proposing means of sublimation. It is merely that he ought not to be guided by his own desires, but rather by a patient's capacities, which are in most instances limited.

I return to the issue of psychotherapy as moral therapy in the final chapter of this project.

We may now sum Freud's "recommendations" during therapy:

- A therapist concerns himself with the volume of information in his daily sessions through use of the fundamental rule—meeting a patient unconscious to unconscious.
- A therapist should not take notes during a session.
- A therapist should not concern himself with treating his sessions as case-studies.
- A therapist, following the principle of neutrality, should adopt the cool indifference of a surgeon.
- A therapist should be guided by assessment of a patient's capacities before suggesting means of sublimation to a patient.

# Additional Issues in Therapy

## Role of Dreams in Psychotherapy

Therapists today still use analysis of dreams in therapy, but oneiric analysis does not have the significance that it had for Freud, who boldly stated that dreams were the "royal road to . . . the unconscious." He writes that the dreams of neurotics, like their slips of tongue, are significant clues of underlying pathology. "The study of dreams therefore becomes the most convenient means of access to knowledge of the repressed unconscious, of which the libido withdrawn from the ego forms a part" (1917, *S.E.*, XVI: 456).

Some critics today maintain that Freud's emphasis on the importance of dreams in therapy was merely a vestige of his early topographical model. With the migration to the structural model and the emphasis on transference, they assert, analysis of dreams ceased to be so important to Freud.[10] It is a claim, I think, whose truth is less, than more, probable.

## Statistical Justification of Therapy

Freud was not shy, at times, about vaunting the unquestioned therapeutic successes of psychoanalysis. He states unabashedly in "Analytic Therapy," "I emphasized the fact that under favorable conditions we achieve successes which are second to none of the finest in the field of internal medicine; and I can now add something further—namely that they could not have been achieved by any other procedure" (1917, *S.E.*, XVI: 458).

A long-standing criticism of Freud's clinical data has been that they seem to confirm psychopathological theory all too readily, even though no systematic studies of Freud's analytic successes have been conducted. Writes Sydney Hook in 1958 of the need for statistical justification of Freud's generalizations: "Since psychoanalysis does claim to function as a therapy, its clinical successes and failures seem to me to be highly relevant in evaluating the truth of its theories. If it has no clinical successes and if it is not confirmed by experimental findings, then it has no more scientific standing than any other consistent mythology." He adds that the clinical data are at best ambiguous. Furthermore, what successes psychoanalysis has had may be the result of suggestion, not sound methodology and respectable theoretical claims. Thus, if psychoanalysis wishes to be considered a science, like any other legitimate science, it must find ways to eliminate competing hypotheses like suggestion.[11]

Michael Scriven agrees that Freud's and other therapists' successes could be due to some accidental feature of the therapeutic environment, such as "being able to discuss personal problems with an interested or noncensorious listener, or, at a later stage, the need to terminate the heavy financial burden of analysis." Recovery could also come about spontaneously over time.[12] He sums glumly, "Claims about the curative effect of psychoanalysis are therefore entirely speculative until some figure for spontaneous recovery rate of comparable patients can be established." Even if psychoanalysis should prove itself slightly superior to spontaneous recovery, there would remain the issues of whether that slight superiority was worth the financial and temporal costs and of permanence of the cure. "Cure" is a slippery term.[13]

Freud himself addresses the issue of "cure" in "Analytic Therapy," where he questions the relevance of statistical data.

> Friends of analysis have advised us to meet the threatened publication of our failures with statistics of our successes drawn up by ourselves. I did not agree to this. I pointed out that statistics are worthless if the items assembled in them are too heterogeneous; and the cases of neurotic illness which we had taken into treatment were in fact incomparable in a great variety of respects. Moreover, the period of time that could be covered was too short to make it possible to judge the durability of the cures. And it was altogether impossible to report on many of the cases: they concerned people who had kept both their illness and its treatment secret, and their recovery had equally to be kept secret. But the strongest reason for holding back lay in the realization that in matters of therapy people [presumably, Freud's critics] behave highly irrationally, so that one has no prospect of accomplishing anything with them by rational means (1917, *S.E.*, XVI: 461).

Here Freud defends psychoanalysis from critics by noting that the associations gleaned in therapy are too heterogeneous, that the various cases are too heterogeneous, that cure can only be decided over a very long period of time, and that many cases have "secretive" elements.[14] Finally, as he is often wont to do when his scientific reputation is called into question through disaffirmance of psychoanalytic findings, he appeals to resistance by his critics. Such critics are behaving highly irrationally, and so any attempt to defend psychoanalysis by rational means will fall on deaf ears and be bootless. I offer a critical analysis of Freud's apologia in chapter 4.

## Psychoanalysis vs. Psychiatry

In "Psycho-Analysis and Psychiatry," Freud argues that psychiatry and psychoanalysis are complementary, not competing sciences.

> Psycho-analysis is related to psychiatry approximately as histology is to anatomy: the one studies the external forms of the organs, the other studies their construction out of tissues and cells. . . . To-day . . . anatomy is regarded by us as the foundation of scientific medicine. But there was a time when it was as much forbidden to dissect the human cadaver in order to discover the internal structure of the body as it now seems to be to practice psycho-analysis in order to learn about the internal mechanism of the mind. It is to be expected that in the not too distant future it will be realized that a scientifically based psychiatry is not possible without a sound knowledge of the deeper-lying unconscious

processes in mental life (1917, *S.E.*, XV: 254-5).

Freud forthwith goes on to state that psychoanalysis, in spite of its avowed limits, is justified therapeutically. What psychical states, like delusional states, psychoanalysis cannot cure, it can study and essay to understand, for understanding, even when cure is out of the question, is a great scientific gain (1917, *S.E.*, XV: 255). I cannot underscore Freud's emphasis that understanding is itself great scientific gain, because, as I argue in the second part of this book, it seems to be much of his motivation for tackling group issues psychoanalytically.

Elsewhere, his estimation of the worth of the psychiatric treatment of his day was not so roseate. In "Beginning of Treatment," he maintains that psychotherapy is riskier business that psychiatry. For psychotherapists, diagnostic mistakes have deleterious results that challenge the value of psychoanalytic therapy; for psychiatrists, diagnostic mistakes are merely theoretical errors that bring no discredit to psychiatrists (1913, *S.E.*, XII: 124-5).

In "Parapraxes," Freud offers a criticism of the purely descriptive, non-etiological methods of psychiatrists:

> It is true that psychiatry, as a part of medicine, sets about describing the mental disorders it observes and collecting them into clinical entities; but at favourable moments the psychiatrists themselves have doubts of whether their purely descriptive hypotheses deserve the name of a science. Nothing is known of the origin, the mechanism or the mutual relations of the symptoms of which these clinical entities are composed; there are either no observable changes in the anatomical organ of the mind to correspond to them, or changes which throw no light upon them. These mental disorders are only accessible to therapeutic influence when they can be recognized as subsidiary effects of what is otherwise an organic illness (1916, *S.E.*, XV: 20-1).

## The End of Therapy

Finally, I return to a topic introduced at the end of the previous chapter: How is an able therapist to know that his constructions all along have been correct? The answer to that question relies on his answer to the question: How is an able therapist to know that analysis is at an end?

Freud addresses the issue of the end of analysis in another late paper—"Analysis Terminable and Interminable" (1937). I quote at length.

> We must first decide what is meant by the ambiguous phrase "the end of an analysis." . . . This happens when two conditions have been approximately fulfilled: first, the patient shall no longer be suffering from his symptoms and shall have overcome his anxieties and his inhibitions; and secondly, that the analyst shall judge that so much repressed material has been made conscious, so much that was unintelligible has been explained, and so much internal resistance conquered that there is no need to fear a repetition of the pathological processes concerned. If one is prevented by

external difficulties from reaching this goal, it is better to speak of an *incomplete* analysis rather than of an *unfinished* one.

The other meaning of the "end" of an analysis is much more ambitious. In this sense of it, what we are asking is whether the analyst has had such a far-reaching influence on the patient that no further change could be expected to take place in him if his analysis were continued. It is as though it were possible by means of analysis to attain to a level of absolute psychical normality—a level, moreover, which we could feel confident would be able to remain stable, as though, perhaps, we had succeeded in resolving every one of the patient's repressions and in filling in all the gaps in his memory (1937, *S.E.,* XIX: 219-20).

The two senses of "end of analysis" might be summed:

**End of Analysis$_1$:** These two conditions must be met (approximately):
1. A patient is no longer suffering from his symptoms and has overcome his anxieties and his inhibitions;
2. The analyst judges that so much repressed material has been made conscious, so much that was unintelligible has been explained, and so much internal resistance conquered that there is no need to fear a repetition of the pathological processes concerned.
**End of Analysis$_2$:** The analyst has had such a far-reaching influence on his patient that no further change can be expected to take place in him through further analysis.

In the first definition, remission of symptoms must be accompanied by an analyst's assurance that the symptoms cannot reappear. Yet here again we are stopped by paralipsis. Freud fails to say how an analyst can be assured of non-remission of symptoms. Yet one cannot help but think that he has the jigsaw-puzzle argument, or something equally as gossamery, in mind.

The second definition is of greater concern, for it makes inordinate demands on a therapist, as it bespeaks the promise of some sense of complete therapeutic success. Analytic therapy, he says, offers the theoretical promise of "absolute psychical normality" as well as its maintenance. Once again, the guarantee reminds one of the jigsaw-puzzle argument—especially because of Freud's use of the phrase, "filling in all the gaps in his memory." Freud never explicitly says that the second definition can be met, but merely asks readers to consult experience to see whether the theoretical promise is practicable or capable of approximation.

Appeal to experience, Freud asseverates, shows that neuroses comprise both constitutional and accidental factors. Constitutional factors are critical: The more they come into play, the less probable is therapeutic success.

Only when a case is predominantly traumatic will analysis succeed in doing what it is so superlatively able to do; only then will it, thanks to having strengthened the patient's ego, succeed in replacing by a correct solution the inadequate decision made in his early life. Only in such cases can one speak of an analysis having been definitely ended. In them, analysis has done all that it should and does not need to be continued (1937, *S.E.,* XXXIII: 220).

Complete therapeutic success is possible, so long as constitutional factors do not predominate in a neurosis.

To illustrate the operose nature of psychoanalytic treatment, Freud follows with two examples of seemingly complete successes that turned sour years later. Such "failures" might give pause to skeptics and optimists, but Freud's own sanguineness is unshaken, with three key reservations. First, it might not be possible to resolve any conflict between the ego and a drive for all time. Second, resolution of one conflict is not necessarily inoculation against another at some future time. Last, an analyst might not have the capacity to stir up a pathogenic conflict in a patient as a means of prophylaxis (1937, *S.E.,* XXIII: 221-3). It follows that complete cure in the second sense of "end of therapy," though possible, is not to be expected from proper psychoanalytic therapy.

That seems to be the earlier view Freud held in "Analytic Therapy." In distinguishing between nervous health (i.e., therapeutic success) and neurosis in the latter, he adds that environmental, not biological factors, might decide the issue.

> The distinction between nervous health and neurosis is thus reduced to a practical question and is decided by the outcome—by whether the subject is left with a sufficient amount of capacity for enjoyment and of efficiency. It probably goes back to the relative sizes of the quota of energy that remains free and of that which is bound by repression, and is of a quantitative not of a qualitative nature. I need not tell you that this discovery is the theoretical justification for our conviction that neuroses are in principle curable in spite of their being based on constitutional disposition (1917, *S.E.,* XVI: 457).

Though he allows for the possibility of a complete cure, he advises caution apropos of practicability. Constitutional factors are never inert. As always, quantitative factors are at play—some mobilized toward success and some in defense of failure—and, with quantities of energy at war, advantage is correlated with size, though victory is seldom ever complete. As Freud says elsewhere, "God is on the side of the big battalions" (1940, *S.E.,* XXIII: 182).

Overall, "end of analysis" is itself a greasy term. No therapist can be confident that any cure will be enduring or that no other form of neurosis will rear its unsightly head in the future—i.e., end-of-analysis$_2$ is a pipe-dream. The final analytic assessment of a therapist, even one of the first rank, is always assailable. In acknowledging that, however, Freud is merely acknowledging fallibility, and fallibility is characteristic of every empirical science, honestly conducted.

# Notes

1. Conditions unaffected by this method are paranoia, melancholia, and dementia praecox.

2. Precisely the mistake Freud made in his haste to convince Dora, whom he began treating in October 1900, that his interpretation of her hysterical symptoms, mostly oral, were of a complex sexual nature (1905, *S.E.,* VII).

3. Freud might have in mind here his own case study of Dora in 1905.

4. Freud immediately cautions that the analogy is limited, because neurotics often slow their stride, because of resistance.

5. Cf. Freud's letter to Arnold Zweig: "A proper analysis is a slow process. In some cases I myself have only been able to uncover the core of the problem after many years, not, it is true, of continuous analysis, and I was not able to say where I had gone wrong in my technique. It is the exact opposite of a mountebank like O. Rank who travels around maintaining that he can cure a severe obsessional neurosis in four months! But partial and superficial analyses, such as you are having, are also fruitful and beneficial. The main impression one gets is of the marvelous quality of the life of the psyche. But it is a scientific undertaking rather than an easy therapeutic operation." Sigmund Freud and Arnold Zweig, *The Letters of Sigmund Freud & Arnold Zweig,* ed. Ernst L. Freud (New York: New York University Press, 1970), 107–8.

6. It is not clear that Freud would have shared their view, given that he said only physio-chemical therapies are *true* causal therapies in "Transference."

7. Not to mention Freud's astonishing admission to Fliess in an 1888 letter that he would sleep through his afternoon sessions (Introduction, xiv, fn. 6).

8. Freud was not consistent with his own "recommendations." See Frank J. Sulloway, "Reassessing Freud's Case Histories: The Social Construction of Psychoanalysis," 153–92, and Paul Roazen, "Freud's Patients: First-Person Accounts," 289–305, in *Freud and the History of Psychoanalysis,* ed. Toby Gelfand and John Kerr (Hillsdale, NJ: The Analytic Press, 1992). In a 1989 letter to Fliess, Freud even stated that he slept through his afternoon sessions, which explains in part his reluctance to face patients. Sigmund Freud and Wilhelm Fleiss, *The Complete Letters of Sigmund Freud to Wilhelm Fliess: 1887–1904,* ed. Jeffrey Moussaieff Masson (Cambridge: Harvard University Press, 1985), 303.

9. September 5, 1930. Sigmund Freud and Oskar Pfister, *Psychoanalysis & Faith,* 137.

10. For more on this issue, see Steven J. Ellman, *Freud's Technique Papers: A Contemporary Perspective* (Northvale, NJ: Jason Aronson, 1991), 134–37.

11. Sydney Hook, "Science and Mythology in Psychoanalysis," in *Psychoanalysis, Scientific Method, and Philosophy,* ed. Sydney Hook (New York University Press, 1958), 219–20.

12. Michael Scriven, "The Experimental Investigation of Psychoanalysis," *Psychoanalysis, Scientific Method, and Philosophy,* ed. Sydney Hook (New York University Press, 1958), 228.

13. Michael Scriven, "The Experimental Investigation of Psychoanalysis," 231.

14. Strangely, he maintains in a letter to Adler, "There should not be any doubt that the psychoanalytic method can be learned. It will be possible to learn it once the arbitrariness of individual psychoanalysts is curbed by tested rules." Hermann Nunberg and Ernst Federn (eds.), *Minutes of the Vienna Psychoanalytic Society, Vol. 1,* trans. M. Nunberg with H. Collins (New York: International Universities Press, 1962, 237.

# Chapter 4
# Efficacy of *Individualpsychologie*

"The unhappiness that our work of enlightenment may cause will after all only affect some individuals. . . . [A]ll the energies which are to-day consumed in the production of neurotic symptoms serving the purposes of a world of phantasy isolated from reality, will, even if they cannot at once be put to uses in life, help to strengthen the clamour for the changes in our civilization through which alone we can look for the well-being of future generations." Sigmund Freud, "Future Prospects of Psycho-Analytic Therapy"

S CHOLARS AND CRITICS OF FREUD often take for granted the worth of psychotherapy as clinical practice ($\Psi A_2$). Their censures aim at what Freud professed to do outside the clinic. They chide Freud for insisting that psychotherapy has itself become a full-fledged science ($\Psi A_3$) and for Freud's use of it as a method for treating group problems—war, technology, pedagogy, and other pressing problems of humanity—i.e., applied psychoanalysis.

Nonetheless, Freud himself, especially late in his life, came to acknowledge problems with individual therapy. Acknowledgement of those problems was likely at least a small part of his shift to group-psychology issues in his later publications.

This final chapter of part I is a critical analysis of Freud's own verdict on the value of psychotherapy as individual therapy. I argue that Freud was, toward the end of his life, guardedly optimistic at best about the curative capacity of psychotherapy as individual therapy. He came to see that psychotherapy had a limited effect on solving individuals' pathological problems, once deep-seated. Its chief merit lay in its capacity to understand and explain human behavior—both "normal" and "abnormal."[1] The "successes" here, as we shall see in the second part of this project, gave Freud the pluck and tools he needed to move toward understanding and explaining the more pressing, extra-clinical problems facing groups of individuals—humanity as a whole, being one.

Thus, the overall value of Freudian psychoanalysis, for Freud, was not its ability to solve human problems, but to prevent them from occurring in the first place by giving humans deeper insight into the human condition. In short, Freud slowly came to see that psychoanalysis was foremost not a curative, but a prophylactic therapy, both for individual and for group pathology. In short, Freud was moving, and moving with full cognizance, from $\Psi A_2$ to $\Psi A_3$—a complete scientific explanation for human behavior within and without social contexts.[2]

This chapter, beginning with a summary of Freud's appraisal of the worth of psychotherapy, is an assessment of the scientific merits of psychoanalysis as individual therapy.

## Cathartic Therapist as Father-Confessor

The aim of psychoanalytic therapy was to give back to each patient, suffering from neurosis, that part of his mental life over which he had lost control. Gaining control was a matter of reclaiming for the ego a fuller possession of self—viz., allowing the patient to see himself once again as a historical being. As Joachim Scharfenberg neatly states: "The ill suffer from memories that have been repressed and are no longer accessible. Therefore they cannot be open to the future but must project the past into the future in a constant 'compulsion to repeat.' They have become ahistorical."[3] Gaining control was also a matter of empowering and freeing the ego to face the demands of the id, super-ego, and reality.

As we have seen from chapter 1, the beginnings of psychoanalysis were modest. In his collaborative work with Breuer, Freud found that hysterical symptoms seemed to be treatable in a manner that ignored organic etiology. Breuer discovered that hypnosis could be used to reproduce the first instant of an event that presumably caused a specific hysterical symptom and that that reproduction was sufficient for removal of the hysterical symptom. Treatment amounted, in part, to a course of narrating or retracing the occurrence of a symptom in reverse order—from symptom as effect to underlying pathogenic memory as cause.

Problems with the cathartic method were several and those did not escape Freud's notice. Below, I rehash the main problems, fully addressed in chapter 2.

- The cathartic method, being symptomatic and not causal, can remove present symptoms, but cannot prevent new ones from emerging.
- The cathartic method is time- and labor-intensive.
- The cathartic method might not remove all symptoms of hysteria.
- The cathartic method might be helpless in cases of acute hysteria.
- The cathartic method is too cognitive.
- The cathartic method ignores the role of transference.

Limits of the method notwithstanding, it led to two results that Freud would never disavow: that hysterical symptoms had a pathogenic meaning and that the removal of the symptom required disclosure of that pathogenic meaning (1922, *S.E.*, XVIII: 235-6).

Freud sums the benefit of cathartic therapy in an analogy—the analyst as father confessor, *inter alia*.

> But lastly—and this remains the strongest lever—we must endeavour, after we have discovered the motives for his defence, to deprive them of their value or even to replace them by more powerful ones. This no doubt is where it ceases to be possible to state psychotherapeutic activity in formulas. One works to the best of one's power, as an elucidator (where ignorance has given rise to fear), as a teacher, as the representative of a freer or superior view of the world, as a father confessor who gives absolution, as it were, by a continuance of his sympathy and respect after the confession has been made (1895, *S.E.*, II: 282).

What is the result of cathartic "absolution"? Consistent with the dour optimism he advocates in later works, Freud replies somberly that one will be able to trade hysterical misery for common unhappiness.[4]

> When I have promised my patients help or improvement by means of a cathartic treatment I have often been faced by this objection: "Why, you tell me yourself that my illness is probably connected with my circumstances and the events of my life. You cannot alter these in any way. How do you propose to help me, then?" And I have been able to make this reply: "No doubt fate would find it easier than I do to relieve you of your illness. But you will be able to convince yourself that much will be gained if we succeed in transforming your hysterical misery into common unhappiness. With a mental life that has been restored to health you will be better armed against that unhappiness" (1895, *S.E.*, II: 305).

## The Virgin's Rare Appearances

In the "Future Prospects of Psycho-Analytic Therapy," Freud complains about difficulties in getting psychoanalysis off the ground. The difficulties, generated by the ill-will of opponents of psychoanalysis, have led to an overall skepticism of psychoanalysis and its clinical methods of psychical cure. The problem he compares to that of a Turkish gynecologist, who has to make gynecological diagnoses through feeling the pulse of women's arms, extended through a hole in the wall. Opponents of psychoanalysis in the West, he asserts, want to allow psychoanalysts no more access to people's minds than has the Turkish gynecologist to the bodies of his female patients (1910, *S.E.*, XI: 147).

The problem, Freud says, is that psychoanalysis has made an enemy of society because it has shown that society is in large part responsible for human unhappiness. Thus, society will not sanction a discipline that not only is critical of it, but also destroys its "happy" illusions.

That notwithstanding, Freud maintains psychoanalysis will have its say in time.

Powerful though men's emotions and self-interest may be, yet intellect is a power too—a power which makes itself felt, not, it is true, immediately, but all the more certainly in the end. The harshest truths are heard and recognized at last, after the interests they have injured and the emotions they have roused have exhausted their fury. It has always been so, and the unwelcome truths which we psycho-analysts have to tell the world will have the same fate. Only it will not happen very quickly; we must be able to wait (1910, *S.E.,* XI: 147-8).

Resistance notwithstanding, Freud then gives his verdict on the overall influence of psychoanalysis. He speaks of a "very remarkable therapeutic constellation." Turning to the unquestioned successes of psychoanalytic therapy for individuals through insight given such individuals, he then asks us to consider society in the manner of a sick person, who has a general recognition of his own pathology. "The success which the treatment can have with the individual," he asserts, "must occur equally with the community."[5] Freud here is not essaying to tackle social issues through recognition of group neurosis, as he does in later works, but rather he advances the simple notion that the insights patients gain through psychoanalytic therapy and cure are themselves invaluable social benefits.

If this hope seems Utopian to you, you may remember that neurotic phenomena have actually been dispelled already by this means, although only in quite isolated instances. Think how common hallucinations of the Virgin Mary used to be among peasant girls in former times. So long as such a phenomenon brought a flock of believers and might lead to a chapel being built on the sacred spot, the visionary state of these girls was inaccessible to influence. To-day even our clergy have changed their attitude to such things; they allow police and doctors to examine the visionary, and now the Virgin makes only very rare appearances (1910, *S.E.,* XI: 149).

Freud then offers a somewhat crude analogy to illustrate the mild utopianism psychoanalysis has to offer. Suppose a number of men and women in good society have gone out picnicking. The women, of polite disposition, announce among themselves that their message for going off to relieve themselves will be that they must go off to pick flowers. A scalawag gets wind of the secret and writes it on the program of the picnic so that it is accessible to everyone. Once that secret is out, it seems reasonable that the group will shun future secrets and merely speak truthfully and openly. Thereafter ladies in need of relieving themselves will simply announce that they have to relieve themselves. Similarly, psychoanalysis offers assistance to those, saddled with troublesome conflicts, who take flight in neurosis. It encourages them to face both truth and their troubles and to fight for mental wellness. Gradual social acceptance of psychoanalysis, due to its successes, will doubtless lead to tolerance of individuals' illnesses (1910, *S.E.,* XI: 149-50). He sums:

The unhappiness that our work of enlightenment may cause will after all only affect some individuals. The change-over to a more realistic and creditable attitude on the part of society will not be brought about too dearly by these sacrifices. But above all, all the energies which are to-day consumed in the production of neurotic symptoms serving the purposes of a world of phantasy isolated from reality, will, even if they cannot at once be put to uses in life, help to strengthen the clamour for the changes in our civilization through which alone we can look for the well-being of future generations (1910, *S.E.*, XI: 150-1).

Freud sees a capacity for rapid changes in social attitudes toward mental illness through scientific advances. Psychoanalysis is, as it were, in the trenches and at the very front-line of the fighting for such advances. The sentiment here is that psychoanalysis is making a modest, but significant contribution toward human betterment.

## Morality and Individual Therapy

### Morality as Individual Neurosis

In a letter to colleague Wilhelm Fliess, dated May 31, 1897, Freud notes that he will "very soon discover the source of morality" (1897, *S.E.*, I: 253). In a subsequent letter (1897, *S.E.*, I: 268-71), he elaborates on that source, which is organic: the bodily sexual zones. The onset of morality, he says, begins when these zones—the anus, mouth, and throat—no longer offer a release for sexual impulses in normal ways. First, the thought and sight of them no longer produces sexual excitation. Second, the internal sensations arising from them fail to contribute to libido as do the sexual organs. The result is repression, which leads, during the waves of a child's development, to piety, shame, and other moral sentiments. The subsequent "choice" of neurosis—hysteria, obsessional neurosis, or paranoia—depends critically on the stage of development at which repression occurs. Morality, in consequence, has its source in repressed sexuality. Freud writes, "What we call the character of the person is built up to a large extent from the material of sexual excitations; it is composed of impulses fixed since infancy and won through sublimation and of such structures as are destined to suppress effectually those perverse feelings which are recognized as useless" (1905, *S.E.*, VIII: 233-4). Freud's thoughts foreshadow the sort of repressive forces that are needed for the development of the super-ego, which he introduces formally almost twenty years later.

Much of the philosophical resistance to psychoanalysis centers on its notion of morality as nothing other than the result of repressed sexuality. In an earlier letter, Freud characterizes morality as the cause, not the result, of sexual repression.

> We shall be plunged deep into psychological riddles if we enquire into the origin of the unpleasure which seems to be released by premature sexual stimulation and without which . . . a repression cannot be explained. The most plausible answer will appeal to the fact that shame and morality are the repressing forces and that the neighbourhood in which the sexual organs are naturally placed must inevitably arouse disgust along with sexual experiences. Where there is no shame (as in a male person), or where no morality comes about (as in the lower classes of society), or where disgust is blunted by the conditions of life (as in the country), there too no repression and therefore no neurosis will result from sexual stimulation in infancy[6] (1896, *S.E.,* I: 221-2).

By the release of unpleasure during sexual activity, pleasure is not the only thing that eradicates moral sensibility. Unpleasure, through build-up of libido, also results in the eradication of moral sensibility. Still, the link of sexual activity and shame is deeper. Morality, thus grasped, is often recognized to be the repressing force in therapy (1896, *S.E.,* I: 222 and 226).

Freud's *Jokes and their Relation to the Unconscious* in 1905 speaks of the insubstantiality of morality through an illustration of every person's grasp, at some time or another, of the truth of *"Carpe diem"* through jokes.

> In reality each of us has had hours and times at which he has admitted the rightness of this philosophy of life and has reproached moral doctrine with only understanding how to demand without offering any compensation. Since we have ceased any longer to believe in the promise of a next world in which every renunciation will be rewarded by a satisfaction—there are, incidentally, very few pious people if we take renunciation as the sign of faith—*"Carpe diem"* has become a serious warning. I will gladly put off satisfaction: but do I know whether I shall still be here tomorrow? (1905, *S.E.,* VIII: 109)

The whispered message of those jokes, Freud says, can be said aloud: Human wishes have a right to be accepted along with the rigid and inflexible rules of morality. Such rules, he adds, might just be those of the rich and powerful, who burke the wishes of common persons but express readily their own. Thus, a person binds his life to others through identification, so that the ephemerality of his life can be overcome, and those wishes he cannot legitimately fulfill must remain unfulfilled, in the effort to change social order (1905, *S.E.,* VIII: 109-10). Morality, à la Nietzsche, is the neurosis of those who do not have the privileges of the rich and powerful. Such persons, having few outlets for their most basic wishes, due to constraints imposed by those with power and wealth, can at best seek compromises for them.

Freud's mature views on morality are sketched in *The Future of an Illusion.*[7] He begins by mentioning the threefold function of the gods: to exercise the terrors of nature, to reconcile men to cruel Fate, and to compensate them for their sufferings and privations. Their perceived role in human affairs came about in the following way. First, Fate—following Greek mythology—was deemed to stand above the gods and direct their destinies. As nature became more independent of the gods, men's expectations turned toward the gods as a source of morality. It was now the tasks of the gods to even out the defects and ills of civilization, to attend to the self-imposed sufferings of men, and to protect the precepts of civilization. "Those precepts themselves were credited with a divine origin; they were elevated beyond human society and were extended to nature and the universe." He adds:

> And thus a store of ideas is created, born from man's need to make his helplessness tolerable and built up from the material of memories of the helplessness of his own childhood and the childhood of the human race. It can clearly be seen that the possession of these ideas protects him in two directions—against the dangers of nature and Fate, and against the injuries that threaten him from human society itself.

In such a manner, the moral laws, guiding human civilization, are built into the fabric of the universe and maintained by a court of divine justices, with extraordinary power and consistency. All good is rewarded; all evil is punished. "In this way all the terrors, the sufferings and the hardships of life are destined to be obliterated" (1927, *S.E.*, XXI: 18-9).

Soon, the attributes of the gods of antiquity were conveniently condensed into one God, and people's relationship to that deity recovered the intensity of a child's relationship to his father. Thus, everything in the world, according to Freud, is the result of the intentions of a superior intelligence that orders everything for the best, though his ways are inscrutable. Providence protects humans from nature and even death, from which it promises them escape, and acts with the love of an omnipotent father (1927, *S.E.*, XXI: 18-9).

In the course of people's psychosexual development, the Oedipal impulses of childhood are repressed and the result of repression is formation of the superego, one's sense of moral self, formed mostly through identification with the father.

## Organic Source of Moral Rules

In "Disillusionment of the War" in 1915, Freud asks how it is that a person raises himself to a high measure of morality. A reasonable reply might be that one eliminates wicked tendencies, through education and through exposure to a civilized environment, and supplants them with good tendencies. Were that the case, however, one would not expect evil to reemerge, and often with great force, in anyone brought up in that manner. Codswallop, Freud asserts. It is impossible to eradicate evil, because evil has an organic, biological base.

> Psychological—or, more strictly speaking, psycho-analytic—investigation shows instead that the deepest essence of human nature consists of instinctual impulses which are of an elementary nature, which are similar in all men and which aim at the satisfaction of certain primal needs. These impulses in them-

selves are neither good nor bad. We classify them and their expressions in that way, according to their relation to the needs and demands of the human community. It must be granted that all the impulses which society condemns as evil—let us take as representative the selfish and the cruel ones—are of this primitive kind (1915, *S.E.*, XIV: 280-1).

How do moral principles form? The primitive impulses are inhibited through human development toward adolescence. They find expression through sublimation, become commingled, and then turn against their possessor. Often through reaction-formation, impulses change content and find expression in contrary symbols or actions. Love finds expression as hatred and hatred finds expression as love, and each does so commonly in the same objects. These vicissitudes of impulses shape a person's character and his morality so that young sadists and animal tormenters often turn out to be humanitarians and animal-rights activists in later life (1915, *S.E.*, XIV: 282).

"Bad" drives are transformed in two ways. Internally, eros-drives mingle with ego-drives to allow for social sensitivity. Externally, there is education, fashioned in the mold of one's culture. Culture, in turn for educating its members, demands renunciation of drives, and renunciation functions to bind people to their culture. As a person develops psychically, external compulsions are increasingly reshaped into internal compulsions. As a rule, then, morality is partly innate and partly learned (1915, *S.E.*, XIV: 282-3).

External compulsions of upbringing and environment work toward altruism from egoism. Yet compulsions do not act alone. Rewards and punishments also contribute to the transition. Therefore, right actions by themselves cannot show when a person is acting because of drive-related inclinations or merely because of incentives motivating selfishness (1915, *S.E.*, XIV: 283-4).

The demands of civilization, asking renunciation of drive energy through tightened moral standards, are psychically unhealthy. Increased sexual suppression results in increased neurosis or other unhealthy non-neurotic malformations of character.

> Anyone thus compelled to act continually in accordance with precepts which are not the expression of his instinctual inclinations, is living, psychologically speaking, beyond his means, and may objectively be described as a hypocrite, whether he is clearly aware of the incongruity or not. It is undeniable that our contemporary civilization favours the production of this form of hypocrisy to an extraordinary extent. One might venture to say that it is built up on such hypocrisy, and that it would have to submit to far-reaching modifications if people were to undertake to live in accordance with psychological truth (1915, *S.E.*, XIV: 284).

He adds that some amount of cultural hypocrisy is probably needed for the maintenance of culture. Moral precepts and piety, it seems clear, are part of that hypocrisy—poor solatium for renunciation.

## Phylogenetic Inheritance

Morality has more than just an ontogenetic explanation for Freud: It must also be explained phylogenetically. That explanation first occurs in Freud's *Totem and Taboo* (1913), which essays to explain the origin of religiosity.[8]

Following social-contract theorists on the origins of society, Freud's phylogenetic explanation takes him back to the primal horde—the ancestral origin of all humanity. In this horde, the primal father, because he was the leader and the strongest male, gave free reign to his sexual impulses to the dismay of the lesser males. The impeded sexual impulses of the lesser males eventually provoked them to form a pact to kill the primal father—the first social deed.[9] They did just that. On killing the father, they disposed of the corpse in a cannibalistic feast. The magnitude of the deed was so great that it stayed with the lesser males, the killers, in the form of a "forgotten" memory, passed on to subsequent generations (1913, *S.E.*, XIII: 140-6) in Lamarckian fashion.

Freud's phylogenic story was an attempt to square psychoanalytic research with biology, but it was also an attempt to explain the origins of morality through religiosity and religious rituals—specifically, Christianity, which Freud often took to be representative of all religions, and its rituals—and, the genesis of the concept "God." Given that Christ died on the cross for mankind's sins and given *lex talionis* (i.e., an eye for an eye), it follows that the deed for which Christ had to pay with his life must have been a murder—the killing of the primal father. This deed also explains the Christian communion, a repetition of the "sons'" cannibalistic feast, and how the Christian notion of original sin in each person is passed on through inheritance (1913, *S.E.*, XIII: 153-5).

In *Totem and Taboo*, Freud says there are "grave difficulties" with his "deduction" to the primal deed (1913, *S.E.*, XIII: 158), but by the time of *Moses and Monotheism*, more than twenty-five years later, the grave difficulties are gone and the deed now must have been committed numerous times in early human history.[10] "Since the emergence of the idea of evolution no longer leaves room for doubt that the human race has a prehistory, and since this is unknown—that is, forgotten—a conclusion of this kind [i.e., the primal deed] almost carries the weight of a postulate" (1939, *S.E.*, XXIII: 80). Hereafter, Freud sets the stage axiomatically for the emergence of morality through the guilt that was phylogenetically transmitted from early primal deeds, sexually motivated.

## Psychotherapy as Moral Therapy

Given that morality has both ontogenetic and phylogenetic explanations that are rooted in human lust, it seems clear that Freud thought little of it as a collection of rational principles with normative merit. Did he, however, believe that all morality was swept away with his two genetic explanations?

The answer is no. Freud took psychotherapy to be a moral therapy of sorts. I turn to "Transference" from his *Introductory Lectures on Psycho-Analysis*.

In "Transference," Freud defends psychoanalysis against the charge of sanctioning sexual licentiousness. Failing to advocate a full sexual life does not amount to advocacy of conventional (i.e., Christian) morality. Patients, he says, get through psychoanalytic therapy an "education to truth":

> [W]e are reformers but merely observers; nevertheless, we cannot help observing with a critical eye and we have found it impossible to side with conventional sexual morality or to form a very high opinion of the manner in which society attempts the practical regulation of the problems of sexual life. We can present society with a blunt calculation that what is described as its morality calls for a bigger sacrifice than it is worth and that its proceedings are not based on honesty and do not display wisdom. We do not keep such criticisms from our patient's ears, we accustom them to giving unprejudiced consideration to sexual matters no less than to any others; and if, having grown independent after the completion of their treatment, they decide on their own judgement in favour of some midway position between living a full life and absolute asceticism, we feel our conscience clear whatever their choice. We tell ourselves that anyone who has succeeded in educating himself to truth about himself is permanently defended against the danger of immorality, even though his standard of morality may differ in some respect from that which is customary in society (1917, *S.E.,* XVI: 434).

The passage above shows—and there are many more illustrations to add[11]— is that psychoanalysis is itself an "education to truth," a way of self-knowing that prepares one to live as best one can in reality, not fantasy. Though itself a modest normative claim, that claim is still a normative claim, which shows that psychoanalytic therapy has an inescapable normative dimension.

There is more to say, which applies to all forms of psychological counseling. No therapist worth his salt can be entirely indifferent to a patient's moral status—especially insofar as clinical treatment aims at psychical health and there can be no viable conception of psychical health without some conception, however minimal, of moral wellbeing.[12] No analyst of any persuasion would conscionably adapt clinical methods to established social mores, if those mores are morally suspect. For instance, a therapist who could conscionably adapt his therapy to the aims of a genocidal culture would not at the same time be aiming at the psychical betterment of his client. His aim, rather, would be a patient's mere adaptation or survival in an inhospitable social setting, not his wellbeing. Freud, late in life, by leaving Vienna, then under Hitler's control, showed that he was neither a moral relativist nor indifferent to moral concerns. His departure showed moral opposition to and moral condemnation of Nazi totalitarianism. Thus, it is impossible to believe that he could advocate relativism or be pococurante in clinical therapy.

# Psychoanalysis and Education

## Education as Sublimation

Education is an issue that Freud touches on in many places in his corpus, though it is not the exclusive topic of any one work. One reason for Freud's reluctance to devote any one work to education is that the German word for education, *"Erziehung,"* is much broader in meaning than the American grasp of the English term. Whereas Americans understand "education" to connote formal schooling, the German word, in keeping with the ancient Greek notion of *"Paideia,"* much more sensibly applies to one's overall upbringing. Thus, there may have been no need to write specifically on applications of psychoanalysis to education: Freud's psychoanalytic insights throughout his corpus have rather clear implications for proper upbringing and, thus, are manifestly educative.

Another reason is that Freud was likely keenly aware of the resistance with which he would have been greeted were he to sketch out a formal-schooling program for children. That would surely have to include suggestions for proper routes of sublimation for sexual impulses in early life to ensure adequate Oedipal resolution—an issue that most would certainly find objectionable. He writes at the end of the fourth of his "Five Lectures":

> During the time at which repression is making its selection among the component instincts, and later, when there should be a slackening of the parents' influence, which is essentially responsible of the expenditure of energy on these repressions, the task of education meets with great problems, which at the present time are certainly not always dealt with in an understanding and unobjectionable manner (1910, *S.E.,* XI: 48).

The suggestion here, elsewhere made explicit (e.g., 1905, *S.E.,* VII: 177), is that formal schooling, as practiced in Freud's day, is in part responsible for individuals' neurosis.

In "Explanations and Applications" from Freud's *New Introductory Lectures on Psychoanalysis,* Freud turns to the topic of education—specifically, to the first task of education.

> Let us make ourselves clear as to what the first task of education is. The child must learn to control his instincts. It is impossible to give him liberty to carry out all his impulses without restriction. To do so would be a very instructive experiment for child-psychologists; but life would be impossible for the parents and the children themselves would suffer grave damage, which would show itself partly at once and partly in later years. Accordingly, education must inhibit, forbid and suppress, and this it has abundantly seen to in all periods of history. But we have learnt from analysis that precisely this suppression of instincts involves the risk of neurotic illness. . . . Thus education has to find its way between the

Scylla of non-interference and the Charybdis of frustration (1933, *S.E.*, XXII: 148-9).

The solution to that problem, Freud asserts, involves deciding just how much to allow and how much to disallow. It also involves different educational means for different types of persons, as young persons have "very different constitutional dispositions." Consistent with his mature notion that neurosis is the result of a feeble or enfeebled ego, the first task of education, then, is to bolster the ego to meet the internal and external obstacles it will surely face in time.

In *Three Essays on Sexuality*, Freud says that the period of latency, roughly between the ages of six and twelve, is critical for a healthy upbringing that encourages sublimation—a mechanism for socially accepted means of channeling impulses.

> It is during this period of total or only partial latency that are built up the mental forces which are later to impede the course of the sexual instinct and, like dams, restrict its flow—disgust, feelings of shame and the claims of aesthetic and moral ideals. . . . What is it that goes to the making of these constructions which are so important for the growth of a civilized and normal individual? They probably emerge at the cost of the infantile sexual impulses themselves. Thus the activity of those impulses does not cease even during this period of latency, though their energy is diverted, wholly or in great part, from their sexual use and directed to other ends. Historians of civilization appear to be at one in assuming that powerful components are acquired for every kind of cultural achievement by this diversion of sexual instinctual forces from sexual aims and their direction to new ones—a process which deserves the name of "sublimation." To this we would add, accordingly, that the same process plays a part in the development of the individual and we would place its beginning in the period of sexual latency of childhood (1905, *S.E.*, VII: 177-8).

The mechanism of sublimation occurs thus. As the reproductive functions have been deferred, the sexual impulses lie dormant. Yet those impulses, arising from erotogenic zones, are naturally taken to be perverse and, consequently, they arouse feelings of unpleasure—i.e., disgust, shame, and moral resentment. Educators, he asserts, seem to grasp the moral significance of infantile sexuality, but they turn from it with dread.

> In so far as educators pay any attention at all to infantile sexuality, they behave exactly as though they shared our views as to the construction of the moral defensive forces at the cost of sexuality, and as though they knew that sexual activity makes a child ineducable: for they stigmatize every sexual manifestation by children as a "vice," without being able to do much against it. We, on the other hand, have every reason for turning our attention to these phenomena which are so much dreaded by education, for we may expect them to help us to discover the original configuration of the sexual instincts (1905, *S.E.*, VII: 178-9).

The overall task of an educator is large. He has to recognize the different constitutions of students, draw inferences from minute clues about what is going on internally, and balance children's need for love with the right amount of distanced authority. In short, each teacher must be a trained and practiced psychotherapist, who has himself been psychoanalyzed (1933, *S.E.,* XXII: 149).

In *Phobia in a Five-Year-Old Boy,* Freud says a problem for educators is that psychoanalysis can draw no clear distinction between neurotics and "normal people." All a psychoanalyst can say is that the latter have suitable means of discharge for impulses, while the former do not. Education, therefore, should not aim at distinguishing the well-adjusted from the maladjusted. Instead, it should focus on prophylaxis—i.e., in finding socially acceptable outlets for impulses to prevent maladjustment.

Thus far, education has been in the service of controlling or suppressing human drives. That usually plays to the favor of those few persons who have a small number of restrictions of impulses and against the many other persons who do not. Yet, he adds, the aim ought not to be control, but instead sublimation.

> Supposing now that we substitute another task for this one, and aim instead at making the individual capable of becoming a civilized and useful member of society with the least possible sacrifice of his own activity; in that case the information gained by psycho-analysis, upon the origin of pathogenic complexes and upon the nucleus of every nervous affection, can claim with justice that it deserves to be regarded by educators as an invaluable guide in their conduct towards children (1909, *S.E.,* X: 146).

Freud acknowledges the educative benefits of psychoanalytic therapy for individuals, which he calls a sort of "after-education." He states:

> An analytic treatment demands from both doctor and patient the accomplishment of serious work, which is employed in lifting internal resistances. Through the overcoming these resistances the patient's mental life is permanently changed, is raised to a high level of development and remains protected against fresh possibilities of falling ill. This work of overcoming resistances is the essential function of analytic treatment; the patient has to accomplish it and the doctor makes this possible for him with the help of suggestion operating in an *educative* sense. For this reason psycho-analytic treatment has justly been described as a kind of *after-education* (1917, *S.E.,* XVI: 451).

## Discontents and their Civilization

The difficulties of educators are enhanced by problems of civilized living, which is largely responsible for human unhappiness. It offers humans protection from the vagaries of nature and even some measure of protection from other human beings, but the price is human unhappiness through construction of artificial rules, comprising shame and disgust, aimed at suppression of drives. When the gains of civilization become greater, human unhappiness and individuals' neuroses become greater.

"Civilization" Freud describes as "the whole sum of the achievements and the regulations which distinguish our lives from those of our animal ancestors and which serves two purposes—namely to protect men against nature and to adjust their mutual relations." "Cultural" relates to "all activities and resources which are useful to men for making the earth serviceable to them, for protecting them against the violence of the forces of nature" (1930, *S.E.*, XXI: 89-90).

Happiness, for Freud, is consequently an economic problem, as it relates to the economics of each individual's libido. Two questions are relevant. First, how greatly do I desire to satisfy my impulses? Second, how much libidinal energy do I have at work for me (1930, *S.E.*, XXI: 83)?

Before answering those questions, Freud notes "a piece of our own psychical constitution" lies behind our suffering. We arrive at the following paradox.

> This contention holds that what we call our civilization is largely responsible for our misery, and that we should be much happier if we gave it up and returned to primitive conditions. I call this contention astonishing because, in whatever way we may define the concept of civilization, it is a certain fact that all the things with which we seek to protect ourselves against the threats that emanate from the sources of suffering are part of that very civilization (1930, *S.E.*, XXI: 86).

In short, in protecting humans from the vagaries of nature, humans wind up exposing themselves to their greatest danger—themselves.

Yet science is not without its technology, and education is a means of fostering advances in technology, aimed at human betterment. Might not science, then, safeguard humans from themselves?

Long ago, Freud adds, humans had the ideals, generated by their wishes of omnipotence and omniscience, which they fused in fulfillment of their wishes into one God—an idealized father figure. Today, with their technological advances in the service of human betterment, humans themselves have come very close to their divine ideal. Humans have become "prosthetic gods" and they look magnificent in that role. Yet, they are not happy (1930, *S.E.*, XXI: 91-2).

Consequently, given Freud's mature views on civilized living and the unhappiness it brings, the chief task of education is to find a mean between the constraints of civilized living and the need for expression of impulses. That is a topic I return to in the final chapter of this undertaking, as it relates more to Freud's contribution to group psychology.[13]

### "Liberated Nonsense"

A final, but greatly significant contribution to education as a means of sublimation is humor. Freud was very fond of humor and thought that humor through jokes offered another proof of the existence of the unconscious. He writes:

I can appeal to the fact that there is an intimate connection between all mental happenings—a fact which guarantees that a psychological discovery even in a remote field will be of an unpredictable value in other fields. We may also bear in mind the peculiar and even fascinating charm exercised by jokes in our society. A new joke acts almost like an event of universal interest; it is passed from one person to another like the news of the latest victory (1905, *S.E.,* VIII: 15).

Life is serious and children are exposed to that seriousness all too rapidly. Young children delight in word games, rhythm, and rhymes. As they grow, they are exposed to increased restrictions in the use of words. "[T]here is far more potency in the restrictions which must establish themselves in the course of a child's education in logical thinking and in distinguishing between what is true and false in reality; and for this reason the rebellion against the compulsion of logic and reality is deep-going and long-lasting." They utilize games and imagination to withdraw from the pressures of conformance to reality and critical thinking. Such pleasure in "liberated nonsense" does not show itself often enough (1905, *S.E.,* VIII: 125-6).

At college, a young student rebels against the dual compulsions of logic and reality by wearing "rags" and engaging in *Bierschwefel*—the blather of persons under the spell of beer or other intoxicants. As a man, he behaves professionally at a scientific congress, after which he engages in *Kneipzeitung,* where what was seriously discussed is reduced to nonsense. Such beneficial retreats, especially where alcohol is involved, allow for some degree of discharge of repressed pleasure.

A change in mood is the most precious thing that alcohol achieves for mankind [as a] cheerful mood, whether it is produced endogenously or toxically, reduces the inhibiting forces, criticism among them, and makes accessible once again sources of pleasure which were under the weight of suppression. . . . Under the influence of alcohol the grown man once more becomes a child, who finds pleasure in having the course of his thoughts freely at his disposal without paying regard to the compulsion of logic (1905, *S.E.,* VIII: 127).

Reasonably enough, games like *Bierschwefel* and *Kneipzeitung* are for Freud not only proof of the repressions linked to civilized living, but also proof of the need for some rebelliously playful relief from logic and reality. Thus, education, which has as its chief aim accommodation of individuals to reality, must also allow for some playful escape from that reality, if it is to enjoy success. Freud sums:

It is our belief that civilization and higher education have a large influence in the development of repression, and we suppose that, under such conditions, the psychical organization undergoes an alteration (that can also emerge as an inherited disposition) as a result of which what was formerly felt as agreeable now seems unacceptable and is rejected with all possible psychical force. The repressive activity of civilization brings it about that primary possibilities of enjoyment, which have now, however, been repudiated by the censorship in us, are lost to us. But to the human psyche all renunciation is exceedingly difficult, and so we find that tendentious jokes provide a means of undoing the renunciation and retrieving what was lost (1905, *S.E.,* VIII: 101).

## Psychoanalysis as Clinical Therapy

One of the themes of this book is that Freud's early clinical successes with patients, in conjunction with his theoretical speculations and his "purchases" from other sciences, in some measure emboldened him to branch out and address broader issues of global significance. Just how successful were these early clinical successes?

### Freud on his Clinical "Successes"

Freud's introduction to the possibility of psychical cure came with his collaboration with Breuer and their cathartic method, which was symptom-oriented, time- and labor-intensive, often ineffective for removing all the symptoms of hysteria, and powerless against acute hysteria.

Freud's mature thinking was that hysteria was the result of a feeble or enfeebled ego that was unable to orient an organism to reality in light of the demands of the id and super-ego and the restrictions of reality. Cure involved recapitulating the presumed causal nexus from neurotic symptoms (e.g., observable behavioral oddities, parapraxes, symbols in dreams, and the material in jokes) to disclose the underlying, unconscious pathogen. The pathogen was believed to be relevantly suitable as a causal determinant and of sufficient traumatic force. It also had an unconscious and sexual etiology, rooted in childhood. Success of treatment entailed not only disclosing the mnemonic trace of this pathogen, but also playing out the affective link through the transference relationship with an analyst. Freud writes in "Analytic Therapy":

> The distinction between nervous health and neurosis is thus reduced to a practical question and is decided by the outcome—by whether the subject is left with a sufficient amount of capacity for enjoyment and of efficiency. It probably goes back to the relative sizes of the quota of energy that remains free and of that which is bound by repression, and is of a quantitative not of a qualitative nature. *I need not tell you that this discovery is the theoretical justification for our conviction that neuroses are in principle curable in spite of their being based on constitutional disposition* (1917, *S.E.,* XVI: 457).

In spite of Freud's "theoretical justification," it is important to ask this question: What was Freud's estimation of the actual effectiveness of his clinical treatments?

Freud was never shy about the indispensability of psychoanalytic treatment as a method of curing neurosis. He states with cockalorum in "Analytic Therapy," "I emphasized the fact that under favorable conditions we achieve successes which are second to none and are of the finest in the field of internal medicine; and I can now add something further—namely that they could not have been achieved by any other procedure" (1917, *S.E.,* XVI: 458). He adds five years later, "In one of the most difficult spheres of medical activity [psychoanalysis] is the only possible method of treatment for certain illnesses and for others it is the method which yields the best or the most permanent results—though never without a corresponding expenditure of time and trouble" (1922, *S.E.,* XVIII: 250). These two statements offer additional confirmation of Grümbaum's dual theses of his Tally Argument (at least, for this stage of Freud's career)— that the analytic worth of psychoanalysis is wholly dependent on cure, which requires correct analytic assessment and which cannot come about through any other method.[14]

In "Analysis Terminable and Interminable," published just two years before Freud's death, Freud speaks skeptically—viz., less optimistically and more soberly—about the prospects of complete analytic success.

[Optimists of psychoanalytic therapy] assume, firstly, that there really is a possibility of disposing of an instinctual conflict (or, more correctly, a conflict between the ego and an instinct) definitely and for all time; secondly, that while we are treating someone for one instinctual conflict we can, as it were, inoculate him against the possibility of any other such conflicts; and thirdly, that we have the power, for purposes of prophylaxis, to stir up a pathogenic conflict of this sort which is not betraying itself at the time by any indications, and that it is wise to do so. I throw out these questions without proposing to answer them now. Perhaps it may not be possible at present to give any certain answer to them (1937, *S.E.,* XXIII: 223).

In "Explanations, Applications and Orientations" four years ealier, he states, "I have never been a therapeutic enthusiast" (1933, *S.E.,* XXII: 151-2).

It is that skeptical line of thought I wish to emphasize and explore more fully in the remainder of this undertaking. I hope to show not so much that Freud lost interest in individual therapy, but instead that he lost hope in it. It remained for Freud to develop his theoretical insights, through new developments in what he called his "metapsychology" (see chapter 5), to combat pressing global concerns in a prophylactic manner.

**Scientific Accessibility to Clinical "Successes"**

In this final section, I turn to criticism of Freudian psychotherapy and its clinical successes.

Perhaps the most pressing criticism of psychoanalysis is that its claims are more pseudo-scientific than scientific. Philosopher Karl Popper made that view famous. In *Conjectures and Refutations,* Popper states: "And as for Freud's epic of the Ego, Super-ego, and the Id, no substantially stronger claim to scientific status can be made for it than for Homer's collected stories from Olympus. These theories describe some facts, but in the manner of myths. They contain most interesting psychological suggestions, but not in a testable form."[15]

The claim that Freudian psychoanalysis is unscientific because it makes no testable claims or that its claims are too threadbare to be refuted, though still vigorously maintained today,[16] has been addressed by Grünbaum in *Foundations of Psychoanalysis*. He writes: "Indeed, the examples of falsifiability that I have already adduced have a quite different moral [than the one Popper gives]: the inability of certain philosophers of science to have discerned any testable consequences of Freud's theory betokens their insufficient command or scrutiny of its logical content rather than a scientific liability of psychoanalysis."[17] Freudian psychoanalysis does make testable claims, Grünbaum asserts, but the data Freud has collected are so contaminated that testing is out of the question.[18]

Yet to show that some claims, like his bipartite thesis on dreams, have testable implications is certainly not sufficient to show psychoanalysis had the status of a science. Many of Freud's substratal concepts—e.g., id, libido, and unconscious—are incontestably vague and metempirical.

What however of the data of Freud's psychoanalysis? It is aidful to repeat that Freud was consistently against the use of statistical data to confirm or disconfirm the theoretical claims of psychoanalysis as a method of therapy. As we saw in chapter 3, he remonstrated that "statistics are worthless" for the following reasons (1917, *S.E.*, XVI: 461).

- My cases-studies are incomparable in a great variety of respects.
- There has not been sufficient time to judge the putative cures to be durable.
- Many case-studies concerned people who had kept their illness, its treatment, and their recovery secret.

What Freud deemed the most important reason I list separately and keep in Freud's words:

- "[I]n matters of therapy people [i.e., Freud's critics] behave highly irrationally, so that one has no prospect of accomplishing anything with them by rational means."

Here it is likely Freud is dissimulating. The real reason, I maintain, was recognition, by Freud and by critics, that psychoanalytic claims were not replicable and, thus, were scientifically questionable. He dodged critics ultimately by adopting the view that psychoanalysis could not be learned through books, but merely through apprenticed experience in properly conducted analytic sessions.

In time, at the urging of Sandor Ferenczi and Ernest Jones, a band of dyed-in-the-wool psychoanalytic adherents, who pledged full allegiance to Freud, formed an *ad captandum* "secret ring" to preserve the sacrosanctity of Freudian psychoanalysis by shielding it from scientific criticism. They decided that the merit in psychoanalysis lay not in its statistical justification, but rather in the therapeutic successes of all those and only those therapists who were personally psychoanalyzed by Freud.[19] Thus, Freud spent roughly the final 20 years of his life analyzing mostly psychotherapists or psychotherapists-in-training.[20] Freudian screening functioned not only to separate Freudian psychotherapists from the charlatan secessionists, but also to make Freud's judgment the ultimate appeal for any psychoanalytic conflict.

In *New Introductory Lectures on Psychoanalysis,* some 16 years later, Freud maintains tendentiously that psychoanalysis has passed the test of time—at least among the scientifically informed. Condemnation still exists in the "facetious contempt of [the conversations and book-writing of] laymen" (1933, *S.E.,* XXII: 138). His verdict here is hasty and incautious, and very likely deceitful. It is sufficient to add that great debate still exists today concerning what is salvageable from Freudian psychoanalytic tenets and methods.

As we have already seen, psychoanalysis is a favorite target for condemnation, Freud often asserts, because it alone is in the service of attacking human repression. The difficulty with that is that any attempt to disconfirm psychoanalytic conclusions can be taken as evidence in their favor—i.e., as evidence of repression. Writes Freud, for instance, "Most of what is brought up against psycho-analysis, even in scientific works, is based upon insufficient information which in its turn seems to be determined by emotional resistances [to it]" (1922, *S.E.,* XVIII: 252). That said, psychoanalysis, unlike other sciences, seems to be immune to refutation and that makes it apple-pie sort of science.

Another tack taken by Freud and psychotherapists today—e.g., Jon Mills[21] and D. P. Spence[22]—is that only a psychotherapist—among Freud's band of disciples, a psychotherapist psychoanalyzed by Freud[23]—is in position to judge a cure to be a cure, because of the length and labor-intensity of and wealth of data and exchanges within clinical sessions. That in effect makes it inaccessible to public criticism and public condemnation. As Michael Scriven rightly noted numerous years ago, that move is casuistic. He says, "[W]e may concede the need of expert advice in making reliable judgments of cure, but we can identify the experts only on the basis of their success in doing some related task that we *can* independently judge."[24] Scientific practice is in essence publicly accessible, and to shut off psychoanalysis from public criticism is to make it a cult-practice, not a science.

"Cure" is more than an empirical issue, Scriven adds. Psychoanalysis as clinical therapy tackles value-of-life issues that take it to a normative dimension.

> I am arguing that one of the problems with a general definition of cure is its essential involvement with moral questions; and with questions of the relative value of, e.g., a creative-nonconformist-anxious pattern of life compared with a noncreative-formist-anxious pattern; and with genetic and empirical questions of an unsettled and nonmedical kind, in short with problems for which psychoanalysis cannot possibly have the right answer since it lacks the data, even if it had

*one* answer to offer. There are serious enough practical problems in judging cases apart from these . . . but these are the ineffable philosophical-empirical barriers which can be scaled only by hard work in the appropriated field, no longer by the amateur. These problems alone give a philosopher the right to work in and a duty to watch the field.[25]

Many of today's psychotherapists, acknowledging the defects of Freud's theoretical assumptions, are still fond of repeating that one can question Freud's views on drives, recapitulationism, psychical determinism, and even his presumed "pansexualism," but not his clinical successes. Psychoanalysis, as a broad scientific discipline ($\Psi A_3$) and having evolved from collected psychological data gleaned from clinical practice, is certainly dubious, but not the clinical practice ($\Psi A_2$), founded on the view of the unconscious—the one theoretical posit, grounded substantially on empirical data, that is indispensable.

Yet Freud himself thought otherwise. In spite of his own enthusiastic defense of $\Psi A_2$ throughout the years, Freud eventually became unenthusiastic about $\Psi A_2$ because of its relative ineffectiveness—a view, for instance, stated flatly in late papers such as "Analysis Terminable or Interminable" and "Constructions in Analysis" and expressed plainly in a 1928 communication to Oskar Pfister. He writes to Pfister, "I have often said that I hold that the purely medical importance of analysis is outweighed by its importance to science as a whole, and that its general influence by means of clarification and the exposure of error exceeds its therapeutic value to the individual."[26]

The reasons for Freud's lack of confidence in and tepidity toward $\Psi A_2$ were many. I list merely three. First, he acknowledged that the quantities of mobile energy that an analyst has at his disposal for therapeutic means are often inferior to the quantities of the warring factions of energies in neurosis.[27] Thus, despite a therapist's best effort, he was often thwarted by quantitative factors, mostly outside of his control. Second, there was his grudging recognition that analytic treatment was not curative. His published case-studies are acknowledged to be "largely unsuccessful" by psychotherapeutic critics[28] and sometimes, as in the case of Dora, even by Freud himself. Sulloway shows that perhaps Freud's most celebrated "success," the case of the Wolf Man, was a colossal failure.[29] Freud published, by his own admission, nothing but problematic cases. That Freud should publish nothing other than problematic cases is telling, in spite of his own insistence that only problematic cases are educative for aspiring analysts.[30] One does not sell a box of Rutgers tomatoes by placing for display several rotting tomatoes.

In short, Freud lost hope in psychotherapy as an effective treatment for individual neurosis and put most of his efforts in later life to $\Psi A_3$, whose focus would be on using psychoanalysis and its theoretical posits to gain insight into the human condition.[31] Psychoanalysis, in his eyes, was now less of a treatment for individual neurosis and more of a large-scale science, based on key theoretical assumptions, which aimed at learning about the motivations of both individual and group human behavior.

Yet Freudian psychoanalysis qua $\Psi A_3$ was becoming increasingly dependent on the sorts of theoretical posits that he claimed were unneeded and of mere heuristic value. It was becoming less of a science, based on experience, and more of a philosophical system, based on intuition and hunches. Hilda Doolittle, a former patient of Freud, quoted him as follows: "My discoveries are not primarily a heal-all. My discoveries are a basis for a very grave philosophy. There are very few who understand this, there are few who are capable of understanding this."[32] Freud's focus turned to the development and defense of $\Psi A_3$—Freudian metapsychology or philosophy, a large part of the second part of this book—and that explains the relative absence of discussion of technical, clinical issues in his publications from 1920 to 1936.

# Notes

1. "Man should not want to eradicate his complexes but rather live in harmony with them; they are the legitimate directors of his behavior in the world," he writes in a letter to Ferenczi (November 17, 1911). Sigmund Freud and Sandor Ferenczi, *The Correspondence of Sigmund Freud and Sandor Ferenczi, Vol. I, 1908–1914,* ed. E. Brabant, E. Falzeder, and P. Giampieri-Deutsch (Cambridge: Harvard University Press, 1993), 314.

2. As I have argued elsewhere, in its capacity to work toward a human utopia. M. Andrew Holowchak, *Freud and Utopia: From Cosmological Narcissism to the Soft Dictatorship of Reason* (Lanham, MD: Lexington Books, 2012).

3. Joachim Sharfenberg, *Sigmund Freud & His Critique of Religion* (Philadelphia: Fortress Press, 1988), 102.

4. Something to which Freud consistently adhered and to which Pfister complained, "If it were part of psycho-analytic treatment to present that despoiled universe to our patients as the truth, I should well understand it if the poor devils preferred remaining shut up on their illness to entering that dreadful icy despoliation." Sigmund Freud and Oskar Pfister, *Psychoanalysis and Faith,* 116.

5. Cf. Ferenczi's comments in a letter to Freud on the social significance of psychoanalysis. Sigmund Freud and Sander Ferenczi, *The Correspondence of Sigmund Freud and Sandor Ferenczi, Vol. I, 1908–1914,* eds. E. Brabant, E. Falzeder and P. Giampieri-Deutsch (Cambridge: Harvard University Press, 1993), 153.

6. In his *Project,* written one year earlier, Freud says that incapacity of infants to discharge $Q\eta$ without the help of an adult leads to a secondary path of discharge enabled through the help of another. Thus, he says "the initial helplessness of human beings is the primal source of all *moral motives*" (1895, *S.E.,* I: 317–18).

7. A view succinctly expressed in a letter to Pfister: "[E]thics are created by patients' demands for ethical values; ethics are not based on an external world order but on the inescapable exigencies of human cohabitation. I do not believe that I behave as if there were 'one life, one meaning in life,' . . ." Sigmund Freud and Oskar Pfister, *Psychoanalysis and Faith,* 129.

8. M. Andrew Holowchak, "The 'Soft Dictatorship' of Reason: Freud on Science, Religion, and Utopia," *Philo,* Vol. 13, No. 1, 2010, 29–53.

9. Indicative of strength in numbers.

10. Writes Roazen of this primal deed, "Freud seems not quite able to accept his own theory of the power of psychic realities; since he had not completely convinced himself of the strength of fantasies, he had to have a 'real' trauma, a 'real' murder of the primal father." Paul Roazen, *Freud: Political and Social Thought* (New York: Alfred A. Knopf, 1968), 155.

11. E.g., *The Future of an Illusion* and "On the Question of a *Weltanschaung.*"

12. Freud writes, "A different view had now to be taken of the task of therapy. Its aim was no longer to 'abreact' an affect which had gone on to the wrong lines but to uncover repressions and replace them by acts of judgement which might result either in the accepting or in the condemning of what had formerly been repudiated. I showed my recognition of the new situation by no longer calling my method of investigation and treatment *catharsis* but *psycho-analysis*" (1925, *S.E.,* XX: 30).

13. For a fuller account, see M. Andrew Holowchak, "Technology and Freudian Discontent: Freud's 'Muffled Meliorism' and the Problem of Human Annihilation," *Sophia,* Vol. 49, No. 1, 2010, 95–111.

14. Cf. Roazen: "[E]arly in his career Freud was very concerned with the therapeutic removal of particular symptoms; by the end of his life he considered symptomatic improvements a mere by-product of a properly conducted psychoanalysis. Clinical success can never be more than a dubious test of any theoretical view; a great variety of psychiatric techniques have cures to their credit." Paul Roazen, *Freud,* 282.

15. Karl Popper, *Conjectures and Refutations: The Growth of Scientific Knowledge* (New York: Routledge, 2002), 49–50.

16. The list is tiresomely long and the thesis is, I believe, humdrum. I list two examples. Frank Cioffi, *Freud and the Question of Pseudoscience* (Chicago: Open Court, 1998), and Richard Webster, *Why Freud Was Wrong: Sin, Science, and Psychoanalysis* (New York: Basic Books, 1995).

17. Adolf Grünbaum, *Foundations of Psychoanalysis,* 113.

18. Adolf Grünbaum, *Foundations of Psychoanalysis,* 127. See also Robert Holt, "The Current Status of Psychoanalytic Theory," in *Freud Reappraised: A Fresh Look at Psychoanalytic Theory* (New York: The Guilford Press, 1989), 324-362.

19. This group also functioned to discriminate genuine psychoanalytic therapy from that of noteworthy secessionists like Adler and Jung.

20. See Phyllis Grosskurth, *The Secret Ring: Freud's Inner Circle and the Politics of Psychoanalysis* (Addison-Wesley Publishing Company, 1991) and Frank J. Sulloway, "Reassessing Freud's Case Histories: The Social Construction of Psychoanalysis," in *Freud and the History of Psychoanalysis,* ed. Toby Gelfand and John Kerr, 153–92.

21. Jon Mills, "A Response to Grünbaum's Refutation of Psychoanalysis," in *Psychoanalytic Psychology,* Vol. 24, No. 3, 207.

22. D. P. Spence, "Freud's Forgotten Evolutionary Project," *Psychoanalytic Psychology*, Vol. 23, No. 2, 2006, 420–29.

23. See fn. 14.

24. Michael Scriven, "The Experimental Investigation of Psychoanalysis," in *Psychoanalysis, Scientific Method, and Philosophy,* ed. Sydney Hook (New York: New York University Press, 1959), 240.

25. Michael Scriven, "Experimental Investigation of Psychoanalysis," 246–47.

26. Sigmund Freud to Oskar Pfister, January 18, 1929. Sigmund Freud and Oskar Pfister, *Psychoanalysis and Faith.*

27. Sigmund Freud and Oskar Pfister, *Psychoanalysis and Faith,* 120.

28. E.g., Seymour Fisher and Roger P. Greenberg, *The Scientific Credibility of Freud's Theories and Therapy* (New York: Basic Books, 1977), 285.

29. At least, if the testimony of the patient himself on the worth of his sessions with Freud is to count. "In reality," says the patient, "the whole thing looks like a catastrophe. I am in the same state as when I first came to Freud, and Freud is no more." Frank J. Sulloway, "Reassessing Freud's Case Histories," 167–70, esp. 169.

30. It is fair and proper to criticize Freud's clinical mistakes and exaggerations of successes, but those criticisms should be made with an appropriate grasp of the inefficacy of alternative therapies for hysteria of Freud's day—e.g., hydrotherapy, electrotherapy, magnetic therapy, and, of course, hypnosis. See Hannah S. Decker, "Freud's 'Dora' Case in Perspective: The Medical Treatment of Hysteria in Austria at the Turn of the Century," in *Freud and the History of Psychoanalysis,* ed. Toby Gelfand and John Kerr (Hillsdale, NJ: The Analytic Press, 1992), 271–87.

31. See M. Andrew Holowchak, "Technology and Freudian Discontent: Freud's 'Muffled' Meliorism and the Problem of Human Annihilation."

32. Steven J. Ellman, *Freud's Technique Papers: A Contemporary Perspective* (Northvale, NJ: Jason Aronson, 1991), 287–88.

# PART II

# PSYCHOANALYSIS AS GROUP THERAPY

## Chapter 5
# Toward *Massenpsychologie*

"The use of analysis for the treatment of the neuroses is only one of its applications; the future will perhaps show that it is not the most important one." Sigmund Freud, *Question of Lay Analysis*

*T*HE GERMAN TERM *MASSE* (PL., *MASSEN*) IS AS AMBIGUOUS as its English equivalent "mass." Both can mean "lump," "stuff," "bulk," or "substance" as well as "a large (unspecified) amount of something" and "crowd." In *Group Psychology and Analysis of the Ego*, Freud is clear that a person's relations to his family members, love object, friends, and physician are group relations, but they are best left under the umbrella of individual-psychology, because the individual's investment of impulses is large and they are easily covered in the clinic. Group psychology (*Massenpsychologie*), thus, concerns an individual who is simultaneously related to a large number of people that would be strangers to him were it not for something that links them together. It studies individual persons as they are members of a race, nation, caste, profession, institution, or any other such large group (1921, *S.E.*, XVIII: 3-4).

Freud's shift to group psychology and its issues, in one sense, is unremarkable. As individuals are at once members of several social groups, individual psychology cannot be separated from group psychology. Freud elaborates:

Individual psychology . . . is concerned with the individual human being, and it examines the ways in which he tries to satisfy his instinctual drives. But only rarely and under specific exceptional circumstances is it in a position to abstract from this person's relationships with other individuals. In the individual's psychic life, other people usually must be considered as either [*sic*] models, objects, helpers or opponents. Thus, from the beginning, individual psychology is simultaneously group psychology—in this extended but legitimate sense (1921, *S.E.*, XVIII: 65).

Psychoanalysis, thus, is in the practice of analyzing individuals, but only exceptionally does it do so by abstracting them from their various social roles. Following Plato, Aristotle, and the Greek and Roman Stoics, individuals are fundamentally social creatures for Freud. As Graham McFee writes, for Freud, as agentive persons, we are not atoms that are separable from each other, but instead social creatures, and our agency depends on "sets of values which antedate us, and into which we grow."[1]

Yet in another sense, which I aim to flesh out in the remainder of the undertaking, Freud's shift to group psychology is remarkable, as it involves different psychoanalytic tools and a broad employment of them.

A complete grasp of Freud's shift to group psychology in later years involves a grasp of three Freudian purchases, which I elsewhere[2] more fully cover: Comtean progressivism, biological recapitulationism, and metapsychological explanation. These three Freudian purchases enabled Freud and psychoanalysis to move from the clinical setting and address group issues. They also gave psychoanalysis, qua $\Psi A_3$, broad explanatory power—at least in the eyes of Freud.

What sort of explanatory power did Freud believe $\Psi A_3$ had? One can envision two primary sorts— "weak normativity" and "strong normativity"—each of which has broad application, due to Freud's universalist intentions.

- To say that an explanation is *WEAKLY NORMATIVE* is to say that it is widely applicable and it may be put to no or little use to affect the course of human events.
- To say that an explanation is *STRONGLY NORMATIVE* is to say that it is widely applicable and it may be put to great use to affect the course of human events.

To say that Freud believed $\Psi A_3$ was *weakly normative* is to say that it could help people to grasp the various impulse-driven motives of human actions, but could not offer much in the way of corrective remedies for social problems. To say that Freud believed $\Psi A_3$ was *strongly normative* is to say that it could not only help people to grasp the various impulse-driven motives of human actions, but it could also offer corrective remedies for social problems.

Did Freud perceive psychoanalysis qua $\Psi A_3$ to be weakly or strongly normative, or somewhere in between the two? I defend the thesis that the sort of explanatory power that Freud thought psychoanalysis had was of or more near to the weakly normative sort. Psychoanalysis gave persons the tools to understand why they behaved the way they did as individuals and in groups, but could do little to change that behavior. Biological factors—e.g., quantities of libido and aggression—were at play, and most persons' ego was ill-equipped to hold in check such biological factors by finding suitable outlets for them. Still understanding was no small beer, for no problem could be addressed until it was correctly seen to be what it really was.

I begin this chapter by expatiating on each of Freud's three purchases— Comtean progressivism, biological recapitulationism, and Freud's own metapsychology. I turn afterward to the development of group psychology, which had its roots in Freud's metapsychological examination of the primary and secondary processes.

## Freud's Three Metempirical Purchases

In *Freud: The Reluctant Philosopher,* Alfred Tauber defends the thesis that the shift to metapsychology and social issues is due to Freud being a "frustrated philosopher." He writes, "I broadly regard such extensions of psychology as representing the expression of a frustrated philosopher, and while these speculations may have many sources, each contributes to a more general humanist commitment whose origins are evident from Freud's youth."[3] Psychoanalytic therapy itself is a confluence of commitments to Kantian autonomy, Nietzschean liberation, and Spinozan freedom-in-fate.

I have argued in *Freud and Utopia* that Freud was a dyed-in-the-wool Positivist throughout his life. Though he paid mouth honor to philosophy and embraced many metempirical concepts, at no time did he ever don the hat of philosopher or construe psychoanalysis or any part of it—e.g., his foray into group-psychology issues like war and contagion—as philosophical. He waxes philosophical many times—when he essays to defend psychoanalysis as a science or when he explains how knowing is possible—but he never takes himself to be doing anything but science.

### Comte's "Great Fundamental Law"

One of Freud's metempirical purchases is "a great fundamental law, to which the mind is subjected by an invariably necessity." He writes, "[E]ach branch of our knowledge, passes in succession through three different theoretical states: the theological or fictitious state, the metaphysical or abstract state, and the scientific or positive state."[4] Upon what is this great law of the mind founded? Experience, he vaunts. "This general revolution of the human mind can," writes Comte, "be easily verified today in a very obvious, although indirect, manner, if we consider the development of the individual intelligence. The starting point being necessarily the same in the education of the individual as in that of the race, the various principal phases of the former must reproduce the fundamental epochs of the latter."[5] All persons can readily see themselves as theologian in childhood, metaphysician in youth, and natural philosopher in adulthood. What applies to individuals applies too to the species.[6] He appeals to all persons' experience of the development of their own minds over time, but the notion of a similar path to the species is inductively gratuitous and the notion that all minds are subject to this law by "an invariable necessity" is *de trop* and tendentious.

> **Comte's Principle of Progress:** Each branch of human knowledge passes successively and inevitably through, first, a theological or fictitious theoretical state, second, a metaphysical or abstract theoretical state and, last, a scientific or positive theoretical state.

In *Totem and Taboo*, Freud writes in a manner strikingly similar to Comte:

The human race, if we are to follow the authorities [i.e., Comte], have [*sic*] in the course of ages developed three such systems of thought—the three great pictures of the universe: the animistic (or mythological), religious and scientific. Of these, animism, the first to be created, is perhaps the one which is most consistent and exhaustive and which gives a truly complete explanation of the nature of the universe. . . (1913, *S.E.*, XIII: 76-7).

There is no reason to doubt Comte is one of the "authorities" to which he refers.

Further evidence of such a purchase comes through his mention of three blows to human narcissism—one by Copernicus, one by Darwin, and the last and "most wounding" by Freud himself. He writes, doubtless with rodomontade:

In the course of centuries the naïve self-love of men has had to submit to two major blows at the hands of science. The first [Copernican blow] was when they learnt that our earth was not the centre of the universe but only a tiny fragment of a cosmic system of scarcely imaginable vastness.... The second blow [of Darwin, Wallace, and predecessors] fell when biological research destroyed man's supposedly privileged place in creation and proved his descent from the animal kingdom and his ineradicable animal nature.... But human megalomania will have suffered its third and most wounding blow from the psychological research of the present time [i.e., from Freud himself] which seeks to prove to the ego that it is not even master in its own house, but must content itself with scanty information of what is going on unconsciously in its mind[7] (1917, *S.E.*, XVI: 284-5).

Psychoanalysis, he says elsewhere, has made two discoveries. First, the sexual drives cannot be wholly mastered. Second, "mental processes are in themselves unconscious and only reach the ego and come under its control through incomplete and untrustworthy perceptions." He sums, "*[T]he ego is not master in its own house*" (1917, *S.E.*, XVII: 141-3).

## Haeckel's Biogenic Law

Freud's second metempircal purchase on the road to group psychology, given in Comte's justification of his great discovery, is recapitulationism—the view that individual embryological development (ontogeny) retraces the same developmental pattern of its species (phylogeny)—more economically, that "ontogeny recapitulates phylogeny." Ernst Haeckel elaborates:

[T]his history of the embryo (ontogeny) must be completed by a second, equally valuable, and closely connected branch of thought—the history of race (phylogeny). Both of these branches of evolutionary science, are, in my opinion, in the closest causal connection; this arises from the reciprocal action of the laws of heredity and adaptation . . . ontogenesis is a brief and rapid recapitulation of phylogenesis, determined by the physiological functions of heredity (generation) and adaptation (maintenance).[8]

Haeckel's articulation of recapitulationism is biological and Freud essays to give it historical and psychological expression and validity. The mental life of children, he asserts, displays the same archaic factors of primeval days of human civilization. A child merely repeats the course of human history in truncated form (1926, *S.E.*, XX: 212). Years later, in *Moses and Monotheism*, he adds, "[T]here is an almost complete conformity in this respect between the individual and the group: in the group too an impression of the past is retained in unconscious memory-traces" (1939, *S.E.*, XXIII: 94). In a letter to Abraham, Freud explains his phylogenetic approach to incest in contrast to the view of Rank. "My explanation was historical, social, phylogenetic," states Freud. "I deduced the incest barrier from the primordial history of the human family and thus saw in the actual father the real obstacle that re-creates the incest barrier in each new individual. Here Rank departs from me. He refuses to enter the phylogenetic field and makes horror of incest a direct repetition of birth anxiety...."[9] In "Short Account of Psycho-Analysis," Freud says of the development of individual psychology and of the subsequent branching out of psychoanalysis to the study of groups:

> If the psychological discoveries gained from the study of dreams were firmly kept in view, only one further step was needed before psycho-analysis could be proclaimed as the theory of the deeper mental processes not directly accessible to consciousness—as a "depth-psychology"—and before it could be applied to almost all the mental sciences. This step lay in the transition from the mental activity of individual men to the psychical functions of human communities and peoples—that is, from individual to group psychology. . . (1924, *S.E.*, XIX: 205).

The step to group psychology enabled Freud to move, at one extreme, from individual psychology ($\Psi A_2$), considering only individuals with neuroses as patients, to psychoanalysis considered as a full-fledged and broad-ranging science ($\Psi A_3$), at another extreme, considering at times all of humanity as a patient. The key was Freud's foundational work in depth psychology or $\Psi A_1$.

*Moses and Monotheism*, published the year of Freud's death, explains how $\Psi A_3$ moved Freud beyond $\Psi A_2$. First, there was the lining up of philology and psychoanalysis through Abel's work on the antithetical meaning of words, on which I elaborate fully in chapter 8. Next, there were Freud's discoveries of the unconscious, a collective and universal attribute of all humans, and of the "perfect correspondence" between obsessive actions of patients and religious rituals. Both steps illustrate that the psychical precipitates of the early-horde period, manifest in the symbolism from the period of development of speech of all peoples of all languages, became unconscious and continue to be passed on from generation to generation today as unconscious precipitates of the super-ego (1939, *S.E.*, XXIII: 67 & 132-3).

In "Short Account of Psycho-Analysis," Freud speaks of his reliance on $\Psi_1$ as an investigative tool for gleaning information about issues that transcend the clinic.

> If we may assume that the most general features of unconscious mental life (conflicts between instinctual impulses, repressions and substitutive satisfactions) are present everywhere, and if there is a depth-psychology which leads to a knowledge of those features, then we may reasonably expect that the application of psycho-analysis to the most varied spheres of human mental activity will everywhere bring to light important and hitherto unattainable results.

What follows is recognition that the antecedents of this excessively long compound conditional statement is true, which allows for expectation of even greater psychoanalytic insights into social issues (1924, *S.E.,* XIX: 206-7).

Freud then gives a brief summary of the chief motivation for the transition of humans from asocial living to communal living—control over the external world.

> [T]he main motive force towards the cultural development of man has been real external exigency, which has withheld from him the easy satisfaction of his natural needs and exposed him to immense dangers. This external frustration drove him into a struggle with reality, which ended partly in adaptation to it and partly in control over it; but it also drove him into working and living in common with those of his kind, and this already involved a renunciation of a number of instinctual impulses which could not be satisfied socially. With further advances of civilization the demands of repression also grew. Civilization is after all built entirely on renunciation of instinct, and every individual on his journey from childhood to maturity has in his own person to recapitulate this development of humanity to a state of judicious resignation (1924, *S.E.,* XIX: 207).

Unsatisfied unconscious wishes have numerous outlets, two of which he mentions. First, there are the normal Oedipal outlets that become manifest during human psychosexual development. Second, there are artistic creations, myths, and imaginative writings, which fulfill wishes through substitutive satisfaction (1924, *S.E.,* XIX: 207-8).

Overall, Freud believes that psychoanalysis, through his work at $\Psi A_1$, has made an uncontestable difference in the advance of the study of group psychology and the larger human issues and it has the capacity for an even greater contribution.

> As a "depth-psychology," a theory of the mental unconscious, it can become indispensable to all the sciences which are concerned with the evolution of human civilization and its major institutions such as art, religion and the social order. It has already, in my opinion, afforded these sciences considerable help in solving their problems. But these are only small contributions compared with what might be achieved if historians of civilization, psychologists of religions, philologists and so on would agree themselves to handle the new instrument of

research which is at their service. The use of analysis for the treatment of the neuroses is only one of its applications; the future will perhaps show that it is not the most important one (1926, *S.E.,* XX: 248).

The tone here seems not that of weak normativism, but rather that of strong normativism—i.e., the potential for a significant revolution in human thinking, given acceptance of psychoanalytic "findings." Nonetheless—given reference to historians of civilization, psychologists of religion, and philologists—it is clear that the sorts of problems that psychoanalysis might help these investigators solve are those that enable humans to have a greater grasp of the human condition by giving them a greater grasp of their past. Freud is not preparing the way for a psychoanalytic utopia. There is nothing to support strong normativism.

## Lamarck's Archaic Memory Traces

A strong belief in recapitulationism also prompted Freud to "deduce" his account of the killing of the primal father, discussed fully in the previous chapter. Given the rough parallels between the developmental paths of individuals and their species over time, Freud essayed to ground his ontogenetic findings with certain phylogenetic findings and to give psychoanalysis biological and historical backing.

An important move was Freud's metempirical purchase of Lamarckianism—specifically, the notion of the inheritance of acquired characteristics, which Freud consistently found indispensable, in spite of disavowal of the principle by most biologists of his time, hence its metempirical status. Freud says in *Moses and Monotheism:*

> On further reflection I must admit that I have behaved for a long time as though the inheritance of memory-traces of the experience of our ancestors, independently of direct communication and of the influence of education by the setting of an example, were established beyond question. . . . My position, no doubt, is made more difficult by the present attitude of biological science, which refuses to hear of the inheritance of acquired characters by succeeding generations. I must, however, in all modesty confess that nevertheless I cannot do without this factor in biological evolution[10] (1939, *S.E.,* XXIII: 99-100).

*Totem and Taboo* asserts that memory-traces require, quite literally, a "collective mind," where there are mental processes just like there are in the psyches of individuals. In this collective mind, the guilt of the primal killing has persisted unconsciously for many thousands of years. The assumption of a collective mind, Freud maintains, makes it possible to smooth out the interruptions of human mental activity that are caused by the death of each individual and that make social psychology possible. Without the continuity of psychical processes from generation to generation, there would be no progress and no development in social psychology (1913, *S.E.,* XIII: 157-8).

Returning to *Moses and Monotheism*, Freud gives three arguments for the existence of memory-traces. I number them for ease of reference.

> (1) If we assume the survival of these memory-traces in the archaic heritage, we have bridged the gulf between individual and group psychology: we can deal with peoples as we do with an individual neurotic. (2) Granted that at the time we have no stronger evidence for the presence of memory-traces in the archaic heritage than the residual phenomena of the work of analysis which call for a phylogenetic derivation, yet this evidence seems to us strong enough to postulate that such is the fact. (3) If it is not so, we shall not advance a step further along the path we entered on, either in analysis or in group psychology. The audacity cannot be avoided (1939, *S.E.,* XXIII: 100).

I offer a word or two on each argument.

The first argument is clearly pragmatic. The assumption of memory-traces allows Freud to analyze groups in the manner of individuals and that in itself is no mere gewgaw, as it allows psychoanalysis access to groups and group problems. Given its pragmatic nature, the argument lacks substance. Yet, Freud might have countered, analysis of groups and their problems holds out the hope for the promise of evidence for memory-traces at some point in the future.

Perhaps acknowledging the weakness of the first argument, Freud comes up with a second argument, which is evidential, not pragmatic. The "residual phenomena of the work of analysis which call for a phylogenetic derivation" are the strongest evidence for memory traces. By "residual phenomena," Freud presumably means those bits of data that cannot be accommodated by individual psychology—e.g., the philological data that seem to corroborate Freud's findings about the nature of the unconscious. Such data, Freud assures his readers, are deemed strong enough to be taken factually, in spite of lack of independent confirmation through other sciences.

Given the evidential strength Freud takes the second argument to have, it is queer that he considers a third argument, which *prima facie* seems to be based on evidence of progress in individual and group psychology. Yet if that were so, one would expect the conditional statement to be phrased counterfactually (i.e., *Were it not so, we would not advance. . .*). It is not—neither in translation nor in Freud's German. Thus, it too must be taken pragmatically, not evidentially. Group psychology, the argument goes, sinks or swims on the existence of archaic memory traces.

Overall, the assumption of memory-traces in humans has another welcome result, though one directed at human narcissism. On the assumption of memory-traces in humans in the form of drives (*Triebe*), there is a further narrowing of the gulf between humans and other animals. Other animals seemingly have instincts (*Instinkten*) that enable them to behave smoothly and regularly, when they encounter novel experiences, and these can only be "preserved memories of what was experienced by their ancestors" as is the case with human drives (1939, *S.E.,* XXIII: 100).

Freud sums, "After this discussion I have no hesitation in declaring that men have always known (in this special way) that they once possessed a primal father and killed him" (1939, *S.E.,* XXIII: 101).

Freud's purchase of Lamarck goes deeper. He mentions in correspondence his "Lamarck idea"—a proposed paper to "put Lamarck entirely on our ground and to show that the 'necessity' accorded to him that creates and transforms organs is nothing but the power of unconscious ideas over one's own body, of which we see remnants in hysteria . . . the 'omnipotence of thoughts.'"[11]

## The Witch Metapsychology

Freud, when pushed formally to justify psychoanalysis as science always falls back on proto-concepts shaped by hard-fought empirical advances. Yet his practice is metempirical. He acknowledges to Jung that the richness of personal experience trumps "books and reports." He adds: "Besides, my interest is diminished by the conviction that I am already in possession of the truths I am trying to prove. . . . I can see from the difficulties I encounter in this work that I was not cut out for inductive investigation, that my whole makeup is intuitive, and that in setting out to establish the purely empirical science of ΨA I subjected myself to an extraordinary discipline."[12]

As I have covered extensively the issue of Freud's metapsychology in *Freud and Utopia,*[13] here I give merely a sketch of my take.

In his 1915 paper titled "The Unconscious," Freud states, "I propose that when we have succeeded in describing a psychical process in its dynamic, topographical and economic aspects, we should speak of it as a metapsychological presentation" (1915, *S.E.,* XIV: 181)—i.e., it concerns forces, places, and quantities. Metapsychological explanation is heuristic, but couched in etiological and neurobiological terms, and aims to:

1. determine the nature of the unconscious,
2. link conscious to unconscious,
3. establish the unconscious as the basic psychical entity,
4. link the mental and the physical, and
5. explain unconscious phenomena in biophysical language in keeping with the desiderata of simplicity, coherence, and comprehensiveness.

I add:

Metapsychology is the speculative superstructure that grew from Freud's clinical data. Thus, he believed it to be consistent with his clinical data and capable of accommodating further psychological discoveries and advances. It is couched, however, in biophysical language and, thus, he believed it to be consistent with current data and models of neurophysiology and capable of accommodating further neurophysiological discoveries and advances. The overall aim for Freud was to provide an etiological framework for psychoanalysis working at the psychical level so as to forge a link with neurobiology.[14]

In that sense, metapsychology for Freud is really $\Psi A_1$, used in a systematic and comprehensive sense, to generate $\Psi A_3$. The question to be resolved is whether $\Psi A_3$, being empirically sensitive, is always open-ended and revisable or is itself the sort of *Weltanschauung* that Freud expressly sought to avoid.[15]

### Three Aspects of Metapsychological Explanation

Howsoever metapsychology is to be grasped, Freud was clear that it comprises three key aspects: a topographical aspect, a dynamic aspect, and an economic aspect.

### *Topographic*

In chapter 7 of *The Interpretation of Dreams*, Freud states: "We are justified, in my view, in giving free rein to our speculations so long as we retain the coolness of our judgement and do not mistake the scaffolding for the building. And since at our first approach to something unknown all that we need is the assistance of provisional ideas, I shall give preference in the first instance to hypotheses of the crudest and most concrete description" (1900, *S.E.,* V: 536).

Freud alludes here to the existence of three "$\psi$-systems"—the systems conscious, preconscious, and unconscious—that "stand in a regular spatial relation to one another, in the same way in which the various systems of lenses in a telescope are arranged behind one another (1900, *S.E.,* V: 537).

"Now let us call 'conscious' the conception which is present to our consciousness and of which we are aware, and let this be the only meaning of the term 'conscious.'" Preconscious designates latent ideas prohibited from consciousness only because of their weakness. Finally, "The term *unconscious* . . . designates not only latent ideas in general, but especially ideas with a certain dynamic character, ideas keeping apart from consciousness in spite of their intensity and activity" (1912, S.E., XII: 260-2). These include not only ontogenetic memories—repressed memories gained through one's personal experiences—but phylogenetic memories—repressed memories of experiences in the early development of the human species that have been passed on through sexual reproduction in Lamarckian fashion.

The topographical model underwent substantial modification, when Freud developed his structural model—id, ego, and super-ego—in *The Ego and the Id* (1923).

We can summarize as follows:

To describe mental agencies *topographically* is to express them in spatial terms, without implying any direct correlation to brain anatomy[16] (1925, *S.E.,*

XX: 32).

## Dynamic

Freud writes of dynamic features of psychical processes in early works such as *Studies on Hysteria* and *The Interpretation of Dreams* as well as in later works (e.g., 1925: *S.E., XX*: 22), but his references to dynamic functioning are always fuzzy, inchoate.

*On the Question of Lay Analysis* tells us the dynamic perspective concerns forces at work in and between psychological elements (1926, *S.E., XX*: 200). In "Psycho-Analysis," he gives what is probably his clearest depiction of the dynamic point of view.

> From the first of these [metapsychological] standpoints the *dynamic* one, psycho-analysis derives all mental processes (apart from the receptions of external stimuli) from the interplay of forces, which assist or inhibit one another, combine with one another, enter into compromises with one another, etc. All of these forces are originally in the nature of *drives*; thus they have an organic origin. They are characterized by possessing an immense (somatic) store of power (*"the compulsion to repeat"*); and they are represented mentally as images or ideas with an affective charge (1926, *S.E., XX*: 265).

"Analysis Terminable and Interminable" shows that dynamic expenditure is costly for the ego in organisms. "The dynamic expenditure necessary for maintaining [the services the ego renders the id], and the restrictions of the ego which they almost invariably entail, prove a heavy burden on the psychical economy" (1937, *S.E., XXIII*: 237).

Thus, we can sum the dynamic perspective:

> To describe mental agencies *dynamically* is to express them as the result of the interplay of internal, organic-based drive-forces with affective charges that are immensely powerful and can be represented pictorially or ideationally.

## Economic

The economic aspect of psychical processes is their economical, quantitative factor. "We have reckoned as though there existed in the mind—whether in the ego or in the id—a displaceable energy, which, neutral in itself, can be added to a qualitatively differentiated erotic or destructive impulse, and augment its total cathexis," Freud writes in *The Ego and the Id*. "Without assuming the existence of a displaceable energy of this kind we can make no headway" (1923, *S.E., XIX*: 44). In "Psycho-Analysis," he adds:

> From the *economic* standpoint psycho-analysis supposes that the mental representatives of the drives have a charge (*cathexis*) of definite quantities of energy, and that it is the purpose of the mental apparatus to hinder any damming-up of

these energies and to keep as low as possible the total amount of the excitations with which it is loaded. The course of mental processes is automatically regulated by the *"pleasure-unpleasure principle"*; and unpleasure is thus in some way related to an increase of excitation and pleasure to a decrease. In the course of development the original pleasure principle undergoes a modification with reference to the external world, giving place to the *"reality principle,"* in accordance with which the mental apparatus learns to postpone the pleasure of satisfaction and to tolerate temporarily feelings of unpleasure (1926, *S.E.*, XX: 266).

Thus, we can sum the economic perspective:

> To describe mental agencies *economically* is to express them as representations of drives with definite quantities of energy, in need of periodic discharge.

Proper mental functioning occurs only when the total amount of excitations are kept as low as possible. Inordinate damming-up of the system can result in neurosis or, in extreme instances, psychosis.

### Freud's Need of Metapsychology

In *The Foundations of Psychoanalysis,* Adolf Grünbaum, taking Freud's commitment to metapsychology as a commitment toward a "speculative superstructure," argues that Freud consistently considered his metapsychology to be superfluous. As he notes, psychoanalysis is founded essentially on his clinical findings ($\Psi A_2$) and he adduces several passages in the Freudian corpus to support his claim. Freud is foremost a scientist and the tool with which he worked was observation, not speculation. Repression itself is founded on observation and his metapsychology is only as good as the data upon which its principles are founded. Grünbaum writes:

> It emerges clearly that when Freud unswervingly claimed natural science status for his theoretical constructions throughout his life, he did so first and foremost for his evolving clinical theory of personality and therapy, rather than for the metapsychology. For he had been chastened in his early reductionistic exuberance by the speedy demise of his "Project." And, once he had repudiated his ephemeral neurobiological model of the psyche after 1896, he perennially saw himself entitled to proclaim the *scientificity* of his clinical theory *entirely on the strength of a secure and direct epistemic warrant from the observations he made of his patients and of himself.* In brief, during all but the first few years of his career, Freud's criterion of *scientificity* was *methodologically* and *not* ontologically reductive. [17]

In short, Grünbaum maintains that the worth of Freudian metapsychology, like any other of Freudian hypotheses or assumptions, is dependent upon the worth of Freud's clinical observations ($\Psi A_2$). The clinical data, then, stand alone: They do not have merit because they are subsumable under some abstract metapsychological superstructure, whose coherence and comprehensiveness are in part measures of its correctness.

Grünbaum is right to insist that Freud always considered himself chiefly a scientist, whose generalizations were open to public criticism and revision and whose concepts were open to clarification or riddance. Freud himself often explicitly states that. Consider, for example, Freud in "Psycho-analysis":

> Psycho-analysis is not, like philosophies, a system starting out from a few sharply defined basic concepts, seeking to grasp the whole universe with the help of these and, once it is completed, having no room for fresh discoveries or better understanding. On the contrary, it keeps close to the facts in its field of study, seeks to solve the immediate problems of observation, gropes its way forward by the help of experience, and is always incomplete and always ready to correct or modify its theories. There is no incongruity . . . if its most general concepts lack clarity and if its postulates are provisional; it leaves their more precise definition to the results of future work (1922, *S.E.,* XVIII: 253-4).

Grünbaum is also correct in asserting that Freud was guarded about his metapsychological superstructure, as he often wrote of it as if it were unnecessary. Freud writes in "On Narcissism":

> One dislikes the thought of abandoning observation for barren theoretical controversy, but nevertheless one must not shirk an attempt at clarification. It is true that notions such as that of an ego-libido, an energy of the ego-instincts, and so on, are neither particularly easy to grasp, nor sufficiently rich in content; a speculative theory of the relations in question would begin by seeking to obtain a sharply defined concept as its basis. But . . . that is just the difference between a speculative theory and a science erected on empirical interpretation. The latter will not envy speculation its privilege of having a smooth, logically unassailable foundation, but will gladly content itself with nebulous, scarcely imaginable basic concepts, which it hopes to apprehend more clearly in the course of its development, or which it is even prepared to replace by others. For these ideas are not the foundation of science, upon which everything rests: that foundation is observation alone. They are not the bottom but the top of the whole structure, and they can be replaced and discarded without damaging it (1914, *S.E.,* XIV: 77).

Grünbaum's claim that the scientific status of psychoanalysis lies squarely, directly, and entirely on the "strength . . . of the observations he made of patients and of himself," if true, means that psychoanalysis for Freud was always fundamentally and, in justification, nothing more than $\Psi A_2$.

Though he did give up the metapsychological reductionism of the discarded *Project*, Freud never gave up hope that metapsychology would somehow corroborate his clinical findings by providing for them a comprehensive and coherent system like that of Newtonian dynamics. Over time Freud came to believe that metapsychology was needed to explain his clinical successes. In "Analysis Terminable and Interminable," he writes:

> [T]he factors which were decisive for the success of our therapeutic efforts were the influence of traumatic aetiology, the relative strength of the instincts which have to be controlled, and something which we have called an alteration of the ego. . . . [I]n connection with [the second factor] we have had occasion to recognize the paramount importance of the quantitative [i.e., economic] factor and to stress the claim of the metapsychological line of approach to be taken into account in any attempt at explanation (1939, *S.E.,* XXIII: 234).

Earlier, in "Autobiographical Study," Freud gives evidence that he cannot do without a metatheoretic superstructure of some sort:

> Later on I made an attempt to produce a "Metapsychology." By this I meant a method of approach according to which every mental process is considered in relation to three co-ordinates, which I described as *dynamic, topographical,* and *economic* respectively; and this seemed to me to present the furthest goal that psychology could attain. The attempt remained no more than a torso; after writing two or three papers . . . I broke off . . . since the time for theoretical predications of this kind had not yet come. In my latest speculative works I have set about the task of dissecting our mental apparatus on the basis of the analytic view of pathological facts and have divided it into an *ego,* an *id,* and a *super-ego* (1925, *S.E.,* XX: 58-9).

Here Freud, referring to the abandoned project *Preliminaries to a Metapsychology,* mentions that the time for metapsychology, "the furthest goal that psychology could attain"—and note his use of "psychology" and not "psychoanalysis"—"had not yet come." Freud here is referring to a metatheoretic superstructure that validates the scientific status of psychoanalysis qua $\Psi A_3$. By 1923, with *The Ego and the Id,* the time had come.

In "Analysis Terminable and Interminable," Freud says that the therapeutic successes of $\Psi A_2$ depend on the "Witch Metapsychology."

> If we are asked by what methods and means this result [of bringing the instincts into harmony with the ego] is achieved, it is not easy to find an answer. We can only say: "*So muss denn doch die Hexe dran!*" ("We must call the Witch to our help after all!")—the Witch Metapsychology. Without metapsychological speculation and theorizing—I had almost said "phantasizing"—we shall not get another step forward.

He adds that what the Witch reveals, neither clearly nor with much detail, is the antithesis between primary and secondary processes (1939, *S.E.,* XXIII: 225), the subject of the final section of this chapter. Here again the justification is clothed pragmatically—metapsychology is it seems a needed heuristic or useful fiction—though it need not and should not be taken thus. Like the arguments for archaic memory-traces, Freud seems to be saying the successes of $\Psi A_2$ can *only* be explained economically—by assuming the existence of unseen quantities of psycho-biological energy that are used by agencies like id and ego. Metapsychological explanation, what I take to be the driving force behind Freud's findings at the level of depth-psychology or $\Psi A_1$, is also the driving force not only behind *Massenpsychologie*, but also *Individualpsychologie*.

Finally, one might note that works such as *Beyond the Pleasure Principle* and *The Ego and the Id* are saturated with metapsychological content. It is difficult to believe that the effort and ti-me spent on such groundbreaking works were not in the service of advancing psychoanalysis as a science, but instead were some pell-mell thoughts on substructure that Freud believed he could readily do without.

Overall, the scientific validation of psychoanalysis as a discipline, $\Psi A_3$ was always chiefly, but not exclusively Freud's clinical data. Freud additionally sought corroborative support for $\Psi A_3$ through non-clinical psychoanalytic "discoveries"—e.g., the killing of the primal father, the reason for Christ's dying on the cross, the paradox of civilization, and human tendency for blood-violence—that were thought to be consistent with data or generalizations of other disciplines, such as biology and history.[18] These discoveries, driven by his inevasible attachment to Comte's progressivism and to biological recapitulationism as well as his own metapsychology, were discoveries of group psychology that were to Freud corroborative support for his clinical findings and his warrant for $\Psi A_3$—a comprehensive and coherent system of unmatched scope and broad explanatory power. Psychotherapist and critic Robert Holt agrees:

> [T]he metapsychological enterprise as a whole seems to have been the partial gratification of Freud's wish for a godlike comprehensiveness of knowledge and for the power that such near-omniscience would entail. . . . Perhaps Freud had to abjure philosophy so vigorously and repeatedly after his adolescent flirtation with it because it came too close to these forbidden infantile fantasies. He may have sensed that to enter seriously on an attempt to solve the great problems of existence—man's place in the cosmos, and the nature of good and evil (committing Adam's sin)—and to do so merely by the exercise of the intellect without the patient collection of data, would threaten to lift his repressive defenses against very early, overweening wishes. Those are transparently Promethean derivatives of the oedipal wishes to kill and replace the father, seizing not only his sexual prerogatives but his seemingly endless power.[19]

In summary, while Freudian psychoanalysis methodologically could not do without metapsychology, Freud personally could not do without metapsychology, because, to his way of thinking, it gave his clinical data vindication through inclusion in a broad-ranging theoretical superstructure, not unlike that of Newtonian dynamics. The theoretical superstructure, he believed, and its varied ties with other sciences gave psychoanalysis credibility and extraordinary explanatory power. Thus, $\Psi A_3$, founded on $\Psi A_1$, began to take on a life of its own. It was becoming what Freud often asserted a science should never be: a *Weltan-schauung*.[20]

# Culture on the Couch

While Freud was a progressivist in the Comtean sense, his "progress" was based on a sort of inveterate ambivalence. Progress toward the sort of scientific utopia, envisaged by Comte, could only come by "mankind . . . 'binding' their unsatisfied wishes" and renouncing human happiness (1913, *S.E.,* XIII: 186) and that was a high price to pay for utopia. Yet because of the development of the ego and the super-ego over time, in response to the ever-increasing demands of civilized living, Freud could not envisage any return to the primitive conditions, whereby humans could sate directly their impulses.

## Two Principles: Pleasure and Reality

For Freud, the Witch "Metapsychology" was based on the notion that there were two systems, primary and secondary processes, and that those systems behaved antithetically—the former concerning itself with pleasure; the latter, with reality. Why was there a need for primary processes? Freud's commitment to determinism bound him to the view that there could be no accidental behaviors and, therefore, those very many behaviors that were not answerable to rational principles—e.g., actions of neurotics and psychotics, dreams, parapraxes, and jokes—were answerable to irrational or unconscious principles.[21]

In his early works, Freud worked under the assumption that the psychical system functioned exclusively to bring about pleasure through release of built-up tension within an organism. That he dubbed the "unpleasure principle" in *The Interpretation of Dreams.* "All other processes in the $\Psi$-systems, including the *Pcs.*, are lacking in any psychical quality and so cannot be objects of consciousness, except in so far as they bring pleasure or unpleasure to perception. We are thus driven to conclude that *these releases of pleasure and unpleasure automatically regulate the course of cathectic processes*" (1900, *S.E.,* V: 600). The difficulty, of course, came in showing how some ideas could be relatively independent of pleasure. His solution in this early work was to link *Pcs.* to speech and thought-processes and consciousness to perceptions (1900, *S.E.,* V: 574).

The defects of that "solution" haunted Freud for years. With *The Ego and the Id* and the introduction of the ego, Freud proposes a more reasonable solution that allows for a greater sense of psychical unity for an organism. Early on, the ego branches out from the id, through the direct effect of the external world on an organism through the system *Pcpt.-Cs.* He describes it topographically as "an extension of the surface-differentiation" that functions to bring reality into consideration. It represents reason and common sense. The id, in contrast, is a reservoir for human passions (1923, *S.E.,* XIX: 22).

The introduction of the ego and explication of its relationship to reality were needed extensions of burgeoning thoughts in that direction. "Formulations on the Two Principles of Mental Functioning" in 1911 is the first big step in that direction and the first occurrence of the terms "pleasure principle" and "reality principle." Every neurosis is in some measure a "loss of *'la function du réel'*" and it is a psychoanalyst's job to bring back reality to bear on the life of his patient.

> In the psychology which is founded on psycho-analysis we have become accustomed to taking as our starting-point the unconscious mental processes, with the peculiarities of which we have become acquainted through analysis. We consider these to be the older, primary processes, the residues of a phase of development in which they were the only kind of mental processes. The governing purpose obeyed by these primary-processes is easy to recognize; it is described as the pleasure-unpleasure [*Lust-Unlust*] principle, or more shortly the pleasure principle (1911, *S.E.,* XII: 218-9).

Peremptory demands of internal needs through wishes disturb equanimity. Hallucinations (e.g., dreams or daydreams) come about to satisfy these disturbances. Abandonment of hallucinations sometimes occurs, when hallucinatory satisfaction of wishes does not occur. He writes, "A new principle of mental functioning was thus introduced; what was presented in the mind was no longer what was agreeable but what was real, even if it happened to be disagreeable. This setting-up of the *reality principle* proved to be a momentous step." With the introduction of the reality principle, consciousness takes up the tasks of attention, notation through memory, impartial passing of judgment, and motor discharge or motor restraint through thinking. This is the preliminary move from primary processes to secondary processes (1911, *S.E.,* XII: 219-21).

For the move from primary processes to secondary processes to occur, libido needs to be liberated from its sole auto-erotic function in early development and must risk attachment to other objects. The risk is sexual frustration. Secondary processes, through the pleasure-ego, allow for delay of real satisfaction of an impulse by imaginary satisfaction through phantasy and the promise of real satisfaction in the future (1911, *S.E.,* XII: 221-3). We can summarize the two principles as follows:

**Pleasure Principle:** The primary-process course of mental events has as its outcome the procurement of pleasure or avoidance of unpleasure.

**Reality Principle:** The secondary-process course of mental events has as its outcome the procurement of pleasure through delay of gratification because of the dictates of reality.

**Group Psychology**

As Peter Gay notes, Freud's Vienna circle was, from its inception, interested in issues of applied psychoanalysis and, thus, Freud needed no special urging to place "culture on the couch,"[22] as he was wont to do in his more mature years. The shift of focus from individual psychology to group psychology began with *Totem and Taboo* in 1913 and took root seven years later in *Beyond the Pleasure Principle*, an abstruse work that gives Freud's metapsychological scaffolding for group psychology. Writes James Strachey:

> In the series of metapsychological writings, *Beyond the Pleasure Principle* may be regarded as introducing the final phase of [Freud's] views. He had already drawn attention to the "compulsion to repeat" as a clinical phenomenon, but here he attributes to it the characteristics of an instinct; here too for the first time he brings forward the new dichotomy between Eros and the death instincts which found its full elaboration in *The Ego and the Id*. In *Beyond the Pleasure Principle,* too, we can see signs of the new picture of the anatomical structure of the mind which was to dominate all Freud's later writings. Finally, the problem of destructiveness, which played an ever more prominent part in his theoretical works, makes its first explicit appearance. The derivation of various elements in the present discussion from his earlier metapsychological works ... will be obvious. But what is particularly remarkable is the closeness with which some of the earlier sections of the present work follow the "Project for a Scientific Psychology," drafted by Freud twenty-five years earlier, in 1895.[23]

One year after *Beyond the Pleasure Principle,* Freud directly tackles the differences between individual and group psychology in *Group Psychology and the Analysis of the Ego.* Though psychoanalysis mainly concerns the relationship of individuals and their paths of instinctual satisfaction—i.e., individual psychology—it also at the same time concerns the relationship of individuals with others—i.e., group psychology. In short, psychoanalysis has both a narcissistic component and a social component (1921, *S.E.,* XVIII: 69).

By "group psychology," Freud means not relations with those in one's nearest social circle—family, intimates, close friends, and one's physician—but instead the simultaneous influence of large groups of people, connected to oneself. "Group psychology is therefore concerned with the individual man as a member of a race, of a nation, of a caste, of a profession, of an institution, or as a component part of a crowd of people who have been organized into a group at some particular time for some definite purpose." He considers the possibility of examining these relations from the vantage-point of some irreducible herd instinct or group mind. That seems implausible. It is more plausible to assume that the "social instinct" is reducible and that it develops out of the family (1921, *S.E.,* XVIII: 70).

The motivation for group psychology is as follows. If psychology can give a relatively complete explanation for the impulses, motives, predispositions, and aims of individuals in relationship to those nearest them, then it would still have before it the herculean task of explaining why it is that individuals think, feel, and act quite differently in or before groups (1921, *S.E.,* XVIII: 72). Overall, the Freudian program here is more in keeping with that of John Stuart Mill than that of Comte, as Mill believed that the laws of society were nothing but the laws that govern individuals, considered in a group.[24]

Following Gustave le Bon's analysis in *The Crowd,* Freud lists three features of groups. First, individuals in groups gain a sense of invincibility, through sheer numbers, that allows them to give themselves up to their impulses. Second, the sentiments and acts in groups are contagious. Third, the sentiments and acts in groups are a product of suggestion, the cause of contagion. From those points, it follows that groups, driven principally by the unconscious, are impulsive, changeable, irritable, credulous, and have a sense of omnipotence. They do not premeditate, persevere in, or delay actions. They think with images and there is no check of those images by reason. In addition, there is no thirsting for truth. In short, in groups, emotions are intensified and intellect is restrained (1921, *S.E.,* XVIII: 74-80).

For Freud, given that individuals lose their individuality—i.e., their continuity, self-consciousness, traditions and customs, and functions and positions—in a group, the problem is one of giving them back something, a different sense of individuation (1921, *S.E.,* XVIII: 86-7).

Psychoanalytic examination takes Freud to his theory of libido—the psychical energy of love, directed toward self and others. The willful giving up of one's identity in a group to suggestion by others in the group is an erotic concession. Groups, thus, are held together by libido (1921, *S.E.,* XVIII: 90-2).

Analysis of artificial groups—e.g., the church and an army—shows the need of an external force to keep them functioning and organized. What holds members in check libidinally is not any common interest—such as race, class, or nation—but their head, viz., god in the church and the commander-in-chief in an army, and the illusion, held by all, that the head loves all with an equal love (1921, *S.E.,* XVIII: 93). As Howard Kaye writes:

> [T]he strength of such bonds [not directed toward the head] paled before those formed on the basis of a shared and intense emotional bond to a powerful leader, even one long dead. Only such love of and fear before a leader reawakens "the idea of a paramount and dangerous personality," associated with both the "primal father" of prehistory and the fantasy father of childhood, and is powerful enough to motivate the transformation of the hostility and envy we otherwise feel toward others into "communal or group feeling."[25]

Dissolution of artificial groups occurs through dissolution of libidinal ties. In an army, it is due to panic, of a magnitude to weaken or destroy libidinal ties, due to common danger or some other cause.[26] In the church, it is due to ruthlessness and hostility, directed toward unbelievers, which are consequences of the libidinal ties of religious institutions[27] (1921, *S.E.,* XVIII: 95-9).

Freud's examination of group psychology ultimately takes him back to individual psychology—specifically, the Oedipal tensions within each family. His focus is a boy's identification with his father and the ambivalence that accompanies it. The boy desires to mold his ego in the manner of his father. Ultimately, identification, as the original form of an emotional tie with another person, becomes a libidinal substitute by introjecting that person into the ego. During latency, part of the ego separates itself and develops into its own faculty, a critical faculty in conflict with the ego called "ego-ideal" (1921, *S.E.,* XVIII: 106-10) or what he would soon call "super-ego."

With the development of the ego-ideal, there is an extraordinary idealization of the sexual object to such extent that one's own ego is self-effaced and neglected. "The object has, so to speak, consumed the ego." He adds, "The criticism exercised by that faculty is silent; everything that the object does and asks for is right and blameless. Conscience has no application to anything that is done for the sake of the object; in the blindness of love remorselessness is carried to the pitch of crime." Ultimately, the sexual object replaces the ego-ideal. Here Freud finds himself in a position to formulate a principle for the libidinal constitution of any primary group that has a leader and that has been able to acquire the characteristics of an individual (1921, *S.E.,* XVIII: 112-6). For Freud:

> A *primary group* is a number of individuals who have substituted one and the same object for their ego ideal and have consequently identified themselves with one another in their ego.[28]

Identification does not paint a complete picture. Many of the characteristics of group behavior—e.g., emotionality, immediacy of gratification, and weakness of intellect—are regressive, but mutually reinforcing. They give signs of being primary, irreducible, and instinctual—characteristics of a herd instinct.[29]

The herd instinct, Freud notes, is observable in young children at school. When each child's primary demand for favored treatment is frustrated, there comes to be a secondary demand, motivated by selfishness, for equal treatment. Each child says, "If I cannot be favored, then no one will be favored." Thus, through reaction-formation, there is justice and equality for all (1921, *S.E.,* XVIII: 118-21).

Psychoanalytic explanation ultimately becomes phylogenetic and takes Freud back to the primal horde and the killing of the primal father—"the 'superman' whom Nietzsche only expected from the future." He states, "The leader of the group is still the dreaded primal father; the group still wishes to be governed by unrestricted force; it has an extreme passion for authority . . . a thirst for obedience" (1921, *S.E.,* XVIII: 123-8).

Freud concludes that surrender to a group is a matter of giving up one's ego-ideal for a group-ideal, embodied in the qualities of the leader. Complete surrender, of the sort one finds in religious extremism, is pathological, but is made plausible by a developmental process that begins narcissistically and works toward some recognition of an outer world and other objects in it that demand equal attention. The egoistic and regressive nature of dreams, humor, and neuroses shows that movement away from narcissism is often deemed intolerable (1921, *S.E.,* XVIII: 129-31).

Nonetheless, civilized living requires that every individual forms many libidinal ties, whether pathological or non-pathological, with groups—i.e., his race, his class, his creed, and his nationality. Freud also makes it plain that, to the extent that any person can be happy, he must raise himself above the collected masses of individuals and develop "a scrap of independence and originality" (1921, *S.E.,* XVIII: 129).

## Upshot

In summary, in spite of the numerous other factors that led him to focus on group issues, Freud's shift to group psychology proved to be a natural extension of his clinical work. Analysis of individuals in therapy gave Freud the needed depth-psychology tools to understand thoroughly human pathology and normalcy. $\Psi A_2$, thus, was shaped in partnership with $\Psi A_1$. Three metempirical purchases—Comtean progressivism, Haeckelian recapitulationism, and Larmarkian inheritance of acquired characteristics—enabled Freud to take psychoanalysis outside the clinic and have something to say vis-à-vis vital social issues. $\Psi A_3$, then, began to emerge from $\Psi A_2$ and $\Psi A_1$.

The thesis that Freud's shift toward larger, more vital social issues reflects a philosophical turn in his thinking is *de trop*. Freud's shift to group-psychology issues is just the application of psychoanalytic principles derived from the interplay of clinical work and theoretical posturing to group-related issues.

## Notes

1. Graham McFee, "Why Doesn't Sports Psychology Consider Freud?" *Journal of the Philosophy of Sport,* 104.

2. M. Andrew Holowchak, *Freud and Utopia.*

3. Alfred I. Tauber, *Freud: The Reluctant Philosopher* (Princeton University Press, 2010), xv.

4. August Comte, *Introduction to Positive Philosophy,* trans. Frederick Ferre (Indianapolis, IN: Hackett Publishing Company, Inc., 1988), 1–2.

5. August Comte, *Introduction to Positive Philosophy*, 4.

6. August Comte, *Introduction to Positive Philosophy*, 4.

7. In "Resistances to Psycho-Analysis," Freud describes the three blows, directed at human narcissism, as "cosmological," "biological," and "psychological" (1925, *S.E.,* XXII: 173). He covers these blows more fully in "A Difficulty on the Path for Psycho-Analysis" (1917, *S.E.,* XVII: 139–43).

8. Ernst Haeckel, *The Riddle of the Universe at the Close of the Nineteenth Century* (Buffalo, NY: Prometheus Books, 1992).

9. February 15, 1924. Hilda C. Abraham and Ernst L. Freud, eds., *A Psycho-Analytic Dialogue: The Letters of Sigmund Freud and Karl Abraham, 1907–1926* (New York: Basic Books, 1965), 347.

10. For more on Freud's Lamarckianism, see Lucy B. Ritvo, *Darwin's Influence on Freud: A Tale of Two Sciences* (New Haven, CT: Yale University Press, 1990), 53–59.

11. Letters to Abraham (October 5, 1917 and November 11, 1917). Hilda C. Abraham and Ernst L. Freud, eds., *A Psycho-Analytic Dialogue*, 158 and 261.

12. December 17, 1911. Freud, Sigmund, and Carl G. Jung, *The Freud/Jung Letters,* ed. William McGuire (Princeton University Press, 1974).

13. M. Andrew Holowchak, *Freud and Utopia,* 23–25.

14. M. Andrew Holowchak, *Freud and Utopia,* 24.

15. The answer to this question invites speculation on philosophy-of-mind issues. Edwin Wallace maintains reasonably that Freud was throughout a consistent materialist, though a methodological (interactional) dualist. Wallace believes one can best accommodate the tension by committing Freud to a dual-aspect monism, where the real objects are material entities and certain material entities have physiological and psychological aspects and where psychological phenomena, to be fully grasped, must be explained both neurobiologically and intentionally. Edwin R. Wallace, "Freud and the Mind-Body Problem," *Freud and the History of Psychoanalysis,* eds. Toby Gelfand and John Kerr (Hillsdale, NJ: The Analytic Press, 1992), 231–69.

16. See also *On the Question of Lay Analysis* (1926, *S.E., XX*: 194).

17. Adolph Grünbaum, *Foundations of Psychoanalysis,* 5–6.

18. Freud's own methods of selection were tendentious. As Sulloway relates, Freud borrowed selectively from biology, but sought to keep his own disciples from following recent developments in that subject. In a letter to Victor Weizsaecker (October 16, 1932), Freud writes, "I had to restrain the analysts from investigations of this kind for educational reasons. Innervations, enlargements of blood vessels, and nervous paths would have been too dangerous a temptation for them. They had to learn to limit themselves to psychological ways of thought." Sulloway, *Freud,* 439. In some sense, it is safe to say that Freud was so insecure about challenges to the scientific status of psychotherapy, that he sought "scientific" corroboration of it wherever he could. For instance, in a letter to friend Oskar Pfister, he writes, "It amused me greatly [in a prior letter] that you objected both to the organic foundations and the metapsychological superstructure [of psycho-analysis]. In reality, of course, one has to work at all levels at the same time." Sigmund Freud and Oskar Pfister, *Psychoanalysis and Faith: The Letters of Sigmund Freud and Oskar Pfister,* eds. H. Meng and E. Freud (New York: Basic Books, 1963), 64.

19. Robert Holt, *Freud Reappraised,* 30–31.

20. Sigmund Freud, "On the Question of a *Weltanschauung*" (1933, *S.E.,* XXII). See M. Andrew Holowchak, "When Freud (Almost) Met Chaplin: The Science behind Freud's 'Especially Simple, Transparent Case,'" *Perspectives on Science,* Vol. 20, No. 1, 2012.

21. Each of them were biologically driven. Symington maintains that psychological determinism was the result of Freud's purchase of classical natural science in the Galilean mould, his deterministic take on Darwinism, and his enchantment with neural-psychology. Paul Symington, "The Unconscious and Conscious Self: The Nature of

Psychical Unity in Freud and Lonergan," *American Catholic Philosophical Quarterly*, Vol. 80, No. 4, 567.

22. Peter Gay, *Freud: A Life for Our Time* (New York: W.W. Norton & Company, 2006), 312.

23. James Strachey, "Editor's Note" (1920, *S.E.*, XVIII: 5–6).

24. John Stuart Mill, *A System of Logic* (London: Longman's, 1970), 572.

25. Because of such strong tendencies to identify with leaders, Freud recognized that it was up to group heads to lead people through the renunciations of civilized living. Howard L. Kaye, "Was Freud a Medical Scientist or a Social Theorist? The Mysterious 'Development of the Hero,'" *Sociological Theory*, Vol. 21, No. 4, 2003, 388–90.

26. In a letter to Breuer, Freud writes: "An officer is a miserable creature; he envies his equals, he bullies his subordinates, and is afraid of the higher-ups; the higher up he is himself, the more he is afraid. I deeply dislike having my value written on my collar, as though I were a sample of some material." Sigmund Freud, *Letters of Sigmund Freud*, ed. Ernst L. Freud (London: The Hogarth Press, 1962), September 1, 1886.

27. Freud's notions of group behavior vis-à-vis the church and dissolution of religious groups is generated from no empirical data. Freud cites only a novel—*When It Was Dark*—that "came into [his] hands" as evidence for or an illustration of his conclusions. For an explication of Freud's misreading of that novel, see Sigmund Diamond, "Sigmund Freud, His Jewishness, and Scientific Method: The Seen and the Unseen as Evidence," *Journal of the History of Ideas*, Vol. 43, No. 4, 1982, 614.

28. See also *New Introductory Lectures* (1933, *S.E.*, XXII: 67).

29. Something Freud earlier rejects (1921, *S.E.*, XVIII: 70). See also "Psycho-analysis" (1922, *S.E.*, XVIII: 257–58).

## *Chapter 6*
# Philosophy, Art, and Religion

"The common man cannot imagine this Providence otherwise than in the figure of an enormously exalted father. Only such a being can understand the needs of the children of men and be softened by their prayers and placated by the signs of their remorse. The whole thing is so patently infantile, so foreign to reality, that to anyone with a friendly attitude to humanity it is painful to think that the great majority of mortals will never be able to rise above this view of life."
Sigmund Freud, *Future of an Illusion*

𝕱REUD'S RENEWED INTEREST IN METAPSYCHOLOGY resulted in his positing the death drives and his structural model of the human psyche, the former proposed in *Beyond the Pleasure Principle* in 1920 and both formally endorsed in *The Ego and the Id* in 1923. Those posits and his analysis of groups in *Group Psychology and the Analysis of the Ego* (1921) were catalysts for the full development of $\Psi A_3$ and applied psychoanalysis, through his exploration and examination of particular types of groups, including the human species, and larger, group issues.

Armed with those new metapsychological posits, Freud in the main turned away from research into individual psychology, as it related to work in the clinic, and turned toward applied psychoanalysis and the frenzy and fanaticism of individuals as members of groups. As biographer Peter Gay notes, "What mattered to him was less what he could learn from art history, linguistics, and the rest than what they could learn from him; he entered alien terrain as a conquistador rather than as a supplicant."[1]

An interest in groups and group issues, without question, could be a healthy way for individuals to find an outlet for sexual and destructive impulses—i.e., sublimation—or it could be a harmful way for an outlet for such impulses—i.e., personal or group neurosis. Four significant groups that preoccupied Freud were those comprising philosophers, artists, religionists, and scientists. This chapter examines the first three; the next chapter, the last through Freud's own analysis of prominent sciences of his day: philology, biology, history, and aesthetics. The aim in these two chapters is expository, not critical, so I have little to say concerning Freud's psychoanalytical critique.

# Freudian Ambivalence

Freud was wont to compare philosophy, art, and religion and treat them as objects worthy of serious psychoanalytic study. At times, his attitude is harmlessly critical in that he aims to shed psychoanalytic light on these disciplines not as pathological phenomena, but rather as socially sanctioned disciplines that are the effects of sublimation. For instance, in "Teaching Psycho-Analysis in Universities," Freud says of the three disciplines:

> In the investigation of mental processes and intellectual functions, psychoanalysis pursues a specific method of its own. The application of this method is by no means confined to the field of psychological disorders, but extends also to the solution of problems in art, philosophy and religion. In this direction it has already yielded several new points of view and thrown valuable light on such subjects as the history of literature, on mythology, on the history of civilizations and on the philosophy of religion. . . . The fertilizing effects of psychoanalytic thought on these other disciplines would certainly contribute greatly towards forging a closer link, in the sense of a *universitas literarum*, between medical science and the branches of learning which lie within the sphere of philosophy and the arts (1919, *S.E.*, XVII: 173).

At other times and often, however, Freud's tone seems censorious, perhaps contemptuous, for someone who claims to be offering nothing more than disinterested analytic insights. For instance, Freud writes in *Totem in Taboo*:

> It might be maintained that a case of hysteria is a caricature of a work of art, that an obsessional neurosis is a caricature of a religion and that a paranoic delusion is a caricature of a philosophical system. The divergence resolves itself into the fact that the neuroses are asocial structures; they endeavour to achieve by private means what is effected in society by collective effort (1913, *S.E.*, XIII: 73).

In the preface to Reik's *Ritual,* he expresses a similar sentiment.

> Thus hysterics are undoubtedly imaginative artists, even if they express their phantasies *mimetically* in the main and without considering their intelligibility to other people; the ceremonials and prohibitions of obsessional neurotics drive us to suppose that they have created a private religion of their own; and the delusions of paranoics have unpalatable external similarity and internal kinship to the systems of our philosophers (1919, *S.E.*, XVII: 261).

Such "discoveries" seem *prima facie* too polished and neat to be accurate representations of reality. There seems to be something superficial about such an elegant categorization of avowedly complex psychical phenomena, as if the categorization is founded on wish-fulfillment instead of impartial discovery. It is worth mentioning that Freud had a penchant for clean categorizations and the cleanliness was often more a product of his system-building than disinterested detection of facts. In an unpublished work called "Overview of the Transference Neuroses," Freud speculates wildly on linking the transference neuroses to certain phylogenetic thoughts in an effort to tie together phylogeny with ontogeny. He gives a summary of his speculations in a letter, dated July 12, 1915, to Sander Ferenczi (my italics throughout).

> There is a series of chronological starting points in patients which runs thus: Anxiety hysteria—conversion hysteria—obsessional neurosis—dementia praecox—paranoia—melancholia-mania.
>
> Their libidinal predispositions run in general in the opposite direction: that is to say, the fixation lies with the former set in very late stages of development, with the latter in very early ones. That statement, however, is not faultless.
>
> On the other hand this series seems to repeat phyologenetically an historical origin. What are now neuroses were once phases in human conditions.
>
> With the appearance of privations in the glacial period men became apprehensive: they had every reason for transforming libido into *anxiety*.
>
> Having learned that propagation was not the enemy of self-preservation and must be restricted they became—still in the time before speech—*hysterical*.
>
> After they developed speech and intelligence in the hard school of the glacial period they formed primal hordes under the two prohibitions of the primal father, their love-life having to remain egoistic and aggressive. *Compulsion*, as in the obsessional neurosis, struggled against any return to the former state. The neuroses that followed belong to the new epoch and were acquired by the sons.
>
> To begin with they were forced to relinquish all sexual objects, or else they were robbed of all libido by being castrated: *dementia praecox*.
>
> They then learned to organize themselves on a homosexual basis, being driven out by the father. The struggle against that signifies *paranoia*. Finally, they overcame the father so as to effect an identification with him, triumphed over him and mourned him: *mania-melancholia*.

Ferenczi advised against publication, as the chronological starting points of the transference neuroses were too elegant and fanciful.[2] Freud ultimately jettisoned the paper.

Overall, Freud's views of art, religion, and philosophy as they relate to science are colored by his purchases of Comtean progressivism and recapitulationism. He says in *Totem and Taboo*:

> If we may regard the existence among primitive races of the omnipotence of thoughts as evidence in favour of narcissism, we are encouraged to attempt a comparison between the phases in the development of men's view of the universe and the stages of an individual's libidinal development. The animistic phase would correspond to narcissism both chronologically and in its content; the religious phase would correspond to the stage of object-choice of which the characteristic is a child's attachment to his parents; while the scientific phase would have an exact counterpart in the stage at which an individual has reached maturity, has renounced the pleasure principle, adjusted himself to reality and turned to the external world for the object of his desires (1913, *S.E.*, XIII: 90).

Religion and science are a part of the quasi-Comtean progressive pattern, while philosophy and art might be fitted into the pattern. The first two stages are driven by the pleasure principle. Animism is entirely narcissistic (ontogenetically, prior to Oedipal resolution; phylogenically, prior to the killing of the primal father and early human societies) and the religious phase is characterized by other-lust (ontogenically, for one's parents; phylogenetically, for others like one's parents or for God—i.e., the primal father). The scientific phase, driven by the reality principle, acknowledges human impulses, but is characterized by what Freud dubs elsewhere the "dictatorship of reason"[3] (1933, *S.E.,* XXII: 171 and 1932, *S.E.,* XXII: 213) and is the realization of the Comtean progressivist scheme. Art, presumably, might be an illusive expression of any stage, while philosophy, he suggests, is a stage between religiosity and science.

One of Freud's finest comparative studies of philosophy, art, and religion is "On the Question of a *Weltanschauung*," written six years after his scathing critique of religiosity in *The Future of an Illusion.* Here Freud examines each of the three disciplines and compares them to science. The question he asks is whether any of these four dsiciplines might justifiably be considered a *Weltanschaaung.*[4]

"*Weltanschauung*," Freud says, is an "intellectual construction which solves all the problems of our existence uniformly on the basis of one overriding hypothesis, which, accordingly, leaves no question unanawered and in which everything that interests us finds a place." Thus, a *Weltanschauung* is one of the ideal human wishes that provides for human security, a plan for human activities, and emotional outlet for human impulses (1933, *S.E.,* XXII: 158).

Are art, philosophy, science, and religion *Weltanschauungen*? Art, *pace* Nietzsche, is an illusion. Yet not pretending to be anything other than an illusion, art is almost always harmless and beneficent, as it stays in the realm of unreality. Philosophy is congenial to science and works much like it by using many of the same methods, but goes astray by "clinging to the illusion of being able to present a picture of the universe which is without gaps and is coherent" and by "over-estimating the epistemological value of [its] logical operations." Though it is pestiferous, its pestiferousness, however, is limited in that it is largely inaccessible to the masses. Science cannot be judged to be a *Weltanschauung*. Rejecting revelation, intuition, and divination, it attempts to fill in gaps in its world-view only through hard-fought empirical advances that are often inconsistent with human wishes. Of the four, only religion presents a true danger, because it is immensely powerful, it holds sway over human emotions, and it paralyzes human reason. It slakes humans' thirst for knowledge through providing answers to all of the most gripping problems that face humans. It tells humans that all of the dangers and vicissitudes of life can be overcome. It issues precepts and prohibitions concerning the conduct of life. In effect, it does everything that only a *Weltanschauung* can do. Science cannot make such promises. "Religion alone," with its immaterial promises, "is to be taken seriously as an enemy [of science]" (1933, *S.E.,* XXII: 160-2).

In the remained of this chapter, I turn to a more vigorous examination of Freud's critique of philosophy, art, and religion.

## Philosophy and Philosophers

### Philosophical Presumptuousness

Freud writes in "On the Question of a *Weltanschauung?*" of the relationship of philosophy to science.

> Philosophy is not opposed to science, it behaves like a science and works in part by the same methods; it departs from it, however, by clinging to the illusion of being able to present a picture of the universe which is without gaps and is coherent, though one which is bound to collapse with every fresh advance in our knowledge. It goes astray in its method by over-estimating the epistemological value of our logical operations and by accepting other sources of knowledge such as intuition.
>
> But philosophy has no direct influence on the great mass of mankind; it is of interest to only a small number even of the top layer of intellectuals and is scarcely intelligible to anyone else (1933, *S.E.,* XX: 160-1).

The passage epitomizes Freud's Positivism by presenting two independent arguments that relate to the practice of the philosophy of his day: the first, concerning the in-principle compatibility of philosophy and science; the second, concerning the in-practice incompatibility of the two.

First, he argues:

1. Philosophy behaves like science and works, in part, by the same methods.
2. So, philosophy is not in-principle opposed to science.

What is troubling is Freud's use of "behaves" and "in part" here. Those terms suggest that he is committed to philosophy not being *in-principle* opposed to science. He seems to be saying that though it looks like science, a closer examination reveals that it really functions quite differently. Freud is not really granting philosophy much here.

That takes us to the second argument.

1. Philosophy clings to the illusion that it can give a completely coherent picture of the universe using intuition and a priori reasoning.
2. This picture, begin non-empirical, must collapse with every fresh advance of scientific knowledge.
3. So, philosophy errs in overestimating the value of a priori reasoning and intuition.

This second argument is difficult to assess. On the one hand, it seems obvious that the first premise, taken universally, is false. On the other hand, if taken (charitably!) as a tendency of many, but certainly not all metaphysicians of his or our day, then of course philosophy resembles a *Weltanschauung*. Following Freud, philosophers, then, suffer from a sort of presumptuousness that scientists, because of their empirical bent, do not. Philosophers, however, would certainly counter that scientists underestimate the value of *a priori* reasoning—i.e., that there can be no coherent justification of a discipline, avowedly completely empirical, without some appeal to what is metempirical. Freud, as a consistent Positivist, does not believe that *a priori* reasoning has any merit and that it can be a source of knowledge. He writes confidently and with rodomontade, "[T]here are no sources of knowledge of the universe other than the intellectual working-over of carefully scrutinized observations—in other words, what we call research—and alongside of it no knowledge derived from revelation, intuition or divination" (1933, *S.E., XXII*: 159).

Again, a letter in 1927 reveals his Positive distaste for philosophical speculation. Metaphysics is the culprit. "I not only have no talent for [metaphysics] but no respect for it, either. In secret—one cannot say such things aloud—I believe that one day metaphysics will be condemned as a nuisance, as an abuse of thinking, as a survival from the period of the religious *Weltanschauung*."[5]

In "Autobiographical Study," Freud expatiates on his eschewal of philosophy, even in times where he felt a non-empirical bent. The reason he cites, without elaboration, is a certain "constitutional incapacity." He says somewhat puzzlingly, "Even when I have moved away from observation, I have carefully avoided any contact with philosophy proper. This avoidance has been greatly facilitated by constitutional incapacity" (1925, *S.E., XX*, 59). Why was there such avoidance? The answer, I maintain in chapter 5, is that Freud was drawn to system-building through metapsychology more than he was ever willing to admit. Yet his penchant for metapsychological explanation was clearly at odds with his Positivism. Freud never reconciled the tension. His metapsychological speculation was to his thinking to be confirmed or corrected with fresh advances in the biological science.

Finally, in "Inhibitions, Symptoms and Anxiety," Freud follows his Positivist leanings and writes of the archaic heritage of philosophy. "[Y]ou will scarcely be able to reject a judgement that the philosophy of today has retained some essential features of the animistic mode of thought—the overvaluation of the magic of words and the belief that the real events in the world take the course which our thinking seeks to impose on them" (1933, *S.E., XX*: 165-6).

Such passages betray decided disrelish for philosophy due to Freud's Positivism.

## Philosophers' Insouciance

In "Some Elementary Lessons," Freud says, "Not everyone is bold enough to make judgements about physical matters; but everyone—the philosopher and the man in the street alike—has his opinion on psychological questions and behaves as if he were at least an amateur psychologist" (1940, *S.E.,* XXIII: 282-3). What is Freud's beef?

It seems clear that the sentence is polysemous. On the one hand, the man on the street and the philosopher can be taken as bookends: The man in the street represents exoteric understanding, while the philosopher represents esoteric understanding. On the other hand, the philosopher, with his "hazy concepts" is not substantially different than the man in the street, when it comes to psychoanalysis. Both speak without grasping that about which they speak. Here the philosopher, with aureate but impenetrable verbiage, fares no better than the man-in-the-street, who has mere exoteric understanding.

Overall, Freud's attitude betrays not merely distaste, but also execration and rancor. In "Claims of Psycho-Analysis to Scientific Interest," Freud states that philosophers are exceptional subjects of psychoanalytic research. "In no other science does the personality of the scientific worker play anything like so large a part as in philosophy" (1913, *S.E.,* XIII: 179). That personality exhibited, through the building of speculative systems, is essentially paranoiac (1913, *S.E.,* XIII: 73 and also 1919, *S.E.,* XVII: 261).

> The complaints made by paranoics also show that at bottom the self-criticism of conscience coincides with the self-observation on which it is based. Thus the activity of the mind which has taken over the function of conscience has also placed itself at the service of internal research, which furnished philosophy with the material for its intellectual operations. This may have some bearing on the characteristic tendency of paranoics to construct speculative systems (1914, *S.E.,* XIV: 97).

The chief demerit of building speculative systems is insensitivity to reality—viz., a sort of philosophical insouciance.

In "Dreams: Difficulties and First Approaches," Freud has a more personal gripe. He complains of philosophers' attitude toward his approach to dreams. "We have nothing to expect from philosophy except that it will once again haughtily point out to us the intellectual inferiority of the object of our study." Moreover, he adds that speculative philosophy, in the manner taught at universities, has edified people nowise about the distinction between mind and body (1916, *S.E.,* XV: 20 and 97-8), whereas psychoanalysis has edified people considerably.

Furthermore, and this perhaps is his main reason for execration and rancor, Freud had continual difficulties with philosophers of his time concerning his notion of unconscious and its relation to sexual repression, which they could not accept. For instance:

> [T]he setting up of the hypothesis of unconscious mental activities must compel philosophy to decide one way or the other and, if it accepts the idea, to modify its own views on the relation of mind to body so that they may conform to the new knowledge. It is true that philosophy has repeatedly dealt with the problem of the unconscious, but, with few exceptions, philosophers have taken up one

or other of the two following positions. Either their unconscious has been something mystical, something intangible and undemonstrable, whose relation to the mind has remained obscure, or they have identified the mental with the conscious and have proceeded to infer from this definition that what is unconscious cannot be mental or a subject for psychology (1913, *S.E.,* XIII: 178).

The passage indicates why most philosophers were inclined to disacknowledge Freud's "unconscious." It demanded of them substantial rethinking of the notion "mind" and its relationship to the body, and philosophers were unwilling to do such rethinking without more compelling empirical reasons for doing so.

Freud's disagreement with philosophers on "unconscious" comes to a head in "Resistances to Psycho-Analysis." The notion of "mental," with which philosophers work, is not empirically grounded and is, thus, scientifically inadequate. Their notion of "mental," founded on "hazy words," is also too narrow to accommodate experience. I quote at length:

> For philosophers were accustomed to putting abstract concepts (or, as unkind tongues would say, hazy words) in the forefront of their explanations of the universe, and it would be impossible that they should object to the extension of the sphere of psychology for which psycho-analysis had paved the way. But here another obstacle arose. The philosophers' idea of what is mental was not that of psycho-analysis. The overwhelming majority of philosophers regard as mental only the phenomena of consciousness. For them the world of consciousness coincides with the sphere of what is mental. Everything else that may take place in the "mind"—an entity so hard to grasp—is relegated by them to the organic determinants of mental processes or to processes parallel to mental ones. Or, more strictly speaking the mind has no contents other than the phenomena of consciousness, and consequently psychology, the science of the mind, has no other subject-matter.
>
> What, then, can a philosopher say to a theory which, like psycho-analysis, asserts that on the contrary what is mental is in itself *unconscious* and that being conscious is only a *quality*, which may or may not accrue to a particular mental act and with withholding of which may perhaps alter that act in no other respect? He will naturally say that anything both unconscious and mental would be an impossibility, a *contradictio in adjecto*, and he will fail to observe that in making his judgement he is merely repeating his own definition of what is mental, a definition which may perhaps be too narrow.

Philosophers, he adds, have no acquaintance with psychoanalytic material. They disregard hypnosis, analysis, as well as interpretation of dreams, obsessions, and delusions. In keeping with Cartesian introspectionism, philosophers know no kind of observation other than self-observation (1925, *S.E.,* XIX: 216-7) and, thus, they are ill-equipped and unjust critics of psychoanalysis.

The difficulty, and it is a genuine difficulty, is that Freud takes unconsciousness to be primary and consciousness to be dependent on it, while philosophers assume, without appeal to empirical investigation, that there is nothing beyond or more fundamental than consciousness.

Leaving aside theoretical difficulties of psychoanalysis, Freud's insistence on the existence of unconscious phenomena and his quarrel with philosophers of his day on it have led to nothing short of a revolution in philosophy of mind and philosophy of the social sciences today. Philosophers in Freud's day pooh-poohed his notion of "unconscious," in the main, because it would have forced them to reconsider and revise philosophical accounts of human intentionality, which were not rich enough to account fully for irrational actions.

Writes Michael Levine:

> There are two principal schools of thought about Freud in contemporary analytic philosophy. There are those who think he has conclusively been shown to be wrong—if not an outright charlatan and cheat. On the other hand, psychoanalytic theory is seen as a source from which to develop approaches to the philosophy of mind, language, theory of meaning, and ethics that are consonant with, and expand upon the work of what some regard as the best and most influential analytic philosophy of our time. Some even see an integration of psychoanalytic theory with philosophy as necessary to both.[6]

Donald Davidson represents the first school of human intentionality. He says charitable ascription of rationality in keeping with our own standards of veridicality must be assumed for human actions and utterances. There is little room for "unconscious" in the Freudian sense of a primary, irrational agency.[7] Roger Grandy represents the second school. Rejecting Davidson's principle of charity, he maintains that human actions and utterances need not always be assumed to be rational. Instead, he opts for intelligibility—i.e., present circumstances or prior conditioning might explain what appears to be irrational behavior.[8]

Thus, philosophers today are open to the notion that human behavior need not always to be explained rationally. "To explain an intentional act is to pick out the practical reasoning process which caused it," states philosopher Brian Faye, "and this process can be illogical and still play its explanatory role. Contrary to rationalism, a commitment to explaining intentional actions by giving the reasons for them does not require that we believe that all actions are rational at some level. Intentional activity is not restricted to the domain of the rational."[9]

One must be guarded however. To say that philosophers of mind are turning to Freud is not to say that they have been ready and willing to take on his conception of "unconscious," as a reservoir for repressions, linked to drive-energy. It is only to say that they are ready to embrace a notion of "mind" that goes beyond the traditional, Cartesian *res cogitans*.

# Art and Artists

## The Mild Narcosis of Art

It is no secret that Freud, like Nietzsche, had a passion for art. That numerous of his writings are about or refer to art is sufficient proof.

Freud acknowledges that he has a layman's, not a connoisseur's, interest in art. The formal and technical qualities of art have little attraction for him. He prefers literature and sculpture to painting. He is unmoved by works of art whose purpose he cannot apprehend. Ultimately, what moves him is the subject matter of works of art and a sufficient depth-grasp of it. He examines a work of art to come to know the artist, not the art. His view is admittedly intellectualist, but intellectualist only in a psychoanalytic manner.

> [W]hat grips us so powerfully can only be the artist's intention, in so far as he has succeeded in expressing it in his work and in getting us to understand it. I realize that this cannot be merely a matter of intellectual comprehension; what he aims at is to awaken in us the same emotional attitude, the same mental constellation as that which in him produced the impetus to create (1914, *S.E.,* XIII: 211-2).

To know a work of art, therefore, is to arrive at the selfsame mental constellation—that admixture of intellect and affect—that drove the creation of the work. Thus, works of art differ nowise from dreams: They too need to be interpreted to be grasped and such interpretation is a matter of working from what is manifest to what is latent.

Art's primary function, its motive force, is to "allay ungratified wishes," both in the artist and his audience. "The artist's first aim is to set himself free and, by communicating his work to other people suffering from the same arrested desires, he offers them the same liberation." Like dreams, works of art fulfill the fantasies of artists through the element of disguise. The finished work is a gentler version of the generative impulses, which are rooted in childhood. "[The artist] represents his most personal wishful phantasies as fulfilled; they only become a work of art when they have undertone a transformation which softens what is offensive in them, conceals their personal origin and, obeying the laws of beauty, bribes other people with a bonus of pleasure." Freud adds that psychoanalytic disclosure of artistic works as reactions to the artist's early childhood impulses[10] is one of the "most attractive subjects of analytic investigation." He sums elegantly, in the manner of interpreting dreams, "Thus art constitutes a region half-way between a reality which frustrates wishes and the wish-fulfilling world of the imagination—a region in which, as it were, primitive man's strivings for omnipotence are still in full force" (1913, *S.E.,* XIII: 187-8).

In *Civilization and Its Discontents,* Freud says that the capacity of art to sublimate offers merely temporary consolation to real-world misery.

> At the head of these satisfactions through phantasy stands the enjoyment of works of art—an enjoyment which, by the agency of the artist, is made accessible to those who are not themselves creative. People who are receptive to the influence of art cannot set too high a value on it as a source of pleasure and consolation in life. Nevertheless the mild narcosis induced in us by art can do no more than bring about a transient withdrawal from the pressure of vital needs, and it is not strong enough to make us forget real misery (1930, *S.E.,* XXI: 80-1).

Works of art, consequently, offer artists and their patrons "transient withdrawal" through mild, insubstantial sublimation.

## Art and Hysteria

Outside of its aesthetic interest for humans and its avowed narcotic effect, art is a valued source of information about artists such as Michelangelo, Leonardo da Vinci, Fyodor Dostoyevsky, and Wilhelm Jensen, about each of whom Freud wrote. Art is also a valued source of information about the development of humans over the millennia, from human prehistory to the present, because portrayals of possession and ecstasy throughout the millennia are preserved in art (1913, *S.E.,* XIII: 1 and 1923, *S.E.,* XIX: 72).

On how he began the psychoanalysis of art and artists, Freud writes:

> At an early stage it was discovered that dreams invented by writers will often yield to analysis in the same way as genuine ones. The conception of unconscious mental activity made it possible to form a preliminary idea of the nature of imaginative creative writing; and the realization, gained in the study of neurotics, of the part played by the instinctual impulses enabled us to perceive the sources of artistic production and confronted us with two problems: how the artist reacts to his instigation and what means he employs to disguise his reactions (1914, *S.E.,* XIV: 36).

In sum, Freud's work in $\Psi A_1$ made possible investigation into creative writing and, thereafter, other forms of creative expression.

In his psychoanalytic investigation of Leonardo da Vinci, Freud notes that art is a means of escaping neurosis. "If a person who is at loggerheads with reality possesses an *artistic gift* (a thing that is still a psychological mystery to us), he can transform his phantasies into artistic creations instead of into symptoms." He thus escapes the "doom of neurosis" and retains some link, however threadbare, to the real world (1910, *S.E.,* XI: 50). Unlike others, who suffer from privation and who find release in meager daydreams, artists learn to work their daydreams into their art so that others might take pleasure in their personal fantasies, tamed down. In short, there is affective contagion in art.

> [H]e possesses the mysterious power of shaping some particular material until it has become a faithful image of his phantasy; and he knows . . . how to link so large a yield of pleasure to this representation of his unconscious phantasy that, for the time being at least, repressions are outweighed and lifted by it. If he is able to accomplish all this, he makes it possible for other people once more to derive consolation and alleviation from their own sources of pleasure in their unconscious which have become inaccessible to them; he earns their gratitude and admiration and he has thus achieved *through* his phantasy what originally he had achieved only in his phantasy—honour, power and the love of women (1917, *S.E.,* XVI: 376-7).

A *coup de main* and key breakthrough for Freud was discovery of a link between artists and hysteria. In the preface to Theodor Reik's *Ritual,* Freud says, "Thus hysterics are undoubtedly imaginative artists, even if they express their phantasies *mimetically* in the main and without considering their intelligibility to other people. . ." (1919, *S.E.,* XVII: 261). In *Introductory Lectures,* he writes:

> An artist is once more in rudiments an introvert, not far removed from neurosis. He is oppressed by excessively powerful instinctual needs. He desires to win honour, power, wealth, fame and the love of women; but he lacks the means for achieving these satisfactions. Consequently, like any other unsatisfied man, he turns away from reality and transfers all his interest, and his libido too, to the wishful constructions of his life of phantasy, whence the path might lead to neurosis. . . . Their constitution probably includes a strong capacity for sublimation and a certain degree of laxity in the repressions which are decisive for a conflict (1917, *S.E.,* XVI: 376).

Yet, as is the case with dreams, one must emphasize that artists keep their wish-impulses at a distance from themselves. As Richard Wollheim writes, "The unconscious appears in Freud's account of art only as providing techniques of concealment or possibilities of play."[11]

Freud underscores the similarities between artistic creations and children's play in *Beyond the Pleasure Principle.* Here, through the compulsion to repeat, artists, like children, find the most painful experiences as highly enjoyable. Like Freud's little nephew, who found pleasure in throwing away toys in order to find them later as a way of dealing with mother loss, artists find a way of working through what is highly unpleasant through their art (1920, *S.E.,* XVIII: 17).

What sort of sublimation does an artist attain? Freud says in *Civilization and Its Discontents,* "A satisfaction of this kind, such as an artist's joy in creating, in giving his phantasies body . . . has a special quality which we shall certainly one day be able to characterize in metapsychological terms." The "finer and higher" satisfaction through sublimation is mild, when compared to the direct satisfaction of primary impulses. Moreover, sublimation is accessible only to those few, who possess special disposition and gifts. Finally, it offers only incomplete protection from suffering (1930, *S.E.,* XXI: 79-80).

**Tragedy and the Primal Father**

I have been arguing throughout that Freud used his metapsychological speculations in spurious ways—e.g., to give it the rudiments of an organic substructure and to tie it with claims of other sciences—to "confirm" his psychoanalytic superstructure ($\Psi A_3$).

One of his most spurious claims is, of course, the killing of the primal father. In *Totem and Taboo,* he claims that if the story is true, then it must have left "ineradicable traces" in human history. They are not hard to find in mythology, but they are also evident in Greek tragedy (1913, *S.E.,* XIII: 155). In this section, I show how Freud used a specific form of art, Greek tragedy, to "confirm" his findings concerning the killing of the primal father.

In Greek tragedy, Freud notes, the Chorus is a group of individuals, dressed alike, that hang on the words and deeds of a central figure—the actor as Hero. Even though other characters were later added to tragedies, the relationship between the Hero and the Chorus remained intimate. The role of the Hero was to suffer and his suffering was the result of rebellion against a human or divine authority. The role of the Chorus was to sympathize with him, hold him back, warn him, sober him, and mourn over him, when his punishment was eventually meted out. Why did the Hero have to suffer? The answer, Freud asserts confidently and tendentiously, is simple.

> [The Hero] had to suffer because he was the primal father, the Hero of the great primaeval tragedy which was being re-enacted with a tendentious twist; and the tragic guilt was the guilt with which he had to take on himself in order to relieve the Chorus from theirs. The scene upon the stage was derived from the historical scene through a process of systematic distortion—one might even say, as the product of a refined hypocrisy. In the remote reality it had actually been the members of the Chorus who caused the Hero's suffering; now, however, they exhausted themselves with sympathy and regret and it was the Hero himself who was responsible for his own sufferings. The crime which was thrown on to his shoulders, presumptuousness and rebelliousness against a great authority, was precisely the crime for which the members of the Chorus, the company of brothers, were responsible. Thus the tragic Hero became, though it might be against his will, the redeemer of the Chorus.

He adds that the unique subject matter of Greek tragedy was the sufferings of the divine goat Dionysus and the lamentations of his fellow goats, which followed and identified with him. The drama was rekindled in the Middle Ages and centered on Christ and his passions (1913, *S.E.,* XIII: 156).

## Religion and Religionists

### That "Oceanic Feeling"

Freud begins *Civilization and Its Discontents* with colleague Raymond Rolland's insistence that a certain "oceanic feeling" drives humans to assent to religious sentiments. This feeling—"a sensation of 'eternity,' a feeling as of something limitless, unbounded"—is not faith-founded and carries no assurance of personal immortality. Yet it is the source of religious energy that fuels religious enthusiasm. To acknowledge this feeling and no other religious beliefs or systems is sufficient to acknowledge one's religiosity[12] (1930, *S.E.,* XXI: 64).

Freud says he is unable to find such a feeling within himself, but he is willing to grant its genuineness by calling it a "subjective fact." He states that one can, from a psychoanalytic perspective, explore the ideational content that is associated with the feeling. It is what a dramatist feels when his hero is about to take his own life—a feeling that may be captured thus through language: "We cannot fall out of this world." Consequently, Rolland's feeling might be more of an "intellectual perception" with accompanying affect. If so, it is capable of psychoanalytic investigation. The remaining question, then, is whether it is the "*fons and origo* of the whole need of religion" (1930, *S.E.,* XXI; 65).

Freud's psychoanalytic explanation for his colleague's oceanic feeling is ontogenetic. Early in the course of normal human development, an infant does not distinguish himself from the external world. Over time, various hedonistic promptings enable him gradually to distinguish his ego from the external world. Thus, it is reasonable to assume that the oceanic feeling is merely the primary ego-feeling of earliest childhood that persists to some degree along the narrower and more sharply defined ego-feeling of maturity. In short, his colleague's "oceanic feeling" is a residue of the sentiment of the helplessness and limitless narcissism of infancy—a desire to return to that stage in the development of the ego, before ego was set in opposition to the id. The link of this primitive narcissism with religion, Freud asserts, occurs later. Therefore, the notion that the feeling is the *fons* and *origo* of religion is covinous (1930, *S.E.,* XXI: 66-72).

## Grounding Religious Beliefs

Freud's most significant contribution to religiosity is *The Future of an Illusion,* written three years prior to *Civilization and Its Discontents.* Religious ideas, Freud says, lay claim to what is most greatly valued for humans, since they "are teachings and assertions about facts and conditions of external (or internal) reality which tell one something one has not discovered for oneself and which lay claim to one's belief" (1927, *S.E.,* XXI: 25). Nonetheless, religious ideas do not differ from other substantial achievements of civilization that answer to the need to defend oneself from the "crushing superiority of nature," which is greatly responsible for human suffering. Unlike other achievements of civilization though, religion promises to rectify the shortcomings of civilization (1927, *S.E.,* XXI: 21).

Does religion keep its promise? That depends on its veridicality. Religionists, of course, cannot entertain the notion of the falsity of their beliefs. They defend religious "truths" in three ways.

First, there is the *ipse dixit* argument:

1. Religious beliefs were entertained by human ancestors.
2. So, religious beliefs must be true.

History shows, Freud counters, that our ancestor's wisdom, if anything, is inferior to our wisdom (1927, *S.E.,* XXI: 26). Therefore, an appeal to ancestral authority is unavailing.

Second, there is the argument from sacrosanctity or inscrutability:

1. Human ancestors' divinely inspired writings are themselves proofs of religious veracity.
2. So, religious beliefs must be true.

The "proofs" of religionists, Freud asseverates, are fraught with revisions, contradictions, and falsification and the "factual confirmations" are unconfirmed speculations, not facts (1927, *S.E.,* XXI: 26). Therefore, this argument is on-a-treadmill.

Finally, there is the argument from sacrilegiousness:

1. It is sacrilegious to call into question the veracity of religious beliefs.
2. So, religious beliefs must be true.

Religious beliefs are no more immune from doubt, Freud says, than are any other beliefs. The argument from sacrilegiousness is more of a threat in the manner of Pascal's Wager—viz., a fallacious appeal to force—than a cogent argument. As such, it betrays the uncertainty and insecurity of the believers behind the beliefs[13] (1927, *S.E.,* XXI: 26).

Overall, no attempts to justify religious beliefs are irrefragable. As archaic teachings from learned ancestors, they have nothing to do with experience or reason. It follows that there is little reason to believe them to be veridical. One must at least be agnostic.

Freud, however, does believe the origins of religious ideas can be traced ontogenetically and phylogenetically.

Ontogenetically, religious ideas are formed in the Oedipal stage of psychosexual development, when the boy renounces his mother as a love-object and identifies with his father. Such identification includes internalization of his father's morality.

Yet that is only half of the explanation. Following the recapitulationism of his day, Freud returns to the story of the acquisition of Oedipal guilt through the killing of the primal father. In the pre-civilized human horde, the primal father lorded over the group and would become the original image of God. As both protector and tyrant of the horde, his authority was absolute. He tyrannized the subordinate males, his "sons," by disallowing them expression of their libidinal impulses. Acting out of sexual frustration, the sons one day ganged up and killed the primal father and disposed of the corpse in a cannibalistic feast, reminiscent of the Christian communion (1927, *S.E.,* XXI: 42, and 1930, *S.E.,* XXI: 100-1 and 131-3).

The magnitude of the deed resulted in a massive sense of guilt, which stayed with the sons and was, à la Lamarck, passed on (unconsciously) to their descendants. Religions and all other products of civilized living are based on the guilt associated with the wicked deed, because they are measures of trying to atone for the killing of the primal father—i.e., the original sin. Freud sums: "We now observe that the store of religious ideas includes not only wish-fulfilments but important historical recollections. This concurrent influence of past and present must give religion a truly incomparable wealth of power" (1927, *S.E.,*

XXI: 42). With the story of the killing of the primal father, the findings of group psychology are made to mesh with those of individual psychology.

## Freud's Great Concession

What ontogenetic and phylogenetic explanations show is that religious beliefs are not evidence- or reason-based, but instead illusion-based. He defines "illusion" thus. "We call a belief an illusion," Freud writes in Feuerbachian fashion in *The Future of an Illusion,* when a wish-fulfilment is a prominent factor in its motivation, and in doing so we disregard its relations to reality, just as the illusion itself sets no store by verification" (1927, *S.E.,* XXI: 30-1). An illusion differs from other beliefs in that it is essentially grounded in human wishes that care nowise for correspondence with reality. He adds disparagingly that there seems to be a correlation between embracing religiosity and weakness of intellect. "When a man has once brought himself to accept uncritically all the absurdities that religious doctrines put before him and even to overlook the contradictions between them, we need not be greatly surprised at the weakness of his intellect" (1927, *S.E.,* XXI: 48). Disparagement notwithstanding, here Freud never claims that religious ideas, explained ontogenetically and phylogenetically, must be false. His attitude, at day's end, is consistently agnostic.

Three years later in *Civilization and Its Discontents,* Freud calls religious ideas "palliative measures" or "auxiliary constructions." He adds:

> The common man cannot imagine this Providence otherwise than in the figure of an enormously exalted father. Only such a being can understand the needs of the children of men and be softened by their prayers and placated by the signs of their remorse. The whole thing is so patently infantile, so foreign to reality, that to anyone with a friendly attitude to humanity it is painful to think that the great majority of mortals will never be able to rise above this view of life. It is still more humiliating to discover how large a number of people living to-day, who cannot but see that this religion is not tenable, nevertheless try to defend it piece by piece in a series of pitiful rearguard actions (1930, *S.E., XXI:* 74).

The religions of mankind are "mass-delusions," which implies their lack of correspondence with reality (1930, *S.E.,* XXI: 81).

Finally, in *Moses and Monotheism,* written nine years after *Civilization and Its Discontents*, Freud speaks of "the compulsion to worship a God whom one cannot see"—a signal that an abstract idea was deemed to have greater veridicality than any sense perception (1939, *S.E.,* XXIII: 112-3). He says, "This remarkable feature [of clinging to religious notions in spite of overwhelming logical objections] can only be understood on the pattern of the delusion of psychotics" (1939, *S.E.,* XXI: 85 and 129). The implication clearly is that religious beliefs are not veridical.

Yet Freud is not stating that religionists are deluded or psychotic, but he is making a great, though ultimately insubstantial, concession to religionists. Freud explains: "The idea of a single god produced such an overwhelming effect on men because it is a portion of the eternal *truth* which, long concealed, came to light at last and was then bound to carry everyone along with it" (1939, *S.E.*, XXI: 129). The explanation seems to presuppose the following argument.

1. The idea of a single god is a portion of long-concealed eternal truth that eventually came to light and had an overwhelming effect on the masses.
2. Only truth can be the cause of such an overwhelming effect.
3. So, it is the truth-value of the idea of a single god that incites belief in it.

Freud writes in reply to the religionists' explanation and the argument implicitly in support of it:

We too would like to accept this [pious] solution. But we are brought up by a doubt. The pious argument rests on an optimistic and idealistic premise. It has not been possible to demonstrate in other connections that the human intellect has a particularly fine flair for the truth or that the human mind shows any special inclination for recognizing the truth. We have rather found, on the contrary, that our intellect very easily goes astray without any warning, and that nothing is more easily believed by us than what, without reference to the truth, comes to meet our wishful illusions. . . . We too believe that the pious solution contains the truth—but the *historical* truth and not the *material* truth (1939, *S.E.*, XXIII: 129).

The "optimistic and idealistic premise" to which Freud refers is what I have made out to be premise 2.

Following a distinction I make in *Freud and Utopia*, we must allow for a distinction between "historical truths" and "material truths," before grasping Freud's concession.

- A truth, $T_H$, is *historical* insofar as it relates to a fragment of an actual state of affairs.
- A truth, $T_M$, is *material* insofar as it corresponds to an actual state of affairs.

We are now in position to grasp the overwhelmingly persuasiveness of religious beliefs. Religious beliefs persuade because they contain a kernel of truth—though merely a historical truth—a collop of a distorted and forgotten past.

In antiquity, there must have been some great male, who was elevated to deity, the memory of whom, though distorted, is still with humans today—i.e., the primal father. Without such a supposition, there can be no explanation of the overpowering influence of the notion of a single god and the remarkable persistence of it in the face of logical inconsistencies (1939, *S.E.*, XXIII: 85 and 128). That concession is huge; it leaves no room for the belief that religious ideas are essentially delusive.

We can also express Freud's intent by saying religious ideas are biologically true, in that they are biologically grounded, given Freud's modified Lamarckianism. The killing of the primal father shows that Freud believed certain psychological characteristics could be acquired and inherited by offspring, if the historical events responsible for their memory should be of sufficient weight.

**Religiosity as Obsessional Neurosis**

In spite of his great concession to religionists—his concession that there is a kernel of (historical, not material) truth to religious ideas—Freud did believe that religiosity was a form of neurosis. In short, neurosis, because it is wish-based, is a form of personal religion and religion, because it is wish-based and shared by members of a group, is a form of group neurosis.

Freud first posited a link between religion and neurosis in his 1907 work "Obsessive Actions and Religious Practices," where he drew parallels between the obsessive nature of certain religious practices and those of obsessive persons. Obsessive persons make certain ceremonial additions, arrangements or restrictions to everyday actions—as if to make the practice of going to sleep every night an activity governed by inviolable and unwritten laws—and they tolerate no deviation from the performance of these activities. These actions become neurotic, when "they are elaborated by small additions or given a rhythmic character by means of pauses and repetitions" (1907, *S.E.,* IX: 118).

The similarities to religious ritual are obvious, but the differences are glaring. First, the actions of obsessive neurotics have a greater degree of variability, whereas those of religionists are stereotyped. Second, the actions of obsessive neurotics are private, whereas those of religionists are public. Finally, the actions of obsessive neurotics seem meaningless, whereas those of religionists seem chock-full of meaning (1907, *S.E.,* IX: 119).

The great contribution of psychoanalysis to the acts of obsessional neurotics is showing that these too are chock-full of meaning, which is unconscious and inaccessible to the agent. Analysis shows that obsession acts begin as mechanisms of defense for the agent—repression of drive-energy, the symptoms of which act as compromise formations between "warring forces of the mind." Freud writes, "As the illness progresses . . . actions which were originally mostly concerned with maintaining the defence come to approximate more and more to the proscribed actions through which the instinct was able to find expression in childhood" (1907, *S.E.,* IX: 123-5).

What is true of obsessional neurosis is true of religious ritual. It too is based on renunciation of impulses, though not exclusively those of a sexual nature. The act of penance, which the confessional conveniently allows, is a sort of obsessional repetition of remedial actions that allows repetition of the deeds—i.e., the sins—that gave rise to them (1907, *S.E.,* IX: 125).

The key psychoanalytic insight to grasp the similarity between obsessional neurosis and religious rituals is the mechanism of displacement. In obsessional neurosis, the everyday and seemingly insignificant rituals, which were mnemonically linked to unconscious thought, push aside and replace those thoughts. So too is it the case with religious rituals. The chief difference, consistent with Freud's early theory of drives, is that obsessional neurosis is exclusively a displacement of sex-impulses, while religious rituals are displacements of ego-impulses. He sums, "[O]ne might venture to regard obsessional neurosis as a pathological counterpart of the formation of a religion, and to describe that neurosis as an individual religiosity and religion as a universal obsessional neurosis" (1907, *S.E.*, IX: 126-7).

In a later work, Freud is clear that religiosity is not a matter of giving sop to Cerberus. Though "it removes their parental complex, on which the sense of guilt in individuals as well as in the whole human race depends, and disposes of it, while the unbeliever has to grapple with the problem on his own"[14] (1910, *S.E.*, XI: 123), there is a price one has to pay for ascribing to religious beliefs and accepting the concomitant renunciation of drive-energy. Though religion protects a person from a personal neurosis, it introduces him to a cultural neurosis. The religionist, then, is spared a personal neurosis by participation in group neurosis. In both cases, the attitude is regressive.

# Notes

1. Peter Gay, *Freud: A Life for Our Time* (New York: W.W. Norton & Company, 2006), 312-3.

2. Sigmund Freud, *A Phylogenetic Fantasy,* ed. Ilse Grubrich-Smitis (Cambridge: Harvard University Press, 1987), 79-81.

3. See M. Andrew Holowchak, *Freud and Utopia: From Cosmological Narcissism to the "Soft Dictatoriship" of Reason* (Lanham, MD: Lexington Press, 2012).

4. For a fuller account, see M. Andrew Holowchak, "When Freud (Almost) Met Chaplin: The Science behind Freud's 'Especially Simple, Transparent Case,'" *Perspectives in Science,* Vol. 20, No. 1, 2012.

5. Sigmund Freud, *Letters,* ed. Ernst Freud (London: Hogarth Press, 1961), 375.

6. Michael P. Levine, ed., *The Analytic Freud: Philosophy and Psychoanalysis* (New York: Routledge, 2000), 2.

7. Donald Davidson, *Actions and Events* (Oxford University Press, 1986), 137.

8. Richard E. Grandy, "Reference, Meaning and Belief," *Journal of Philosophy,* vol. 70, 443.

9. Brian Fay, *Contemporary Philosophy of Social Science: A Multicultural Approach* (Malden, MA: Blackwell Publishing, 1996), 103.

10. See also *Leonardo da Vinci* (1910, *S.E.*, XI: 107).

11. Richard Wollheim, "Freud and the Understanding of Art," *The Cambridge Companion to Freud,* ed. Jerome Neu (New York: Cambridge University Press, 1991), 265.

12. For more on religion and religiosity, see M. Andrew Holowchak, "The 'Soft Dictatorship' of Reason: Freud on Science, Religion, and Utopia," *Philo,* Vol. 13, No. 1, 2010, 29-53, and chapter 2 of *Freud and Utopia.*

13. Cf. "On the Question of a *Weltanschauung*" (1933, *S.E.*, XXII: 169-70).

14. See also 1920, *S.E.*, XVIII: 142.

# Chapter 7
# Psychoanalysis and Other Sciences

"A new joke acts almost like an event of universal interest; it is passed from one person to another like the news of the latest victory." Sigmund Freud, *Jokes*

*L*IKE PHILOSOPHY, ART, AND RELIGION, SCIENCE IS A WAY for scientists to sublimate erotic and destructive impulses. Yet unlike the others, science, given Freud's attachment to Positive progressivism, is an effective way of dealing with the frustrations of human happiness by reality and with the civilizing tendencies of humans. While artists flounder hysterically in Stygian mimesis, philosophers wallow in paranoical delusions, and religionists punctiliously practice obsessional rituals—each out of touch with reality—scientists, howsoever obsessive, avoid the pratfalls of those other disciplines by modestly essaying to disclose the secrets of reality.

This chapter focuses chiefly, but not exclusively, on sections from a much-neglected opuscule titled "Claims of Psycho-Analysis to Scientific Interest," written in 1913. My focus again is more expository than analytical. My concern is more to flesh out Freud's views on such sciences than to analyze them critically. I aim at the sciences that might prove to be of greatest significance for psychoanalysis and psychoanalysts—philology, biology, history, and aesthetics—and Freud's psychoanalytical investigation of them.

## Psychoanalysis and Philology

Freud begins the second part of "Claims of Psycho-Analysis" by "overstepping common linguistic usage" and stating an interest in philology. He understands philology loosely as the discipline concerned with speech, and speech can be a communication that is verbal, written, or gestural. His attention immediately turns to dreams and their relationship to conscious and unconscious phenomena (1913, *S.E.*, XIII: 176).

Freud writes, "The language of dreams may be looked upon as the method by which unconscious mental activity expresses itself." That method uses a queer sort of language and one, following philological analysis, which is archaic and which has a logic of its own. Dreams, for instance, do not express negation.

Also, it is common for contrary concepts to express themselves freely in a dream or for one concept to express itself with contrary meanings. Moreover, dreams are highly symbolic expressions, which often allow for translation without reference to a patient's associations. Thus, the language of dreams has its roots in the earliest phase of linguistic development and, therefore, escapes conscious understanding (1913, *S.E.*, XIII: 177).

The language of dreams, given the preferred use of visual representation, is more comparable to written, than verbal, language. Freud draws from Egyptian hieroglyphs. In dreams as in hieroglyphs, certain elements are not meant to be interpreted, but merely function determinatively to establish the meaning of something else. Hieroglyphs contain the same ambiguity that dreams contain. Hieroglyphs moreover contain relations that can only be grasped implicitly from an understanding of their context, as is the case with dreams. These similarities show that psychoanalysts have much to gain from philological analysis (1913, *S.E.*, XIII: 177).

The reservation, gleaned from a thorough study of psychopathology, is that the unconscious, unlike written language, has many "dialects." Dreams prefer images; hysteria uses gestures; obsessional neurosis uses thought-language; dementia praecox and paranoia use idiosyncratic peculiarities (1913, *S.E.*, XIII: 177-8).

Philological analysis has also anticipated some of the discoveries of psychoanalysis in the links of *faeces* with *money, gift,* and *gold; baby* and *penis;* and *penis* and *little one* (1917, *S.E.*, XVII: 128 and 1933, *S.E.*, XXII: 100).

In *The Psychopathology of Everyday Life,* Freud states that linguistic material makes possible the limits of verbal and written slips (1901, *S.E.*, VI: 222). To grasp the significance of a verbal or written slip, one must use depth-psychology. As with dreams, there are positive and negative elements of slips. Positively, there is an uninhibited stream of associations with each slip. Negatively, there is a relaxation of inhibiting attention. The first depends on the last: Only with the relaxation of inhibiting attention does the stream of associations come into consciousness (1901, *S.E.*, VI: 61).

Freud illustrates with numerous examples. I give only one. A woman in therapy recollects a forgotten childhood memory. When she gets to the part where she mentions a certain section of her body to which a "prying and lascivious hand" had gone, she draws a blank. Immediately thereafter, she brings up the story of a friend and the possibility of her friend's summer residence at the woman's cottage at M. When the friend asks where the cottage is, the woman replies "on the hill-thigh" [*Berglende*] instead of "on the hill-side" [*Berglehne*] (1901, *S.E.*, VI: 63).

## Primal Words

The power of words is undeniable. In *Introductory Lectures on Psychoanalysis,* Freud says:

Words were originally magic and to this day words have retained much of their ancient magical power. By words one person can make another blissfully happy or drive him to despair, by words the teacher conveys his knowledge to his pupils, by words the orator carries his audience with him and determines their judgements and decisions. Words provoke affects and are in general the means of mutual influence among men (1916, *S.E.*, XV: 17).

In an essay of 1910, "Antithetical Meaning of Primal Words," three years prior to "Claims of Psycho-Analysis," Freud looks to philologist Karl Abel's *Philological Essays* to shed light on dreams and the unconscious. What Abel's analysis of Egyptian hieroglyphics shows is that the oddities of dreams seem to have a precedent in early language (1910, *S.E.*, XI" 155).

First, it was common in Egyptian hieroglyphs for one word to have a meaning directly opposite to its commonly understood meaning. That, Abel notes, is the same with German, where "strong" means both "strong" and "weak" and "light" means both "light" and dark" (1910, *S.E.*, XI: 156).

Second, Egyptians made use of compound words, where words with antithetical meaning were combined—compounds such as "old-young," "far-near," "bind-sever," "outside-inside," *inter alia*. The intention here was not to bind antithetical words to come up with a new meaning, but instead to represent one of the two antithetical parts by the compound (1910, *S.E.*, XI: 157).

Abel's explanation of antithetical meaning is that one word, say *ken* ("strong"), originally had one meaning and the opposite meaning at the same time, since for instance "strong" could not be grasped independently of "weak." Over time, there was a phonetic reduction, where the two different but similar words came to represent the different antithetical meanings. *Ken* as "strong-weak"—where the difference in meaning could only be grasped by intonation, gesture, or an additional pictograph—came later to be divided into *ken* as "strong" and *kan* as "weak" (1910, *S.E.*, XI: 158).

Third, Egyptians made ample use of reversal of sound to indicate reversal of meaning. For illustration, were *gut* Egyptian for "good," then it would mean either "good" or "bad" and it would also be expressed as *tug* (1910, *S.E.*, XI: 160-1).

The emphasis on contraries in hieroglyphs suggests that Egyptians preferred the contrary mode of meaning—i.e., reversal of meaning—to negation. That is confirmed in his *Introductory Lectures on Psychoanalysis* (1916, *S.E.*, XV: 178-80).

Freud's conclusion is that the language of dreams is regressive and archaic. Thus, psychotherapists interested in interpreting dreams need a fuller grasp of the origins and development of language (1910, *S.E.*, 1911, 161). Psychotherapists, to do their patients fullest service, need to be philologists.

Freud's insights have an early antecedent in the *Oneirocritica* of the Greek interpreter of dreams Artemidorus of Daldis in the second century A. D. Artemidorus makes use of a variety of techniques to interpret dreams prophetically, including antinomy and converse signification. For instance, he uses antinomy at II.59, where he tells of a dream in which a man sent his son off to earn some money. His son, still abroad, appeared to the man in a dream and said, "*I have 3800 coins.*" It was interpreted that *his son would return home without money* because, in part, "opposite things always turn out [in dreams]." Artemidorus uses converse signification ("what is indicated by something is, in turn, significant of that thing") at IV.24, when he tells of a woman who dreamed that *her eyes were sore* and, soon, *her children became sick*. Another woman, dreaming that *her children took sick, got sore eyes*.[1]

## Prometheus and Fire

Thus far, we have seen that Freud used philology to "confirm" his discoveries of the meaning of dreams and the nature of the unconscious. Now I turn to psychoanalytical interpretations of philological issues.

A fine example of psychoanalytical interpretation of a tale of supreme interest to philologists is the tale of Prometheus in Greek mythology in a 1932 essay of Freud. The thesis Freud defends is that to gain control over fire, men had to control their homosexual desire by putting it out with fire. The mechanism of interpretation Freud uses is that of translating symbols in terms of their opposites.

The myth occurs in *Theogony,* where Prometheus steals fire from the gods in a hollow fennel stalk and takes it to men. There are two prominent considerations for Freud. First, there is a symbolic factor. Given the obvious link of *fennel stalk* with *penis-tube*, Freud asks how the link between *penis-tube* and *preservation of fire* can be established. Yet penis-tube does not harbor fire, but what is needed to quench fire—a stream of urine (*Harnstrahl*). Second, there is a historical factor. Freud notes that the taking of fire is a crime of theft and that is consistent with stories passed down from "different and widely separated peoples." Why here is the acquisition of fire linked with theft?

In the myth of Prometheus's sacrifice of a bull to the gods, there is an answer. Prometheus arranges matters so that he flimflams Zeus and the other gods, capable of the most forbidden libidinal displays, to benefit humans, while he performs the sacrifice. The useless parts are sacrificed to the gods, while the edible, tasty parts are saved for human consumption. "Speaking in libidinal terms, we should say that instinctual life—the id—is the god who is defrauded when the quenching of fire is renounced: the legend, a human desire is transformed into a divine privilege. But in the legend the deity possesses nothing of the characteristics of a super-ego, he is still the representative of the paramount life of the instincts" (1932, *S.E., XXII*: 188-9).

There is another significant feature: the punishment of Prometheus. Prometheus is subsequently chained to a rock, where every day a vulture feeds on his liver and every night the liver is restored—the daily devouring and restoration being representative of erotic desires and the bird devouring being representative of a penis. The significance of the liver, Freud rightly notes, is that it was considered to be the organ wherein the passions existed for the ancients.[2] Thus, it is an appropriate punishment for a crime of passion. However, Prometheus's crime is a crime committed through renunciation for the benefit of human beings at expense of the gods. In such a manner, the acquisition and control of fire presupposes instinctual renunciation (1932, *S.E.,* XXII: 189-90).

A complication occurs with *fire* being a symbol for sexual passion for the ancients and *flame* being a symbol of an erect phallus. The attempt to quench fire with urine, Freud asserts, had the meaning of a "pleasurable struggle with another phallus." Overall, the tale brings to mind the phoenix bird. As often as it is consumed by fire, it emerges rejuvenated. The significance of the phoenix is likely related to the revivified penis more so than the setting and rising of the sun each night and day. The overall significance is the degeneration and regeneration of libidinal desires—i.e., their ultimate indestructibility.

> [T]he historical core of the myth deals with a defeat of instinctual life, which a renunciation of instinct that has become necessary. It is, as it were, the second part of primal man's understandable reaction when he has suffered a blow in his instinctual life: after the punishment of the offender comes the assurance that after all at bottom he has done no damage (1932, *S.E.,* XXII: 191).

The moral of the tale is that sexuality can survive renunciation of libido.

Given the sexual significance of the myth, a third, physiological factor is evident. The male sexual organ has two functions: first, the evacuation of the bladder and, second, the act of love. These functions are as incompatible as are fire and water. Sexual excitation is impossible when there is evacuation of urine. Evacuation of urine is impossible when there is sexual excitation. Freud sums, "The antithesis between the two functions might lead us to say that man quenches his own fire with his own water"—a consideration of which primal man, he says, was doubtless aware (1932, *S.E.,* XXII: 192-3).

## Psychoanalysis and Biology

### Infantile Sexuality

In "Claims of Psycho-Analysis to Scientific Interest," Freud next turns to biology—specifically the biological link of infantile sexuality to normal, adult sexuality. He makes several points. First, the normal sexuality of adulthood is conjoined to childhood sexuality by a series of developments, combinations, divisions, and suppressions that are seldom ever fully achieved and that leave behind predispositions toward regression to childhood—i.e., psychopathology. Second, infantile sexuality is attached to erotogenic bodily zones and to the impulses linked with them. Third, infantile sexuality begins with self-preservation—i.e., nutrition, excretion, muscular excitation, and sensation. These instances, together with the data of psychoanalysis, show that the function of human sexuality goes far beyond reproduction. Libidinal- and ego-interests form an alliance, as it were, only after the course development that involves numerous restrictions of libido. Failure along these developmental lines results in neurosis. He writes: "For the final formula which psycho-analysis has arrived at on the nature of the neuroses runs thus: The primal conflict which leads to neurosis is one between the sexual instincts and those which maintain the ego. The neuroses represent a more or less partial overpowering of the ego by sexuality after the ego's attempts at suppressing sexuality have failed" (1913, *S.E.,* XIII: 180-1).

At once, Freud's reference to drives forces him beyond descriptive psychology and toward metapsychological speculation. Though psychoanalysis is "impartial judgement of the psycho-analytic facts before us," descriptive work takes Freud only so far.

> But after we have completed our psycho-analytic work we shall have to find a point of contact with biology; and we may rightly feel glad if that contact is already assured at one important point or another. The contrast between the ego instincts and the sexual instinct [i.e., Freud's first theory of drives], to which we have been obliged to trace back to the origin of the neuroses, is carried into the sphere of biology in the contrast between the instincts which serve the preservation of the individual and those which serve the survival of the species (1913, *S.E.,* XIII: 182).

Freud adds that he cannot proceed psychoanalytically without borrowing terminology from biology. "Drive" (*Trieb*)—customarily mistranslated by Strachey as "instinct"—is needed to link the frontier between the psychological and biological spheres. So too are "masculine" and "feminine" needed to describe active and passive qualities of the aims of the drives (1913, *S.E.,* XIII: 182). The link, of course, that Freud takes himself to be forging between psychoanalysis and biology—Freud's metapsychology—is gratuitous.[3]

## Teleological Language

In *Three Essays on Sexuality*, Freud writes, "Visual impressions remain the most frequent pathway along which libidinal excitation is aroused; indeed, natural selection counts upon the accessibility of this pathway—if such a teleological form of statement is permissible—when it encourages the development of beauty in the sexual object" (1905, *S.E.,* VII: 156). Here he uses teleological language to describe the tendency of organisms to be sexually stimulated by the visual impressions of beauty.

Later, when Freud turns to the topic of infantile sexuality, he adds:

> The sexual aim of the infantile instinct consists in obtaining satisfaction by means of an appropriate stimulation of the erotogenic zone which has been selected in one way or another. This satisfaction must have been previously experienced in order to have left behind a need for its repetition; and we may expect that Nature will have made safe provisions so that this experience of satisfaction shall not be left to chance.

In a footnote, he adds that teleological phrasing is almost necessary in biological discussions, though the possibility of error always lurks with its use (1905, *S.E.,* VII: 184). In both passages, Freud's use of teleological language is uninjurious and used in a manner no different than that of Darwin.

In "Contributions to a Discussion on Masturbation," Freud responds to Rudolf Reitler's criticisms of his teleological views on infantile masturbation in the 1905 and 1910 versions of *Three Essays on Sexuality*. Freud's reply, in part, is that the criticisms are misguided, because Reitler presupposes an anthropomorphic teleology that, although natural, aims at one end, which Freud disavows. Nature, Freud says, is multitelic, not monotelic, and it regulates this multitelicity effectively. Freud sums his view on nature's teleology: "The use of teleology [even] as a heuristic hypothesis has its dubious side: in any particular instance one can never tell whether one has hit upon a 'harmony' or a 'disharmony.' It is the same when one drives a nail into the wall of a room: one cannot be certain whether one is going to come up against lath and plaster or brick-work" (1912, *S.E.,* XII: 247-8). Freud's cautionary words are perhaps fatidic—indicative of the struggles he would shortly face in essaying to proffer a metapsychological (i.e., quasi-biological) substructure to his science of psychoanalysis ($\Psi A_3$).

## Psychoanalysis and History

### Dreams and Social Institutions

In "Claims of Psycho-Analysis to Scientific Interest," Freud makes two points concerning the psychoanalytic contribution to the history of civilization: one apropos of dreams and the other apropos of the cultural institutions of civilized societies.

First, the psychoanalytic studies of dreams and neuroses have shed light on the cryptic meaning of myths and fairy tales. It has long been presumed that the changes and transformations of those stories is the key to their underlying meaning. Studies of dreams and neuroses have also gleaned the obfuscous motives behind the changes in meaning of myths and fairly tales over the years. Dreams and neurotic symptoms are products of the same motives that have generated the mythic construction, by which natural phenomena become explicable and cult observances and usages that are today incomprehensible become intelligible (1913, *S.E.,* XIII: 184).

Second, as we have already seen, psychoanalysis has been able to shed light on cultural institutions such as religion, justice, morality, and philosophy. The keys have been to analyze the primitive psychological conditions that provided the motivation for such institutions and to supplant superficial explanations with the new insights gleaned (1913, *S.E.,* XIII: 184).

An investigation of primitive peoples shows mankind caught up . . . in a childish belief in its own omnipotence. A whole number of mental structures can thus be understood as attempts to deny whatever might disturb this feeling of omnipotence and so to prevent emotional life from being affected by reality until the latter could be better controlled and used for purposes of satisfaction. The principle of avoiding unpleasure dominates human action until it is replaced by the better one of adaptation to the external world. *Pari passu* with men's progressive control over the world goes a development in their *Weltanschauung*, their view of the universe as a whole. They turn away more and more from their original belief in their own omnipotence, rising from an animistic phase through a religious to a scientific phase. Myths, religion and morality find their place in this scheme as attempts to seek a compensation from the lack of satisfaction of human wishes (1913, *S.E.,* XIII: 186).

Through reference to Comtean progressivism, Freud notes that humans developed compensatory schemes—viz., myths, religion, and morality—as means of rationalizing their unhappiness in their development from the complete narcissism of animism, where impulses found immediate satisfaction, or nearly so.

Freud tells us that the neuroses are attempts at individual solutions to unsated wishes. In addition, social institutions are attempts at social solutions for the same problems. He ends, "The recession of the social factor and the predominance of the sexual one turns these neurotic solutions of the psychological problem into caricatures which are of no service except to help us in explaining such important questions" (1913, *S.E.,* XIII: 186-7). Thus, group psychology in this relatively early work shows that such caricatures of social institutions enable humans to trade off individual neurosis for group neurosis.

## Historical Truths

As we saw in the previous chapter, Freud distinguishes between "historical truths" and "material truths"—the former relates to stories, based on a fragment of actual truth; the latter relates to a correspondence with the actual states of material affairs. In this section, I mention two sorts of "historical truths" that psychoanalysis has disclosed: one of a phylogenetic sort, the other of an ontogenetic sort.

Freud, in *Moses and Monotheism,* addresses the notion of the existence of a single god. The pious maintain that the notion of a single god is an advance in intellectuality. It grips men, because it is a "portion of eternal truth"—a phylogenetic historical truth—that has come to light. Freud writes:

> We too would like to accept this [pious] solution. But we are brought up by a doubt. The pious argument rests on an optimistic and idealistic premise. It has not been possible to demonstrate in other connections that the human intellect has a particularly fine flair for the truth or that the human mind shows any special inclination for recognizing the truth. We have rather found, on the contrary, that our intellect very easily goes astray without any warning, and that nothing is more easily believed by us than what, without reference to the truth, comes to meet our wishful illusions. . . . We too believe that the pious solution contains the truth—but the *historical* truth and not the *material* truth.

Psychoanalysis, he adds, does not believe in a single great god, but rather a cynosure, who appeared huge and  as elevated to deity over time in early history—the primal father (1939, *S.E.,* XXIII: 29).

In *Leonardo da Vinci* and *Autobiographical Study,* Freud states that a person's conscious memories of his maturity are comparable to a chronicle of current events, while a person's conscious memories of his childhood are comparable to the "history"—i.e., the legends and myths—of the earliest years of a nation that has been compiled for tendentious reasons, much later. These conscious memories of childhood, these "screen memories," are therefore ontogenetic historical truths, not material truths (1910, *S.E.,* XI: 84 & 148 and 1925, *S.E.,* XX: 72).

Freud stretches the notion of ontogenetic historical truth to include the paranoic's interpretation of chance events in *Psychopathology of Everyday Life* and the compulsive beliefs linked to delusions in "Constructions in Analysis." These too contain a portion of historical truth from infantile sources. "The transposing of material from a forgotten past on to the present or on to an expectation of the future is indeed a habitual occurrence in neurotics no less than in psychotics." When a neurotic follows his anxiety to the expectation of some terrible event, he is following some repressed memory of an early event. An analyst's task is to disentangle the fragment of historical truth from its permutations and current attachments back to its genesis. Freud concludes that psychoanalysis can glean valuable information about psychotics in such a manner, even if it leads to no therapeutic success (1932, *S.E.,* XXIII: 267-8).

Overall, the phylogenic reconstruction in *Moses and Monotheism* is based on a straightforward application of principles, discovered in the clinic and used on individuals, to groups, treated as individuals. As Freud writes in "Construction in Analysis":

> If we consider mankind as a whole and substitute it for the single human individual, we discover that it too has developed delusions which are inaccessible to logical criticism and which contradict reality. If, in spite of this, they are able to exert an extraordinary power over men, investigation leads us to the same explanation as in the case of the single individual. They owe their power to the element of historical truth which they have brought up from the repression of the forgotten and primaeval past (1932, *S.E.,* XXIII: 269).

## Psychoanalysis and Aesthetics

Freud's contribution to aesthetics, broadly construed to include not only art and literature, but also humor, is ponderous. James Strachey lists twenty-two separate works that directly concern aesthetics (1930, *S.E.,* XXI: 213-4).

Following philosophers of his day, Freud considers the aesthetic to be a sort of contemplative enjoyment that has no aim other than itself (1905, *S.E.,* VIII: 95). *Civilization and Its Discontents* considers the pronouncement that happiness is to be sought chiefly in enjoyment of the beauty of human forms and gestures, natural objects and landscapes, and artistic and scientific creations. Though an aesthetic attitude shields us little against suffering, enjoyment of beauty, which has no use and has no clear cultural need, offers us great compensation. Moreover, while aestheticians investigate the conditions under which things are felt to be beautiful, they have not been able to explain the origin and nature of beauty through their "flood of resounding and empty [philosophical] words." What the aestheticians have missed is the derivation of beauty from sexuality. "'Beauty' and 'attraction,'" Freud states flatly, "are originally attributes of the sexual object," though not of the genitals, which are scarcely ever judged beautiful, but of secondary sexual characteristics (1930, *S.E.,* XXI: 82-3).

## Artistic Creation

Art is merely the human contribution to the aesthetic. As I have shown in the previous chapter, Freud's general attitude toward art is intellectual. To understand a work of art is a matter of getting inside the head of its artist—viz., of understanding the motives and intentions behind the work. Disclosure of intention, however, only comes after interpretation of a work through disclosure of its meaning and content (1914, *S.E.,* XIII: 212). In this regard, works of art, considered psychoanalytically, differ nowise from dreams. To understand completely a work of art, one must psychoanalyze its creator.

Fullest understanding of works of art, a proper psychoanalytic grasp of intentions, requires explanation by unconscious, childhood, sexual causes—the sort of explanation given in his psychoanalytic analysis of Leonardo da Vinci in his work of the same name. He begins, "If a biographical study is really intended to arrive at an understanding of its hero's mental life it must not—as happens in the majority of biographies as a result of discretion or prudishness—silently pass over its subject's sexual activity or sexual individuality" (1910, *S.E.,* XI: 69). His analysis leads to two main conclusions: Leonardo's especial tendency toward sexual repression and his uncommon capacity for sexual sublimation. Overall, after psychoanalytic investigation of Leonardo's works, it seems that only someone who had the type of childhood that Leonardo had, could have painted the *Mona Lisa* and the *Virgin and Child with St. Anne.*

However, psychoanalytic assessments, in bringing people in touch with reality, are botherations to people. They feel hurt that a just and kindly providence does not protect them better from fate. "[W]e are all too ready to forget that in fact everything to do with our life is chance, from our origin out of the meeting of spermatozoon and ovum onwards—chance which nevertheless has a share in the law and necessity of nature, and which merely lacks any connection with our wishes and illusions" (1910, *S.E.,* XI: 136).

Like other social practices, artistic creations are efforts to satisfy ungratified wishes, both through the creativity of artists and in appreciation of what is created by their audience. As artists intend to liberate themselves in some measure from the underlying tensions within them, they offer their audience the same release, which comes through concealment—i.e., a softening of what is offensive in them. Artists' works, then, are nothing else than reactions to their early childhood experiences. It constitutes a region—wishes fulfilled halfway in imagination and wishes frustrated in reality—where early man's striving for omnipotence are still operative. As a halfway region between fantasy and reality, art is without question an attractive subject for psychoanalytic investigation (1913, *S.E.,* XIII: 187-8).

## Jokes and the Aesthetic

Freud says that jokes too are subject to aesthetic analysis, because philosophers subsume jokes under the comic and the comic under aesthetics (1905, *S.E.,* VIII: 95).

Freud begins the analytic part of *Jokes and their Relation to the Unconscious* by noting that jokes are of equal interest to psychologists and aestheticians. He then cites the available literature on jokes for his time. Kuno Fisher relates that comics are concerned with an aspect of what is ugly. To emphasize ridiculous and comic contrasts and to make them accessible to aesthetic consideration, judgment is needed to illuminate thoughts. A joke is just such a judgment. He defines a joke thus, "A joke is a judgement which produces a comic contrast; it has already played a silent part in caricature, but only in judgement does it attain its peculiar form and the free sphere of its unfolding." Later he adds, "[I]t is a *playful* judgement," just as aesthetic freedom is the playful contemplation of things. When one contemplates things playfully, there is freedom for comic contrast. Jean Paul Richter adds, "Joking is merely playing with ideas." Theodor Visher defines joking as the capacity to unite, with rapidity, several ideas that are alien to each other in content and nexus. Emile Kraeplin defines a joke as "the arbitrary connecting or linking, usually by means of a verbal association, of two ideas which in some way contrast with each other." Theodor Lipps says, "A remark seems to us to be a joke, if we attribute a significance to it that has psychological necessity and, as soon as we have done so, deny it again." For instance, we make sense of nonsense or we discover truth in something that should not admit of truth (1905, *S.E.,* VIII: 10-2).

Jokes have the features of bewilderment and illumination as well as that of brevity. Whereas Immanuel Kant noted that the bewilderment lasts only momentarily, Heymans and Lipps add that illumination inevitably follows bewilderment and that produces comic effect. Richter says, "*Brevity* is the body and soul of wit, it is its very self." He adds: "A joke says what it has to say . . . in *too* few words—that is, in words that are insufficient by strict logic or by common modes of thought and speech. It may even actually say what it has to say by not saying it" (1905, *S.E.,* VIII: 13-4).

All these insights—activity, relation to the content of thinking, playful judgment, coupling of dissimilar things, contrasting ideas, sense in nonsense, bewilderment followed by enlightenment, disclosure of the hidden, and brevity of wit—are mere *disjecta membra,* Freud asserts brashly. "When all is said and done, they contribute to our knowledge of jokes no more than would a series of anecdotes to the description of some personality of whom we have a right to ask for a biography" (1905, *S.E.,* VIII: 14-5).

Like dreams and slips, jokes require psychoanalytic interpretation to be grasped fully. For Freud, jokes have an aim rooted in human impulses—the procurement of libidinal release. The indispensable satisfactions derived from jokes show they are activities that aim at deriving pleasure from mental processes. Jokes provide satisfaction of impulses by removing, if only for a while, the external and internal obstacles of aesthetic culture. The economy of jokes, then, is not merely in saying as much as is possible in as few words as is possible, but in allowing a "pleasure in economy [that relates to] economy of psychical expenditure" (1905, *S.E.,* VIII: 120). In short, the best jokes are those that do the most work—viz., give the greatest yield of pleasure—as economically as possible.

Aesthetic economy is also facilitated associatively by what Freud calls the "principle of assistance," which I sum below.

> **Principle of Assistance:** When the possibility of some pleasure, P, supervenes in a situation where another lesser pleasure, P', is obstructed, P allows for a release of the possibility of P' and P' becomes an incentive bonus for P and the corresponding release of pleasure, the result of P' and P, is greater than P' or P alone.

He illustrates by a desire to insult another that would result in a certain pleasure P'—suppressed because of aesthetic sensitivity. The would-be insulter then considers a joke, derived from the words and thoughts of the insult that has its own corresponding pleasure, P. The joke, then, allows for a veiling of the insult and the release of *both* P' and P. The scenario Freud describes quasi-algorithmically is a sort of fore-pleasure that relates to joking of the same sort that relates to sexual experiences (1905, *S.E.,* VIII: 136-7).

## The Uncanny

Another concept subject to aesthetical and psychoanalytic analyses is the uncanny (*das Unheimliche*), which Freud addressed in 1919. The "uncanny" relates to what is frightening and that has not been a proper subject for aestheticians, who have preferred to study its opposite—what is sublime, beautiful, and attractive. The "uncanny is that class of the frightening which leads back to what is known of old and long familiar" (1919, *S.E.,* XVII: 219-20).

Freud begins with "The Sand Man," a story by E. T. A. Hoffman. The story begins with Nathaniel, thinking back to his youth, when he would hear a story at night about the coming of the Sand Man, a dreadful person who would throw sand into the eyes of boys and girls that would not go to bed. Heads bleeding from the sand, the children would then be thrown into sacks and carried to the Half-Moon as food for his children. The children of the Half-Moon, with hooked beaks, would then sit in their nest and peck at the eyes of the naughty children in bird-like fashion (1919, *S.E.,* XVII: 230-1).

Psychoanalytic experience of patients shows, for Freud, that the fear of losing one's eyes is derived from the fear of castration. Such a connection is needed, he adds *ad hoc*, to tie together elements of the story that otherwise would appear meaningless (1919, *S.E.,* XVII: 232).

A peculiarity of the story is the repetition of features, character traits, crimes, and names over generations. That doubling, shown by Rank to be an insurance against death, takes on new meaning for Freud. There is also a doubling of the ego for Freud—the development of a critical agency that sets itself apart from and presides over the ego (i.e., the ego-ideal, or super-ego later)— and that is at least partly responsible for the factor of repetition (1919, *S.E.,* XVII: 234-6).

Another peculiarity of the story is the involuntary repetition of something inescapable or fateful. Referring to *Beyond the Pleasure Principle,* Freud writes:

> It is possible to recognize the dominance in the unconscious mind of a "compulsion to repeat" proceeding from the instinctual impulses and probably inherent in the very nature of the instincts—a compulsion powerful enough to overrule the pleasure principle, lending to certain aspects of the mind their daemonic character, and still very clearly expressed in the impulses of small children; a compulsion, too, which is responsible for a part of the course taken by the analyses of neurotic patients.

It is the compulsion to repeat unpleasant experiences—a sort of confirmation of destructive impulses—which is perceived to be uncanny (1919, *S.E.,* XVII: 238).

From here, Freud posits a new hypothesis, comprising two theses (1919, *S.E.,* XVII: 241), which I dub the principles of recurrence and alienation.

**Principle of Recurrence:** There is a class of frightening things where the frightening element is something repressed that recurs (i.e., the uncanny).

**Principle of Alienation:** The uncanny is something familiar and old that is established in the mind and that has become alienated from it through repression.

Freud then states that it is necessary to test his new hypothesis, but does so in a tendentious way—through "one or two more examples of the uncanny," as if *illustrations* of some hypothesis can be proffered as evidence for it.[4] Freud, in his final example, says that neurotic men often find the female genitalia to be uncanny, as it represents a Cimmerian place where each man once lived. The uncanny here is symbolic of home-sickness. Thus, to dream of a *foreign place* and find it uncannily familiar is to dream of *one's mother's genitals or body.* Those examples "show" that the uncanny occurs most noticeably when the distinction between reality and fantasy is effaced (1919, *S.E.,* XVII: 244).

The psychoanalytic formula that the uncanny is something familiar that is repressed finds numerous instances of contradiction. Yet as all of such instances are to be found in literature, Freud finds it profitable to distinguish the uncanny that one experiences from the uncanny that one finds in literature. The uncanny that one experiences fits perfectly well the psychoanalytic definition. It is when infantile repressions are revived by some impression or when primitive beliefs that have been discarded seem to be once again confirmed. The uncanny one finds in literature is paradoxical: Much that is not uncanny in fiction would be uncanny in real life and there are many more opportunities for the effects of the uncanny in fiction (1919, *S.E.*, XVII: 249).

## Creative Writing and Play

Freud compares the creative writer to a child at play in "Creative Writers and Day-Dreaming." Like a child at play, a creative writer creates a world of fantasy, which he takes seriously while working, as he invests his efforts with prodigious affect.

> Language has preserved this relationship between children's play and poetic creation. It gives the name of *"Spiel"* ["play"] to those forms of imaginative writing which require to be linked to tangible objects and which are capable of representation. It speaks of a *"Lustspiel"* or *"Trauerspiel"*; ["comedy" or "tragedy": literally, "pleasure play" or "mourning play"] and describes those who carry out the representation as *"Schauspieler"* ["players": literally, "show-players"] (1908, *S.E.*, VI: 144).

Overall, the result is the same as that of dreams—i.e., a childhood wish is fulfilled. The creative writer indulges himself in diurnal fantasies; he is a professional and consummate day-dreamer. "Language, in its unrivalled wisdom, long ago decided the question of the essential nature of dreams by giving the name of 'day-dreams' to the airy creations of phantasy" (1908, *S.E.*, VI: 148).

Referring to works of fiction, in which all characters are split into good and bad, Freud notices one commonality. Like the hero of every daydream, "His Majesty the Ego," the hero of fiction is invincible. If he is wounded in one chapter, he will doubtless be nursed to health in the next. If he is on a sinking ship in one chapter, he will doubtless be rescued miraculously in the next. In addition, the hero is fated to have spiked the erotic interests of all the women in the book (1908, *S.E.*, VI: 149-50).

In short, the raw material of creative writing is the same raw material that is responsible for the generation of dreams—unconscious childhood fantasies, mostly of a sexual sort. The writer's talent is in his ability to affect in readers the feeling of pleasure through catharsis. As with dreams, "The writer softens the character of his egoistic day-dreams by altering and disguising it, and he bribes us by the purely formal—that is, the aesthetic—yield of pleasure which he offers us in the presentation of his phantasies." The yield of pleasure Freud dubs "fore-pleasure," again comparable to the foreplay of sexual activity (1908, *S.E.*, VI; 152-3). Unlike with dreams, however, this fore-pleasure occurs not pictorially, but with words. The hircine suggestion, which Freud does not address here, is that child's play too may be a sort of sexual fore-play—an anticipation of the greater libidinal yield of future days.

# Notes

1. See M. Andrew Holowchak, *Ancient Science and Dreams: Oneirology in Greco-Roman Antiquity* (Lanham, MD: University Press of America, 2002).

2. E.g., Plato, *Plato's Timaeus,* trans. Francis M. Cornford (New York: Macmillan Publishing Company, [1959] 1987), 70d-72d.

3. See M. Andrew Holowchak, *Freud and Utopia: From Cosmological Narcissism to the "Soft Dictatorship" of Reason* (Lanham, MD: Lexington Press, 2012), 22-32.

4. For more on the distinction between "illustration" and "evidence," see M. Andrew Holowchak, *Critical Reasoning and Philosophy: A Concise Guide to Reading, Evaluating, and Writing Philosophical Works* (Lanham, MD: Rowman & Littlefield, 2011), 90-1.

# Chapter 8
# Efficacy of *Massenpsychologie*

"Life is impoverished, it loses in interest, when the highest stake in the game of living, life itself, may not be risked. It becomes as shallow and empty as, let us say, an American flirtation, in which it is understood from the first that nothing is to happen, as contrasted with a Continental love-affair in which both partners must constantly bear its serious consequences in mind." Sigmund Freud, "Thoughts for the Time on War and Death"

*T*HE CATALYST FOR FREUD'S WORK in group psychology was, in large part no doubt, the brutal behavior exhibited by humans in World War I, which forced him to rethink his metapsychology and introduce the death drive. This chapter looks at Freud's analysis of group-psychology issues, such as human discontent, technology, war, death, and even psychoanalysis itself, considered as a group phenomenon. At chapter's end, I argue that Freud's own behavior directed toward protecting psychoanalysis as science, by making it immune to public criticism by non-psychoanalysts and by dissidents, is itself a manifestation of the sort of pathology that Freud insists characterizes artificial groups. Like leaders of strong artificial groups, Freud is an ectype of the primal father.

## The Paradox of Civilization

Though psychoanalysis was concerned at first exclusively with investigation of the pathology of individuals, it became over time, at least in the eyes of its founder, a method for analyzing the emotional basis of the relations of individuals to society. As Freud states in *Totem ￼nd Taboo*, neuroses in general are asocial in that they aim to push individuals out of their social setting and into a sort of monastic seclusion made possible by their illness. The mechanism for this isolation is guilt—a social modification of neurotic anxiety (1913, *S.E.,* XIII: 188). Yet as Freud states years later in *Group Psychology and the Analysis of the Ego, The Future of an Illusion,* and *Civilization and Its Discontents,* persons can involve themselves in groups, like military groups and religious organizations, which function to displace their neurosis, as it were, by sparing them individual neurosis at the price of group neurosis. The trade-off is convenient for individuals but pricy for cultures that aim at progress through abandonment of narcissism and a heightened grasp of reality. This section is an examination of that trade-off and

its potentially dangerous implications for humans through a focus on the paradox of civilization in *Civilization and Its Discontents*.

Under the pleasure principle, Freud states that gratification of impulses is
responsible for human happiness and that there are three impediments to
gratification—the decay of our bodies over time, the unpredictability of the
external world, and our failed relationships with others.[1] The last—the most
frustrating of all, because it seems like the one that is most controllable—has
been the focus of the book (1930, *S.E.,* XXI: 76-7).

Humans' posture toward such hindrances ultimately is defensive. Intoxication, isolation, illusion, suppression of drives, hedonism, and sublimation are
mechanisms of "coping." Intoxication enables them to achieve endogenous
pleasure at expense of withdrawal of reality. Isolation keeps them physically
away from the dangerous taboos of civilized living and allows for a private
release of drive-energy; illusion functions similarly, though in a mental manner.
A voluptuary lifestyle allows for the possibility of intense satisfaction of
impulses, though it places humans completely at the mercy of reality, which
might refuse to participate in their aesthetic attitude. Last, sublimation grants
indirect and mild satisfaction of impulses in a socially acceptable manner, but
amounts to a gold-for-bronze exchange (1930, *S.E.,* XXI: 77-82).

Humans' defensive posture amounts to solatium due to the constraints of
civilization. Civilization refuses direct and immediate satisfaction of impulses,
but it offers humans security. Technological gains, as civilization advances,
protect humans and adjust their mutual relations, but the cost is ponderous—
human happiness.

Happiness Freud cashes out hedonistically. It is experience of pleasure and
freedom from pain—in a nutshell, gratification of the needs of humans' most
primitive mental apparatus, the id, and the frustration of all such things that
might prevent gratification. "What we call happiness in the strictest sense,"
Freud writes dynamically and economically, "comes from the (preferably
sudden) satisfaction of needs which have been dammed up to a high degree, and
it is from its nature only possible as an episodic phenomenon" (1930, *S.E.,* XXI:
76). With the maturation of the human mental apparatus in civilized society over
time, other agencies—i.e., the ego and the super-ego—have developed to delay
or frustrate opportunities for libidinal discharge through a regard for reality and
morality. Unhappiness results.

That leads to the paradox of civilization. Civilization protects people and
regulates their mutual relations at the expense of their own happiness. Society
demands that humans live by rules, but rules—promoting order through par-
simony, cleanliness, and order—in turn, impose severe restrictions for outlets of
expression of impulses, both libidinal and aggressive.[2] The tension seems irremediable for Freud: individuals' demand for freedom of expression of impulses
versus the regulations of civilization that prohibit such expression, imposed by
the group (1930, *S.E.,* XXI: 95). The upshot is that society thrives at the expense
of the psychical health of the individuals in it. As civilized societies "progress,"
their individuals become increasingly neurotic.

Overall, humans would be much happier if they could abandon civilized living and return to their primitive, precivilized lives. That, unfortunately, is not an option. The structural maturation of the human psyche—i.e., the development of ego and super-ego from id—disallows such a movement, which would be tantamount to a phylogenetic retrogression (1930, *S.E.,* XXI: 86 and 96-7).

Experience shows there is no happy, once-and-for-all solution to the imbroglio. Defensive postures like intoxication, illusion, and suppression are what they are—defensive postures. Of them, only sublimation, which thrives on renunciation and displacement of impulses that are most appropriately directed toward other human beings, holds out some degree of hope for success (1930, *S.E.,* XXI: 94-7). Humans can divert libido into philanthropy, artistic creation, scientific study, religion, or philosophy, and divert aggression in professional athletics or military service. Such economical solutions, however, give sop to Cerberus. Without them, individuals would surely suffer the price of psychical debilitation. Yet as manifestations of a defensive posture, they are anything but economically availing. One imagines the "relief" offered an overburdened dam, about to break, through drilling several small holes in it.

Civilization is a paradoxical byproduct of displaced drive-energy. It utilizes libido to build social bonds, whose very rules function to suppress libidinal expression. While individuals have a goal of happiness, civilization has a goal of unification. At once, we find an explanation for neurosis. Neurosis occurs because people cannot tolerate the amount of frustration of drive-energy that civilized living imposes on them. In sum, civilization binds people at the expense of their own psychical health.

## The "Cheap Enjoyment" of Progress

Humans' civilizing is signified by technological advance. In need of some degree of control over nature, through science, they have gained a remarkable degree of control.

> Today [man] has come very close to the attainment of this ideal [viz., protection from nature]; he has almost become a god himself. Only, it is true, in the fashion to which ideals are usually attained according to the general judgment of humanity. Not completely; in some respects not at all, in other only half way. Man has, as it were, become a kind of prosthetic God. When he puts on all of his auxiliary organs he is truly magnificent; but those organs have not grown on to him and they still give him much trouble at times. . . . Future ages will bring them new and probably unimaginably great advances in this field of civilization and will increase man's likeness to God still more.

Were Freud alive today—given the extraordinary advances in medicine, computer technology, astronomy, and biology, *inter alia*—he would doubtless say the final sentence is understated. Apropos of humans' cosmological grasp of the universe, even deity it seems is no longer needed. Consider what noted physicists Stephen Hawking and Leonard Mlodinow write in *The Grand Design*: "Because there are laws such as gravity, the universe can and will create itself from nothing. It is not necessary to invoke God to light the blue touch paper and set the Universe going."[3]

As prosthetic gods, humans have gained perhaps immeasurable protection from the vagaries of nature. Freud however warns, "[P]ower over nature is not the *only* precondition of human happiness, just as it is not the *only* goal of cultural endeavor. . . ." He continues in a stirring passage that must be appreciated *in toto*, if at all:

> Is there then no positive gain in pleasure, no unequivocal increase in my feeling of happiness, if I can, as often as I please, hear the voice of a child of mine who is living hundreds of miles away or if I can learn in the shortest possible time after a friend has reached his destination that he has come through the long and difficult voyage unharmed? Does it mean nothing that medicine has succeeded in enormously reducing infant mortality and the danger of infection for women in childbirth, and, indeed, in considerably lengthening the average life of a civilized man? And there is a long list that might be added to the benefits of the kind which we owe to the much-despised era of scientific and technical advances. But here the voice of pessimistic criticism makes itself heard and warns us that most of these satisfactions follow the model of the "cheap enjoyment" extolled in the anecdote—the enjoyment obtained by putting a bare leg from under the bedclothes on a cold winter night and drawing it in again. If there had been no railway to conquer distances, my child would never have left his native town and I should need no telephone to hear his voice. If traveling across the ocean by ship had not been introduced, my friend would not have embarked on the sea-voyage and I should not need a cable to relieve my anxiety about him (1930, *S.E.*, XXI: 88).

Ultimately, the satisfaction of technological advances is inconsequential—i.e., no greater than "putting a bare leg from under the bedclothes on a cold winter night and drawing it in again." As is often the case, Freud's use of analogy to illustrate the point he is making is spot-on.

Every conquest of nature comes with a price. Every technological advance, designed to increase human security by protecting humans from the vicissitudes of nature, fosters another technological advance that threatens humans with greater problems to be faced. Moreover, human aggression through the death drive works to dissolve what *Eros* continually unites. Humans are constantly plagued by war, and technological advances in weaponry threaten humans with a tenebrous, gloomy prospect—annihilation (1933, *S.E.*, XXII: 177-8). "The element of truth behind all this," Freud writes, "which people are so ready to disavow, is that men are not gentle creatures who want to be loved, and who at the most can defend themselves if they are attacked; they are, on the contrary, creatures among whose instinctual endowments is to be reckoned a powerful share of aggressiveness (1930, *S.E.*, XXI: 111).

Consequently, by the canon of human happiness, technology has nowise improved the human condition. Technological advance brings with it suppression and displacement of human impulses that prefer, so to speak, immediate and direct expression. "At some point . . . the scenario would become insufferable and irreversible, should technology become the principal outlet for libido, which seems increasingly to be the case today," I write in "Technology and Freudian Discontent," "and that is an undeniable sign of severe, perhaps irremediable underlying pathology. In such a pathological society, one would expect passionate, rapid, and most importantly uncritical technological advance in all areas of productive science, which is what humans have today, even more than in Freud's day."[4]

## Freudian *Weltschmerz*

Given Freud's observation of the inverse relationship between civilization and human happiness, no solution seems possible. In spite of Freud's purchase of Comtean progressivism, humans are essentially impulse-driven, not rational creatures. In *The Ego and the Id,* he compares the id to a horse and the ego to its rider. The rider, in light of the superior strength of the horse, has to use skill and cunning to get the horse to take him where he wishes to go. If the horse is unwilling, the rider merely guides it where it wishes to go or gets parted from the horse (1923, *S.E.,* XIX: 25).

If any solution is possible, it must appeal to human reason and gratify human passions, for "instinctual passions are stronger than reasonable interests" (1930, *S.E.,* XXI: 112). The ego, humans' link with reality and their coherent organization of mental processes, is not only in the service of the id, but it is also not even master in its own house.[5] Referring back to the horse-and-rider analogy, in most cases of human agency, the horse (the id) wins. Thus, any appeal to reason alone—reason not in the service of human passions—cannot work. Reason must work toward a solution that accommodates fundamentally human impulses.

In *The Future of an Illusion*, an earlier and decidedly more sanguine work than *Civilization and its Discontents*, Freud offers a clue to a solution. Humans' intellect, he concedes, is "powerless in comparison with his instinctual life." Still, though intellect might be weak, it is unrelenting. "The voice of intellect is a soft one, but it does not rest till it gains a hearing. Finally, after a countless succession of rebuffs, it succeeds." The optimism is posthaste mitigated. He adds, "The primacy of the intellect lies . . . in a distant, distant future, but probably not in an *infinitely* distant one" (1927, *S.E.,* XXI: 53).

Freud does not appeal to experience for the possibility of a solution, because he cannot. There is precious little in human history from which to draw that offers a clue to the continued advance of civilization and the riddance of human unhappiness. If anything, the history of humans is a history of unrelenting belligerence, and the technological advances in military warfare admit the possibility of full-scale annihilation.

How best can human cleverness master aggression to pave the way for the "distant, distant future"? Freud falls back on metempiricism—i.e., on an appeal to speculation and to the "Witch" metapsychology. Vis-à-vis metapsychology, he appeals especially to the notions of the economics and dynamics of libidinal and aggressive drives.

In *Civilization and Its Discontents*, Freud says that reaction-formations, of the sort that incite people into libido-friendly identifications with others, must be cunningly employed such as to hold in check human aggression (1930, *S.E.*, XXI: 113). Here moral and religious precepts, stripped of their metaphysical baggage, ought to be brought into play. It is not that the precepts are right or wrong, good or bad, but instead that the survival of the species is at stake.

Three years later in "Why War?" Freud outlines two generic strategies. First, one can try to bring erotic impulses into play as antagonists to destructive impulses either by universalized love—a suggestion he categorically rejects in *Civilization and Its Discontents*—or by identification with others through shared interests. Second, one can educate the upper stratum of men to subordinate their drives to the dictates of reason for the good of everyone. Should these prove impossible, Freud hints that there are other methods, slow and indirect, of deflecting destructive impulses, yet preterition concerning such methods is a good reason to think Freud believed they too would be unavailing. Freud sums sourly, "An unpleasant picture comes to one's mind of mills that grind so slowly that people may starve before they get their flour" (1933, *S.E.*, XXII, 212-3).

Overall, Freud was not sanguine about the possibility of a convenient solution to the paradox of civilization, if only because metapsychological considerations have an undeniable biological component. Forces and quantities of energy are at play, and the result might just be a matter of strength and numbers. Are humans, on average, endowed with more or less aggression than libido? Whatever the numbers, Freud the realist, following Tacitus, writes with great sobriety in *Outline of Psychoanalysis*: "[T]he final outcome of the struggle we have engaged in depends on *quantitative* relations—on the quote of energy we are able to mobilize in the patient to our advantage as compared with the sum of energy of the powers working against us. Here once again God is on the side of the big battalions" (1940, *S.E.*, XXIII: 182).

## Human Annihilation

Since the advent of World War I and on account of the loss of his daughter Sophie and grandson Heinele and certain intimate friends, death held an aphontic fascination for Freud. No believer in an afterlife, his fascination with death, as is the case with many intellectuals that spend a lifetime in study and amassing information, was no doubt its annihilative capacity. While life is given equally to all humans, not all humans are fated or of a capacity to live equally well. In that regard, some persons fare no better than lower animals. Yet death is the great democratic principle. When it comes, it asks nothing of one's astuteness, intellection, wealth, status, or even virtue. When it comes, it takes everyone in the same manner. When it leaves, everyone's slate is wiped clean—thoroughly clean.

This section explores Freud's thoughts on death and war. I begin by examining death as individual annihilation and then turn to war as the possible harbinger of the annihilation of the species. Due to the war and several personal tragedies, each topic was a disquieting and tenebrous, yet seductive, topic for Freud. Yet both, he realized, were important topics for psychoanalytic penetration. First, humans' fear of the inevitability of death was illustrative of a certain congenital human resistance to mortality—a residue of great significance and evidence of some phylogenetic inheritance. Second, the ease with which the church-going moralist could don himself in military accoutrements during war and annihilate others in different accoutrements was evidence of powerful, psychical ambivalence in all humans—and that ultimately would lead to acceptance of a death drive in opposition to *Eros.*

I focus on "Thoughts for the Times on War and Death"—a 1915 paper, which was certainly seminal for his works, *Beyond the Pleasure Principle* and *Group Psychology,* years later. Consistent with what I take to be Freud's weak normativism—the notion that psychoanalysis for Freud is explanatorily rich, but mostly unavailing in directing or correcting the course of human history—what psychoanalysis, considered as group therapy, has to offer humans is no remedy for fear of death and the bellicosity of human individuals and belligerency of states, considered as large groups of humans. It offers humans insight and understanding, which require maturity of reason, but comprise the first step, according to Freud, toward a solution.

## Death and Individual Annihilation

Humans' attitude toward death is paradoxical, Freud writes. On the one hand, they acknowledge, via appeal to experience, that death is natural, undeniable, and unavoidable. On the other hand, humans tend not to think about death—especially their own. "[A]t bottom no one believes in his own death," Freud states, "or, to put the same thing in another way, that in the unconscious every one of us is convinced of his own immortality" (1915, *S.E., XIV:* 289).

Toward the dead, people emphasize chance—i.e., accident, disease, infection, or advanced age—not inevitability. They adopt an attitude that resembles admiration for having accomplished something arduous or significant, as if all persons, by virtue of having lived, are deserving of praise. They ignore faults of the deceased and praise them through laudatory orations—fittingly called "eulogies"[6]—and through words engraved on tombstones. What is most bewildering is that humans have greater consideration for the dead, no longer in need their kindnesses, than they do for the living, in utmost need of them (1915, *S.E., XIV:* 289-90).

Because they tend not to think about their own death—at least, not as annihilation—all humans are essentially gamblers when it comes to death: Life has little to offer, when one cannot risk it. Freud elaborates in an amusing analogy:

> Life is impoverished, it loses in interest, when the highest stake in the game of living, life itself, may not be risked. It becomes as shallow and empty as, let us say, an American flirtation, in which it is understood from the first that nothing is to happen, as contrasted with a Continental love-affair in which both partners must constantly bear its serious consequences in mind (1915, *S.E.*, XIV: 290).

People take solace in the realm of fiction, where they can die with the tragic hero and yet still live, and then do the same again with another hero in another tragedy. The thrill is gimcrack, however. There is nothing at stake. War brings them back to reality. In wars, people really do die and they die by the thousands. Life again becomes exciting. "To be sure, it still seems a matter of chance whether a bullet hits this man or that; but a second bullet may well hit the survivor; and the accumulation of deaths puts an end to the impression of chance. Life has, indeed, become interesting again; it has recovered its full content" (1915, *S.E.*, XIV: 291).

Freud then looks back to primeval man's ambivalence concerning death. He took seriously the death of enemies, for that was annihilation of someone execrable. Nonetheless, he denied the possibility of his own death or of the death of a loved one.[7] This "law of ambivalence of feeling" still governs human relationships today—especially the most intimate ones (1915, *S.E.*, XIV: 292-3).

Is there a link between recognition of death and the origin of human speculative thinking? Freud corrects the thoughts of certain philosophers, who maintain that rudimentary reflections on death were catalysts for human speculation. It was not every death, Freud adds, but merely the deaths of loved ones that turned humans to speculation. Primitive men posited that loved ones did not fully die; they became spirits. From there, it was a short step to a distinction between body and soul and again to the possibility of a life—though a tenuous, shadowy one—after death, hence the Greek notion of *eidola*. Over time, religion invented a substantive, desirable life after death, an afterlife, and reduced life to mere preparation for that afterlife. Hereafter, it was only natural to extend life backward and form the notion of past lives. So thoroughly did humans in time come to deny death (1915, *S.E.*, XIV: 294-5).

Ethical commandments, the most important of which is "Thou shall not kill," were soon created. At first, that commandment applied to loved ones, but soon it was extended to strangers, even enemies (1915, *S.E.*, XIV: 295).

Ethical prohibitions as powerful as the commandment that prohibits killing must be directed against impulses, equaling their power. In short, the fact of the prohibition, Freud argues compellingly, speaks for an impulse to do just what is prohibited. "So powerful a prohibition can only be directed against an equally powerful impulse. What no human soul desires stands in no need of prohibition," writes Freud. "The very emphasis laid on the commandment 'Thou shalt not kill' makes it certain that we spring from an endless series of generations of murderers, who had the lust for killing in their blood, as, perhaps, we ourselves have to-day." Like the prohibition against killing, all other ethical principles are based on human guilt, which is linked phylogenically to the killing of the primal father and which has been inherited by humans today (1915, *S.E.*, XIV: 296).

How does the primeval attitude relate to the modern one? It is essentially the same, states Freud. Primal ambivalence has been taken up by the human unconscious, which disavows negation, houses contradictions, has no notion of death, and regards itself as invincible. In the unconscious, which is the primal self of each person, people wish for the annihilation of others, though they do not actually carry out such wishes in reality. Such wishes are readily disclosed through interpretation of dreams and analysis of jokes and parapraxes. Freud sums, "And so, if we are to be judged by our unconscious wishful impulses, we ourselves are, like primaeval man, a gang of murderers" (1915, *S.E.*, XIV: 297).

War, Freud asserts, undoes the accretions of civilization and lays bare the primal impulses in each person. Humans declare themselves to be invincible and declare others as enemies that must be exterminated. That, nonetheless, is barefacedly delusive.

> Is it not we who should give in, who should adapt ourselves to war? Should we not confess that in our civilized attitude towards death we are once again living psychologically beyond our means, and should we not rather turn back and recognize the truth? Would it not be better to give death the place in reality and in our thoughts which is its due, and to give a little more prominence to the unconscious attitude towards death which we have hitherto so carefully suppressed? This hardly seems an advance to higher achievement, but rather in some respects a backward step—a regression; but it has the advantage of taking the truth more into account, and of making life more tolerable for us once again. To tolerate life remains, after all, the first duty of all living beings. Illusion becomes valueless if it makes this harder for us (1915, *S.E.*, XIV: 299).

Freud summarizes famously, "If you wish to endure life, prepare yourself for death."

## War and Human Annihilation

People, Freud says, are disillusioned that the great, civilized nations—with an interest in and domination of global affairs, with great control over nature through technological advances, and with high aesthetic and moral standards—have, during times of war, jettisoned the same moral standards that they have demanded of their citizens during times of peace. Of the first great world war, Freud writes:

> Not only is it more bloody and more destructive than any war of other days, because of the enormously increased perfection of weapons of attack and defence; it is at least as cruel, as embittered, as implacable as any that has preceded it. It disregards all the restrictions known as International Law, which in peace-time the states had bound themselves to observe; it ignores the prerogatives of the wounded and the medical service, the distinction between civil and military sections of the population, the claims of private property. It tramples in blind fury on all that comes in its way, as though there were to be no future and no

peace among men after it is over. It cuts all the common bonds between the
contending peoples, and threatens to leave a legacy of embitterment that will
make any renewal of those bonds impossible for a long time to come (1915,
*S.E.,* XIV: 278-9).

What is most astonishing is that one civilized nation can turn against another with such execration that the newly despised nation is thereafter treated as
if it has always been barbaric. The belligerent state allows itself all such violent
actions that any civilized person would consider inhumane. Through
propagandist newspeak, it engages in cozenage not only toward its enemy but
also toward its own citizens. While the belligerent nation demands obedience
and sacrifice from its citizens, it paternalistically keeps the truth from them, as if
they were children. Sober citizens conclude, "[T]he state has forbidden to the
individual the practice of wrongdoing [during times of peace], not because it
desires to abolish it, but because it desires to monopolize it, like salt and tobacco
[during times of war]" (1915, *S.E.,* XIV: 278-9).

Overall, human disillusionment during times of war is founded on two observations: the low morality that states show externally, while they profess internally to be protectors of morality, and the brutality of "civilized" individuals
in the war. That disillusionment is ill-founded. Freud elaborates: "[O]ur mortifi-
cation and our painful disillusionment on account of the uncivilized behaviour
of our fellow-citizens of the world during this war were unjustified. They ware
based on an illusion to which we had given way. In reality our fellow-citizens
have not sunk so low as we feared, because they had never risen so high as we
believe" (1915, *S.E.,* XIV: 285).

Another cause of disillusionment is the lack of insight of the best intellects
of the day during wars. Why should that be so? Intellect, Freud says, only functions reliably when it is at a distance from strong emotional ties that bind it.
"Psycho-analytic experience . . . can show every day that the shrewdest people
will all of a sudden behave without insight, like imbeciles, as soon as the necessary insight is confronted by an emotional resistance, but that they will completely regain their understanding once that resistance has been overcome." The
paralysis of reason that seems to characterize one's fellow citizens during war—
even them of greatest intellect—is a consequence of overwhelming emotional
excitation that is bound to disappear once the source of that excitation disap-
pears (1915, *S.E.,* XIV: 287).

Being able to understand how even the ablest citizens can be swept away by
wartime cozenage, it is readily apprehensible how nations are swept away by
wartime cozenage.

> Having in this way once more come to understand our fellow-citizens who are
> now alienated from us, we shall much more easily endure the disappointment
> which the nations, the collective individuals of mankind, have caused us, for
> the demands we make upon these should be far more modest. Perhaps they are
> recapitulating the course of individual development, and to-day still represent
> very primitive phases in organization and in the formation of higher unities. It

is in agreement with this that the educative factor of an external compulsion towards morality, which we found was so effective in individuals, is as yet barely discernible in them.

Even at this stage of human phylogenetic development, nations more than individuals obey passions more than reason. Reason serves only as a tool for their passions—even passions of the most vitriolic form. It allows nations to satisfy their passions and then provides them with sufficient "rationalizations" for their misdeeds (1915, *S.E.,* XIV: 287-8). Note that Freud recognizes that the behavior of groups is barbaric compared to that of individuals, but offers no explanation of it. The problem would fester in him until *Group Psychology,* six years later, where he offers an explanation of group excitation, contagion, and neurosis.

Why is execration so universal that war seems to be a natural condition for humans? Freud offers merely a consolatory sentiment, consistent with weak normativism and Comtean progressivism. "It may be that only later stages in [biological] development will be able to make some change in this regrettable state of affairs. But a little more truthfulness and honesty on all sides—in relations of men to one another and between them and their rulers—should also smooth the way for this transformation" (1915, *S.E.,* XIV: 288).

## Schopenhauer's Porcupines

Given Freud's purchase of recapitulationism, it comes as no surprise that he would turn attention to larger, more clamant human issues in his mature years. Believing that there were stark parallels between the development of individuals and that of the species over time, it was natural that he would at some point apply the psychoanalytic findings of individual pathology to groups. In that way, therapy that was directed at enabling individuals to gain a greater sense of unity through recapturing their own history, instead of reliving it through repetitive pathological symptoms, could be directed at groups. Thus, the aim of group psychology might be grasped simply as giving all human beings a greater awareness of their own species' history to prevent them, to paraphrase Santana, from repeating it. Writes Joachim Scharfenberg:

> If Freud . . . tried to free the patient from precisely the vicious circle of the constant compulsion to repeat, then that was also true for the phenomenal forms of culture: if history exhausts itself in constant repetition, it maintains a pathological character trait. . . . The liberation of the human race from these compulsions to repeat is, therefore, the real passion of his criticism of religion.[8]

In *Group Psychology,* written as a means of spelling out the new egopsychology he was developing at the time, Freud playfully cashes out the paradox of civilization through an analogy used by philosopher Arthur Schopenhauer. Schopenhauer, Freud relates, writes of porcupines that wished to profit by each other's warmth on a morbidly cold night by huddling together. In huddling together, they soon felt the sting of each other's quills and so they moved apart. In moving apart, they again felt the morbid coldness. This huddling together and moving apart continued for some time until the porcupines discovered a mean distance at which they benefit from each other's warmth, while avoiding each other's quills (1921, *S.E.,* XVIII: 101).

What is the case with Schopenhauer's porcupines is the case with humans, Freud believes. Humans are constitutionally enabled to tolerate only so much of each other as to derive some benefit of those others, without thereby being substantially harmed. Yet as we found in *Civilization and Its Discontents,* people are frustrated more by their fellow humans than by the exigencies of fate or the prospect of death. The reason is the existence of antipodal drives, characterized by libido and aggression. Therefore, they have a need for companionship and keep other humans nearby, but at arm's length.

Thus, Freud's view of the justification of morality can only be contractarian. Moral principles are not god-sent, following Christianity, or duty-based, following Immanuel Kant. They are not to be read in the laws of nature, following the Greek and Roman Stoics. As is the case with Epicurus, morality is nothing in itself, but based on mutual need. Given the existence of both erotic and destructive impulses and given the constraints of civilization, humans willingly embrace ethical prohibitions that work to suppress impulses, not so much as to prevent their harming others, but more to prevent others from harming them.

## The Inevasible Normativity of Psychoanalysis

Freud was fond, I have already noted, of comparing psychoanalytic treatment to surgery. Like a skilled surgeon, a trained analyst takes active measures to overcome a patient's mental "disease." Of his measures, often he is obliged to cause increase in suffering in the short-term, through bringing to consciousness the underlying pathogens, in order to bring about long-term cure. Like a surgeon, he remains completely neutral concerning his patients. He meets them unconscious to unconscious and does what is possible to help them integrate again into their cultural setting. He is not in the practice of offering moral guidance (1910, *S.E.,* XI: 52-3 and 1917, *S.E.,* XVI: 459).

Psychoanalysts with a hermeneutic disposition are wont to note that therapy is essentially ethical, because therapeutic treatment is inevasively evaluative. That claim I take to be obvious and in no need of amplification. What is in need of amplification is the extent to which Freudian psychoanalysis is ethical and the extent to which, if any, Freud was cognizant of that.

Alfred Tauber has recently argued that psychoanalysis—by virtue of identifying persons independently of unwanted repressions, defining autonomous choices and goals, and providing a moral compass to establish values and self-identity—is inescapably a moral discipline. The aim of psychoanalysis, rightly grasped, is hermeneutic—viz., the joint construction between therapist and patient of a healing narrative. "[T]he analysand becomes the protagonist of a psychic drama, playing a character whose history is revealed as a story." The story requires a historical structure, an interpretive framework, a *telos*, and a moral. "[N]arration helps to define and determine anticipated action, orient self-conscious thought, and unify notions of personal identity as a center of agency in relation to others." Tauber sums, "From the hermeneutic point of view, both psychoanalytic theory and practice are seen as conceiving a life history outlining the dynamics of behavior, which follows a logic of its own interiority and whose validity is decided by criteria of its own coherence and veracity."[9]

Tauber skillfully identifies flaws in Freud's take of analytic therapy by fleshing out fully the implications of psychoanalytic therapy, committing Freud willy-nilly to those implications, and noting how those commitments link Freud to Nietzsche, Schopenhauer, and especially Kant. Unlike surgery, psychoanalysis cannot be value-neutral and a therapist cannot be dispassionate. Dispassion is, Tauber thinks, undesirable for proper therapy. Moreover, the insights gleaned in analysis require in great measure self-directed human agency of the sort recognized by Kant and that are inconsistent with strict determinism. Tauber adds:

> The "ethics" of *understanding* drives the quest to know. This moral venture of "seeing"—one developed, exercised, and pursued—becomes an act of self-actualization, an act of self-definition. Psychoanalytic knowledge obviously remains in the employ of that agenda, so Freud's own notion of science belied the more profound purpose of self-knowledge. On this view, scientific knowledge was in the employ of this deeper moral agenda.[10]

There are, however, flaws with Tauber's rendering. First, asserting that psychoanalysis requires a free-choosing moral agent seems *prima facie* reasonable, but it is not—at least, not for Freud. It asserts much more than Freud would have been willing to grant. Except for uncustomary patients, Freud thought little of peoples' capacity for intelligence and self-directed behavior. He noted that most prefer reality to unreality. He nowise ever embraced, even ever entertained, anything like Kant's noumenal self. Second, apropos of science, Freud was a dyed-in-the-wool Positivist. He allowed Kant's phenomenal take on things—that all observable things in the cosmos are completely determined by their circumstances in space and time and the laws governing the physical universe—but never his noumenal take—that there is a sort of free-floating will, somehow independent of space and time, that is rationally capable of self-direction through free choosing—to which Tauber willy-nilly commits Freud. Finally, Freud never would have granted that psychoanalysis was a hermeneutic discipline. In that, Tauber's take on Freud is not different than that of Paul Ricouer and Jürgen Habermas, each of whom write of Freud's own failed grasp of the practice of science.[11] The defects of the psychotherapy-as-hermeneutic thesis make it untenable.

Though Freud likened a trained psychoanalyst to a skilled surgeon and pleaded for a therapist's dispassion—being dispassionate does not imply being pococurante—he never asseverated that therapy ought never to have a normative dimension. Therapy done right is an "education to reality" and that in itself is advocacy of a sort of normative naturalism.

In his 1917 essay "Transference," Freud writes, "[W]e are reformers but merely observers; nevertheless, we cannot help observing with a critical eye and we have found it impossible to side with conventional sexual morality or to form a very high opinion of the manner in which society attempts the practical regulation of the problems of sexual life." Thus, the notion that sexual expression is taboo is psychically insalubrious. Society's morality—i.e., Christian morality— demands "a bigger sacrifice than it is worth" and is disingenuous and unwise.

> We do not keep such criticisms from our patient's ears, we accustom them to giving unprejudiced consideration to sexual matters no less than to any others; and if, having grown independent after the completion of their treatment, they decide on their own judgement in favour of some midway position between living a full life and absolute asceticism, we feel our conscience clear whatever their choice. We tell ourselves that anyone who has succeeded in educating himself to truth about himself is permanently defended against the danger of immorality, even though his standard of morality may differ in some respect from that which is customary in society (1917, *S.E.,* XVI: 434).

In *The Future of an Illusion* 10 years later, Freud takes education to reality outside the clinic. Humanity itself is a patient, and psychoanalysis in the largest sense, qua $\Psi A_3$, is offered as therapy. Humans from antediluvian times, he asserts, have learned much—especially through advances in science. Science, psychoanalysis especially, is teaching them to make the best use of their resources to adjust themselves to the vicissitudes of nature and to human pettifoggery. What they cannot overcome, they can bear with foursquare resignation. "[Humans'] scientific knowledge has taught them much since the days of the Deluge, and it will increase their power further. And, as for the great necessities of Fate, against which there is no help, they will learn to endure them with resignation" (1927, *S.E.,* XXI: 49-50). The tone is manifestly Stoical.[12]

In consequence, the pure Positivism Freud advocates vis-à-vis the practice of science is not practicable for psychoanalysis, whether as individual therapy or group therapy. In that regard, advocacy of education to reality makes psychoanalysis a queer sort of science—one with a normative dimension. $\Psi A_3$, then, is an ethics of sorts, in which Comtean progressivism is facilitated by the insights of depth psychology and its metapsychologcial dimension. In short, $\Psi A_3$ offers aidful insight into the human condition and can be used for human progress toward what Freud calls the "soft dictatorship of reason" (1932, *S.E.,* XXII: 171 and 1932, *S.E.,* XXII: 213). Freud's fault is his failure to recognize three things: that $\Psi A_2$ has a normative dimension, that $\Psi A_3$ is a naturalistic discipline with a normative dimension, and that $\Psi A_3$ does amount to a *Weltanschauung.*

Why should individual and group therapies as education to reality— education to truth—be moral therapies? As Bernard Williams has persuasively argued in *Truth and Truthfulness,* truth is a value—a human good—and therapy with an eye to truth is therapy with a moral dimension.

Williams demonstrates by assuming his own genealogy, an imaginary one, which begins with an admittedly fictive prior state of nature. This imaginary genealogy is merely a means of setting reasonable guidelines for a possible genealogy of truth.

In the state of nature, people will combine their beliefs so that there will be a pool of shared information. For that, there has to be dispositions toward sincerity and accuracy.

> Sincerity basically involves a certain kind of spontaneity, a disposition to come out with what one believes, which may be encouraged or discouraged, cultivated or depressed, but is not itself expressed in deliberation and choice. Equally, Accuracy does involve the will, in the uncontentious and metaphysically unambitious sense of intention, choice, attempts, and concentration of effort.[13]

Within this imaginary state of nature, thus, there will be both plain truths, relative to a technology, and those truths, not relative to any technology. The latter truths—e.g., "There is a birch tree in front of the house at 222 Elm Street"—are ones that would never be shelved or discarded with innovations of technology. That is, in effect, to say that certain propositions about everyday objects play a foundational role in language.[14]

For Williams, it is not necessary to ascribe an understanding of space and time to those persons who might live in this state of nature. If they would agree that they lack knowledge, then they would agree "there are things distant from them and earlier in time about which they do not know." It is the same with space or place, as "however far away a place may be, it is at some determinate distance from where they are." Thus, we arrive at a non-local, objective conception of events in space and time. This objective conception of events, necessary in any state of nature, requires truth as a virtue. We can safely conclude, "[T]he State of Nature is itself supposed to be a society, and that no society can get by ... with a purely instrumental conception of the values of truth."[15] He adds: "The concept of truth itself—that is to say, the quite basic role that truth plays in relation to language, meaning, and belief—is not culturally various, but always and everywhere the same. We could not understand cultural variation itself without taking that role for granted."[16] In short, with the acquisition of objectivity, we have moved from an imaginary to a real genealogy.

Thus, Freudian psychotherapy, at the levels of $\Psi A_2$ and $\Psi A_3$, with their aim of education to reality, is an incontestable commitment to truth in an objective sense. Because truth is a human value, a commitment to truth is itself a moral commitment. Freudian psychotherapy, in consequence, is itself moral therapy.

## Freud as the Primal Father

I begin *Freud and Utopia* with an elucidation of four Freudian identifications—Freud and Hercules, Freud and Nietzsche's *Übermensch,* Freud and Oedipus, and Freud and Moses—each of which Freud willingly embraced. In this section, the final section of this book, I make a fifth identification and one of which

Freud was, at least, consciously unaware: Freud and the primal father. I make the claim that Freudian psychoanalysis, more of a *Weltanschauung* than a science, is itself an artificial group, like the army or the church, in which members are affectively linked to a presumed omnipotent leader, whose love for them is presumed unconditional. In short, I use Freud's own critique of artificial groups in *Group Psychology* to assess Freud's psychoanalysis in its largest sense—$\Psi A_3$.

## Freud on Artificial Groups

"Individual psychology must . . . be just as old as group psychology, for from the first there were two kinds of psychologies, that of the individual members of the group and that of the father, chief, or leader. The members of the group were subject to ties just was we see them to-day, but the father of the primal horde was free. His intellectual acts were strong and independent even in isolation, and his will needed no reinforcement from others" (1921, *S.E.,* XVIII: 123). These statements, from *Group Psychology,* could have been from Freud's autobiography, had he written one.

The primal father, we have seen, Freud introduces in *Totem and Taboo* in an effort, following his purchase of recapitulationism, to link his ontogenetic findings, presumed to be derived from his clinical work, with phylogeny. The primal father was the leader of the primitive clan, held together through force by his autocratic "unrestricted authority" and its "thirst for obedience." He relates the oft-told story of how the primal father, preventing libidinal expression of his sons, forced them into abstinence and, thus, into libidinal ties with him and one another. "His sexual jealousy and intolerance became in the last resort the causes of group psychology" (1921, *S.E.,* XVIII: 72). The sons, disallowed libidinal expression other than homosexual acts, banded together at some juncture, killed the primal father, and ate his flesh so as to dispose wholly of the carcass and allow disremembering of the deed.

Artificial groups, such as the church or an army, differ little from the primal clan. "[T]he aim of a group is to equip the group with the attributes of an individual"—viz., identification with the leader and, thus, each other (1921, *S.E.,* XVIII: 25). What binds members of an artificial group is in last resort fear. Members are seduced by the impression that the leader of the group loves all equally and justly (1921, *S.E.,* XVIII: 72-3). So complete is the impression that each member gives up his super-ego and identifies, with wholesale libidinal investment, with the leader. The fear that binds them, consequently, is a child's worst nightmare—loss of love. The scenario of group love and identification with each other is comparable to an older child's love for a younger sibling. He would prefer to put aside his younger sibling, if he could do so without damaging his relationship with his parents. He cannot, so he identifies with his younger sibling to secure whatever parental affection he can (1921, *S.E.,* XVIII: 65-6).

"A group is impulsive, changeable and irritable," writes Freud. "It is led almost exclusively by the unconscious" (1921, *S.E.,* XVIII: 13). Given those claims, the characteristics of such groups must be homomorphic with those of the unconscious, which has no regard for reality. Following Gustave Le Bon and others who have studied groups, Freud notes "weakness of intellectual ability, lack of emotional restraint, the incapacity for moderation and delay, [and] the inclination to exceed every limit in the expression of emotion and to work it off completely in the form of action" are key characteristics of groups (1921, *S.E.,* XVIII: 62). In keeping with those key characteristics, members in groups think the group is omnipotent, do not premeditate, relinquish personal interests, are incapable of persevering and intolerant of delay, have no notion of impossible and so often take action to outrance, are extraordinarily credulous, think through associations of images, have simple and exaggerated feelings, do not doubt, embrace antipodal thoughts without anxiety, are excited only by excess of stimulation, embrace repetition, "know" truth from untruth, are both obedient to and intolerant of authority, respect force (even violence) and regard kindness as weakness, are swept away by contagion, want to be ruled and to fear, have "a deep aversion to all innovations and advances and an unbounded respect for tradition," are capable of high achievements through abnegation, selflessness, and devotion to an ideal, and can exhibit high or low ethical conduct (1921, *S.E.,* XVIII: 6-18).

Of such characteristics, some warrant elucidation. First, because they are motivated almost exclusively by the unconscious, "groups have never thirsted after truth. They demand illusions, and cannot do without them. They constantly give what is unreal precedence over what is real; they are almost as strongly influenced by what is untrue as by what it true" (1921, *S.E.,* XVIII: 16-7). Furthermore, members of a group are especially bewitched by words, which the leader of a group uses hypnotically and with plethoric force. Freud elaborates: "A group . . . is subject to the truly magical power of words; they can evoke the most formidable tempests in the group mind, and are also capable of stilling them. Reason and arguments are incapable of combating certain words and formulas" (1921, *S.E.,* XVIII: 16).

## Psychoanalysis as an Artificial Group

There is little question, in spite of claims of hermeneutic therapists today, that Freud always thought psychoanalysis had the status of a natural science. Nonetheless, when one examines how psychoanalysis established itself through its development over the years, there is little to suggest that its "successes" are the result of hard-fought empirical advances. The history of psychoanalysis is the history of a movement, not a science—an artificial group with an all-powerful, uncompromising leader—a Triton among minnows.

The movement began modestly with the Wednesday Psychological Society in 1902, which would become the Vienna Psychoanalytic Society in 1907. In 1908, there was the first International Psychoanalytic Congress in Salzburg and the *Jahrbuch für Psychoanalytische und Psychopathologische Forschungen* was launched. In 1910, the International Association of Psychoanalysis was founded, Carl Jung was named its president, Karl Abraham formed the Berlin Psychoanalytic Society, and the *Zentralblatt für Psychoanalyse* was founded. In 1911, Abraham Brill formed the New York Psychoanalytic Society, the American Psychoanalytic Society had its first meeting, and *Imago,* a journal that concerns extra-clinical issues, was founded. In 1912, the *Internationale Zeitschrift fur Psychoanalyse* was established. In 1913, Ferenczi founded the Hungarian Psychoanalytic Society, and founded the London Psycho-Analytic Society. In 1919, Jones established the International Psycho-Analytic Press and the *International Journal of Psycho-Analysis.*

All things soon were not roseate. Writes Phyllis Grosskurth, "Freud could not separate his creation, the theory of psychoanalysis, from himself, its creator. Rejection of any part of the theory meant personal rejection of him."[17] Dissenters of canonical psychoanalysis, of which Freud was sole arbiter, were in a manner of speaking ostracized—i.e., barred from its practice.

In 1911, Alfred Adler, one of the most respected psychoanalysts, resigned from the presidency of the Vienna Psychoanalytic Society, from the Vienna Psychoanalytic Society, and from the editorship of *Zentralblatt.* He dared to think independently. He saw the Oedipus complex as symbolic, not literal,[18] and was resentful of Freud's choice of Jung, a non-German, as president of the International Psychoanalytic Association in 1910. Withdrawing, Adler took nine other discontents with him and they formed what would later become the Society for Individual Psychology. Freud writes with rodomontade in a letter to Jung: "Rather tired after battle and victory, I hereby inform you that yesterday I forced the whole Adler gang . . . to resign from the society." He adds, "They have founded a new society for 'free ΨA' as opposed to our own unfree variety."[19] Following the secession of Adler was Stekel in 1912, whom Freud never fully embraced as a competent analyst. In a letter to Jung, he cites Stekel's possible discoveries and misrepresentations, upon leaving his psychoanalytic society, as reasons for tolerating him as a member of the association.[20] The concern here was damage control.

To guard against further dissension and secession, Jones suggested the notion of a secret committee—a small, intimate group of followers, analyzed by Freud and loyal to him, to "represent the pure [psychoanalytic] theory unadulterated by personal complexes"—in a letter to Freud on July 30, 1912. Freud replied:

> What took hold of my imagination immediately is your idea of a secret council composed of the best and most trustworthy among our men to take care of the further development of and defend the cause against personalities and accidents when I am no more. You say it was Ferenczi who expressed this idea, yet it may be mine own shaped in better times, when I hoped Jung would collect such a circle around him composed of the official headman of the local associations. . . . I daresay it would make living and dying easier for me if I knew of such an association existing to watch over my creation.[21]

The committee was to comprise Karl Abraham, Max Eitingon, Sandor Ferenczi, Ernest Jones, Otto Rank, and Hanns Sachs and its express aim—and here the language is revealing—was "to guard the kingdom and policy of their master."[22] Notably absent was Freud's favorite son, Carl Jung, because he too had been showing clear signs of disagreement with canonical psychoanalysis. Freud gave each member of the committee in 1913 a ring.

In 1914, Jung, because of differences with Freud, resigned as editor of the *Jahrbuch* and as president of the International Association of Psychoanalysis. Freud was fonder of Jung than of any other member of his group, but refused to allow him or any other member equal status. Freud always had to be father to his fellow psychoanalysts as sons—especially the most prominent members. For instance, when Freud first showed Jung confidence in 1908 by confiding in him apropos of his failed friendship with Wilhelm Fleiss, Jung replied: "[Y]our relationship with him impels me to ask you to let me enjoy your friendship not as one between equals but as that of father and son. This distance appears to me fitting and natural. Moreover it alone, so it seems to me, strikes a note that would prevent misunderstandings and enable two hard-headed people to exist alongside one another in an easy and unstrained relationship."[23] Over one year later, Freud awarded Jung the status of his "eldest son" and anointed him as his "successor and crown-prince."[24]

Yet upon appointing Jung as successor, Freud became paranoid about Jung, wishing to replace him. Two incidents are telling. In Bremen before Freud was to sail to America with Jung and Ferenczi in 1909, the men together enjoyed a meal. At some point, Jung cavalierly mentioned newly discovered corpses, preserved in peat bogs in Germany. Believing the turn in the conversation to be unconsciously revelatory, Freud interjected that talk of corpses expressed an unconscious death wish against him. Freud then fainted. Freud as primal father was concerned that one of his sons, the eldest and strongest, was about to replace him. Next, on the voyage to America, Freud and Jung passed time by analyzing each other's dreams. Jung pushed for details on one of Freud's dreams. Freud demurred, due to fear of losing authority and power.

Jung was an independent, intractable son. He was incapable of the father-and-son relationship he proposed in 1908—a relationship no doubt egged on by Freud. While Jung was going an independent course, Freud longed for Jung to stay true to psychoanalysis—viz., Freud's own views. Like Adler, Jung objected to the centrality of sexuality in psychoanalysis and psychopathological explanation. Over time, his letters to Freud betray hostility. In 1912, Jung writes a series of impertinent letters, in which he remonstrates about Freud's "playing the father to [his] sons."[25] Yet Freud could have it no other way. Being anything other than the "omniscient father" would, he knew, spell doom for psychoanalysis.[26]

Freud found solace in his secret committee, whose members were committed to Freud and not only tolerated, but embraced the vicissitudes of his developing views on his "science." Their love of their father was unconditional and sycophantic. Letters to Freud often exhibit barefaced obedience and an *ad captandum* jockeying for esteem in Freud's judgment that characterizes children that vie for parental affection. "The members of the Committee constantly spoke of their 'debt' to Freud," writes Grosskurth, "as though they were driven by an inner need to repay him for an inestimable gift." While they were required to appropriate every notion of Freud, he generally turned a deaf ear to their notions. "Freud constantly discouraged the Committee members from burdening him with their ideas on the pretense that he found it difficult to follow another's train of thought. In reality, he believed that cracks would appear in the foundation of his theory if foreign matter was allowed to seep through."[27]

Grosskurth strikingly compares the societies that emerged from the committee to communist cells.

> By insisting that the Committee must be *absolutely secret,* Freud enshrined the principle of confidentiality. The various psychoanalytic societies that emerged from the Committee were like Communist cells, in which the members vowed eternal obedience to their leader. Psychoanalysis became institutionalized by the founding of journals and the training of candidates; in short, an extraordinarily effective political entity.[28]

Grosskurth takes the analogy to outrance, yet it is not without bite or relevance for psychoanalysis today. In "The Impending Death of Psychoanalysis," Robert Bornstein says Freud's extra-analytic "disclosures" gave a sort of unity to psychoanalysis, but that has not led to unification in psychoanalysis through genuine etiological explanation. The raw "data" of the clinic did not lead invariably in the direction Freud wished it would have lead. Instead, they have led to what Robert Bornstein aptly calls the "insularity of psychoanalysts."[29] Today there is classical psychoanalysis as well as object relations psychology, ego psychology, and self psychology—to name the most prominent offshoots of Freudian psychoanalysis and not to mention the great number of offshoots from those offshoots.[30] The offshooting seems the result of independent battling for conceptual space,[31] which is uncharacteristic of an empirical science.

# Upshot

By the time of *Group Psychology* in 1921, the task of a psychoanalyst is now broadened. Given that individual neuroses are in large part determined by universal neuroses—e.g., religious restrictions and disavowals—no longer does a psychoanalyst concern himself exclusively with individual neuroses. He is now a global therapist, whose concern is eradication of animism through eradication of obsessional religiosity and, to a lesser extent, paranoic philosophy, and the substitution of science and its concern for veridicality and reality for them.[32]

Why did Freud turn to group issues? If it is the case that Freudian psychoanalysis is itself, in the mind of its maker, part of the transitional state from the mercurial wish-driven fantasies of religious ideology to the cool neutrality of science in search of truth and human betterment, then it becomes evident why Freud focused on larger social and moral issues in his later years. Freud believed that the problem of individual neuroses was in great part determined by the "obsessional neuroses of humanity." The fight against individual neuroses was best, most efficiently, to be fought against group neuroses, fueled by animism and religious ideology. Animism and religion comprise not only obsessional restrictions, but also a disavowal of reality through hypostatization of wish-based illusions. What made this fight against group neuroses most difficult was that Freud certainly knew that one cannot ask people to give up so much without, in return, giving them back something of equal return, or nearly so.

Freud's solution to group neurosis like individual neurosis was education to reality, which has clear implications for $\Psi A_2$ as well as for $\Psi A_3$. $\Psi A_2$ is a commitment to returning patients to reality in such a manner that they can endure its vagaries. $\Psi A_3$ involves a similar commitment at the level of groups, of which humanity is one.

Can Freudian psychoanalysis be the key harbinger of this education to reality? Given the metempirical nature of much of Freudian psychoanalysis—the topic of numerous publications—and the deceit and ensorcellment used on disciples to keep them true to his principles, psychoanalysis is more a fictive product of Freud's rich imagination and desire for fatherly omnipotence than it is a science, founded on clinical data. It follows that it is ill-suited to be a harbinger of anything related to reality. The influence of Freud on global culture, however, cannot be denied. It is likely that many of Freud's neoterisms or substratal conceptions—super-ego, repression, unconscious, and sublimation, etc.—will be with humans for the foreseeable future.

# Notes

1. Cf. Kant in "Beginning of Human History." Kant says that humans fear the perpetual threat of war, the shortness of human life, and a wish, incapable of fulfillment, to return to the golden age. Immanuel Kant, "On the Beginning of Human History," *Perpetual Peace and Other Essays* (Indianapolis: Hackett Publishing Company, 1983), 58-9.

2. Sex is limited to the genitalia, object-choice is restricted to the other, and incest is strictly prohibited (1930, *S.E.,* XXI: 104-5).

3. Stephen Hawking and Leonard Mlodinow, *The Grand Design* (New York: Bantam, 2010).

4. M. Andrew Holowchak, "Technology and Freudian Discontent: Freud's 'Muffled' Meliorism and the Problem of Human Annihilation," *Sophia,* Vol. 49, 2010, 100-1.

5. Freud wavered on the notion of the ego being an agency whose energy source was independent of the id. In *Ego and the Id* (1923, *S.E.,* XIX: 30fn. 1 & 46), he states baldly that the ego uses borrowed energy to fulfill its functions. In other works—*Beyond the Pleasure Principle* (1920, *S.E.,* XVIII: 50-2), *Autobiographical Study* (1925, *S.E.,* XX: 56), *Anxiety and Instinctual Life* (1933, *S.E.,* XXII: 103), and *Outline of Psychoanalysis* (1940, *S.E.,* XXIII: 150-1)—he says plainly that the ego is the "reservoir of libido."

6. Greek for "good words" or "good accounts."

7. Though deaths of loved ones must also have been causes for rejoicing in that these loved ones, though parts of him, were also strangers to him.

8. Joachim Sharfenberg, *Sigmund Freud & His Critique of Religion* (Philadelphia: Fortress Press, 1988), 121.

9. Alfred I. Tauber, *Freud: The Reluctant Philosopher* (Princeton University Press, 2010), 197-9.

10. Alfred I. Tauber, *Freud,* 213.

11. Jürgen Haberman, *Theory and Practice* (Boston: Beacon Press, 1973), and Paul Ricouer, *Freud and Philosophy* (New Haven, CT: Yale University Press, 1970).

12. For more on Freud's Stoicism, see M. Andrew Holowchak, *Freud and Utopia,* 138-41.

13. Bernard Williams, *Truth and Truthfulness: An Essay in Genealogy* (Princeton: Princeton University Press, 2002), 44.

14. Bernard Williams, *Truth and Truthfulness,* 53.

15. Bernard Williams, *Truth and Truthfulness,* 54-9.

16. Bernard Williams, *Truth and Truthfulness,* 61.

17. Phyllis Grosskurth, *The Secret Ring: Freud's Inner Circle and the Politics of Psychoanalysis* (New York: Addison-Wesley, 1991), 53.

18. See Freud's letter to Ernest Jones, June 25, 1911. Sigmund Freud and Ernest Jones, *The Complete Correspondence of Sigmund Freud and Ernest Jones,* ed. R. Andrew Paskauskas (Cambridge: Harvard University Press, 1993),

19. October 12, 1911. Sigmund Freud and Carl G. Jung, *The Freud/Jung Letters,* ed. William McGuire (Princeton University Press, 1974).

20. Sigmund Freud and Carl G. Jung, *The Freud/Jung Letters,* April 27, 1911.

21. Sigmund Freud and Carl G. Jung, *The Freud/Jung Letters,* August 1, 1912.

22. Sigmund Freud and Ernest Jones, *The Complete Correspondence of Sigmund Freud and Ernest Jones*, August 7, 1912.

23. Sigmund Freud and Carl G. Jung, *The Freud/Jung Letters,* February 20, 1908.

24. Sigmund Freud and Carl G. Jung, *The Freud/Jung Letters,* April 16, 1909.

25. Sigmund Freud and Carl G. Jung, *The Freud/Jung Letters,* December 18, 1912.

26. Phyllis Grosskurth, *The Secret Ring,* 50.

27. Phyllis Grosskurth, *The Secret Ring,* 16-7.

28. Phyllis Grosskurth, *The Secret Ring,* 15.

29. Robert Bornstein, "The Impending Death of Psychoanalysis," *Psychoanalytic Psychology,* Vol. 18, No. 1, 2001, 17-8.

30. They exist as independent institutes. The Association of Autonomous Psychoanalytic Institutes has been recently formed (2001) to rival the American Psychoanalytic Association and has twenty-one member institutes to the thirty-two for the APA.

31. Freud in a letter to Groddeck (June 5, 1917) explained offshooting as the result of "unbridled ambition" (Freud et al., 1961).

32. See Alexander Mitscherlich, "Group Psychology and the Analysis of the Ego—A Lifetime Later," *The Psychoanalytic Quarterly,* Vol. 47. No. 1, 1978, 1-23.

# Bibliography

Beit-Hallahmi, Benjamin. *Psychoanalysis and Theism: Critical Reflections on the Grunbaum Thesis* (Lanham, MD: Jason Aronson, 2010).

Brenner, Charles. *Psychoanalytic Technique and Psychic Conflict* (New York: International University Press, 1976).

Ellman, Steven J. *Freud's Technique Papers: A Contemporary Perspective* (Northvale, NJ: Jason Aronson, 1991).

Fancher, Raymond E. *Psychoanalytic Psychology: The Development of Freud's Thought* (New York: W.W. Norton & Co., 1973).

Fisher, Seymour, and Roger P. Greenberg. *The Scientific Credibility of Freud's Theories and Therapy* (New York: Basic Books, 1977).

Freud, Sigmund. *The Letters of Sigmund Freud,* ed. Ernst L. Freud (London: The Hogarth Press, 1961).

Freud, Sigmund, *A Phylogenetic Fantasy,* ed. Ilse Grubrich-Smitis (Cambridge: Harvard University Press, 1987).

Freud, Sigmund. *The Standard Edition of the Complete Psychological Works of Sigmund Freud*, Vols. I-XXIV, ed. and trans. James Strachey (London: The Hogarth Press, 1976).

Freud, Sigmund, and Karl Abraham. *A Psycho-Analytic Dialogue: The Letters of Sigmund Freud and Karl Abraham, 1907-1926,* ed. Hilda C. Abraham and Ernst L. Freud (New York: Basic Books, 1965).

Freud, Sigmund, and Sandor Ferenczi. *The Correspondence of Sigmund Freud and Sandor Ferenczi, Vol. I, 1908-1914,* ed. E. Brabant, E. Falzeder, and P. Giampieri-Deutsch (Cambridge: Harvard University Press, 1993).

Freud, Sigmund, and Wilhelm Fleiss. *The Complete Letters of Sigmund Freud to Wilhelm Fliess: 1887-1904,* ed. Jeffrey Moussaieff Masson (Cambridge: Harvard University Press, 1985).

Freud, Sigmund, and Carl G. Jung. *The Freud/Jung Letters,* ed. William McGuire (Princeton University Press, 1974).

Freud, Sigmund, and Oskar Pfister, *Psychoanalysis and Faith: The Letters of Sigmund Freud & Oskar Pfister,* ed. Heinrich Meng and Ernst L. Freud (New York: Basic Books, 1963).

Freud, Sigmund, and Lou Andreas Salomé. *Sigmund Freud and Lou Andreas Salomé: Letters,* ed. Ernst Pfeiffer (New York: W.W. Norton & Company, 1972).

Freud, Sigmund and Edward Silberstein. *The Letters of Sigmund Freud to Eduard Silberstein, 1871-1881,* ed., Walter Boehlich (Cambridge: Harvard University Press, 1990).

Freud, Sigmund and Arnold Zweig. *The Letters of Sigmund Freud and Arnold Zweig*, ed. Ernst L. Freud (New York: New York University Press, 1970).

Gay, Peter. *Freud: A Life for Our Time* (New York: W.W. Norton & Company, 2006).

Gelfand, Toby, and John Kerr. *Freud and the History of Psychoanalysis* (Hillsdale, NJ: The Analytic Press, 1992).

Grosskurth, Phyllis. *The Secret Ring: Freud's Inner Circle and the Politics of Psychoanalysis* (Addison-Wesley Publishing Company, 1991).

Grünbaum, Adolf. *The Foundations of Psychoanalysis: A Philosophical Critique* (Berkeley: University of California Press, 1984).

Holowchak, M. Andrew. *Freud and Utopia: From Cosmological Narcissism to the "Soft Dictatorship" of Reason* (Lanham, MD: Lexington Press, 2012).

Holowchak, M. Andrew, ed. *Radical Claims in Freudian Psychoanalysis: Point/Counterpoint* (Lanham, MD: Jason Aronson Press, 2012).

Hook, Sydney, ed. *Psychoanalysis, Scientific Method, and Philosophy* (New York: New York University Press, 1958).

Jones, Ernest. *The Life and Works of Sigmund Freud* (New York: Basic Books, 1953).

Kahn, Michael. *Basic Freud: Psychoanalytic Thought for the 21st Century* (New York: Basic Books, 2002).

Kitcher, Patricia. *Freud's Dream: A Complete Interdisciplinary Science of the Mind* (Cambridge: MIT Press, 1995).

Langs, Robert. *Freud on a Precipice: How Freud's Fate Pushed Psychoanalysis over the Edge* (Lanham, MD: Jason Aronson, 2009).

Levine, Michael P., ed. *The Analytic Freud: Philosophy and Psychoanalysis* (New York: Routledge, 2000).

Masson, Jeffrey M. *The Assault on Truth* (New York: Farrar, Straus & Giroux, 1984).

Neu, Jerome. *The Cambridge Companion to Freud* (New York: Cambridge University Press, 1991).

Ritvo, Lucy B. *Darwin's Influence on Freud: A Tale of Two Sciences* (New Haven, CT: Yale University Press, 1990).

Roazen, Paul. *Freud: Political and Social Thought* (New York: Alfred A. Knopf, 1968).

Smith, Joseph H., and William Kerrigan, ed. *Pragmatism's Freud: The Moral Disposition of Psychoanalysis* (Baltimore: The Johns Hopkins University Press, 1986).

Sulloway, Frank J. *Freud: Biologist of the Mind* (New York: Basic Books, 1979).

Tauber, Alfred I. *Freud: The Reluctant Philosopher* (Princeton University Press, 2010).

Wollheim, Richard, and James Hopkins. *Philosophical Essays on Freud* (London: Cambridge University Press, 1984).

# Index

Abel, Karl, 143
Abraham, Karl, 174–75
Adler, Alfred, 174–75
Aesop, 59
analogical arguments, 46–48
Artemidorus, 42, 143–44

Bernheim, Hippolyte, xv, 4–5, 28–32, 35
Bornstein, Robert, 176, 178
Brenner, Charles, 37–38
Breuer, Joseph, xiii, 5–7, 9, 11, 15, 23n9, 24nn12–13, 28, 36, 72, 86, 119n26
Brill, Abraham, 174

cathartic therapy, 5–9, 28–35, 72–73, 86; abandonment of, 33–35; abreacting and, 28–30; hypnosis and, 5–7, 30–31; limits of, 33, 72–73; mnemonic elements of, 7–9; pressure technique, 28–32
Charcot, Jean-Martin, xv, 3–4, 11, 30
Christ/Christianity, 79–80, 133, 136, 168, 170
Chrobak, Richard, 15
Comte, August, 98–100, 111–12, 115, 117
Comtean progressivism, 98–99, 111, 117, 123–24, 161, 167, 170
Copernicus, Nicholas, 100

Darwin, Charles, 15, 18, 100
Davidson, Donald, 129
Dostoyevsky, Fyodor, 131
dreams. *See* psychoanalysis (dreams)

Ellis, Havelock, 15
Ellman, Stephen, 37
Epicurus, 168

Fancher, Raymond, 38
Fay, Brian, 129
Ferenczi, Sandor, 88, 91n1, 91n5, 123, 174–75
Fisher, Kuno, 151
Fliess, Wilhelm, 4, 9, 11–12, 14–19, 175
Fonagy, Peter, 38
Frazer, J. G., 15
Freud, Sigmund, 99–105, 121–39, 141–54, 157–77; attitude toward art, 122–39; four identifications, 169–70; metempirical purchases, 99–105; as primal father, 171–76; *Weltschmerz*, 161–62

Gill, M. M., 37–38
god(s), 76–77, 79, 84, 144–45, 148–49, 160–61
Grandy, Roger, 129
Grosskurth, Phyllis, 174, 176
Grünbaum, Adolf, 39, 57, 82, 87–88, 108–9
Grunes, Mark, 37–38

Haeckel, Ernst, 100
Haeckel's biogenic law, 100–3, 117
Hawking, Stephen, 160
Hoffman, E. T. A., 152
Holt, Robert, 111
Hungarian Psychoanalytic Society, 174
hypnosis. *See* cathartic therapy, hypnosis and

Scharfenberg, Joachim, 167
Schopenhauer, Arthur, 167–68, 169
Scriven, Michael, 64–65
Stekel, Wilhelm, 40–41, 174
Stoics, 168
Strachey, James, 113–14, 146, 149
structural model, 19–21, 121
Sulloway, Frank, 118n18

Tacitus, 162
Tauber, Alfred, 99, 168–69
truth, historical vs. material, 148–49, 160, 165–73, 176

Vienna Psychoanalytic Society, 173–74
Visher, Theodor, 151

Williams, Bernard, 170–71
Wollheim, Richard, 132

Zweig, Arnold, 69n5

# About the Author

M. Andrew Holowchak teaches philosophy at Rider University in Lawrence-ville, New Jersey. He has published some seventy peer-reviewed papers in areas such as ethics, psychoanalysis, ancient philosophy and science, philosophy of sport, and social and political philosophy and has authored nineteen books including *Freud and Utopia, Extreme Freud, Dutiful Correspondent: Philosophical Essays on Thomas Jefferson, Happiness and Greek Ethics, Critical Reasoning & Philosophy, Ancient Science and Dreams, Philosophy of Sport, Aretism, The Stoics*, as well as two philosophical novels, *Life of a Jellyfish* and *Hotel Bob*. His current research is on philosophical elements in the writings of Thomas Jefferson.

When not teaching, reading, or writing, Holowchak enjoys strength training, biking, gardening, classic and foreign movies, cooking, brewing beer, and polite conversation. He lives in Lindenwold, New Jersey, with his wife, Angela, and their several obstreperous cats.